Can You Be a Catholic and a Feminist?

Can You Be a Catholic and a Feminist?

JULIE HANLON RUBIO

OXFORD
UNIVERSITY PRESS

Oxford University Press is a department of the University of Oxford. It furthers the University's objective of excellence in research, scholarship, and education by publishing worldwide. Oxford is a registered trade mark of Oxford University Press in the UK and certain other countries.

Published in the United States of America by Oxford University Press
198 Madison Avenue, New York, NY 10016, United States of America.

© Oxford University Press 2024

All rights reserved. No part of this publication may be reproduced, stored in a retrieval system, or transmitted, in any form or by any means, without the prior permission in writing of Oxford University Press, or as expressly permitted by law, by license, or under terms agreed with the appropriate reproduction rights organization. Inquiries concerning reproduction outside the scope of the above should be sent to the Rights Department, Oxford University Press, at the address above.

You must not circulate this work in any other form and you must impose this same condition on any acquirer.

Library of Congress Cataloging-in-Publication Data
Names: Rubio, Julie Hanlon, author.
Title: Can you be a Catholic and a feminist? / Julie Hanlon Rubio.
Description: New York, NY : Oxford University Press, [2024] |
Includes bibliographical references and index.
Identifiers: LCCN 2023057304 (print) | LCCN 2023057305 (ebook) |
ISBN 9780197553145 (hardback) | ISBN 9780197553169 (epub)
Subjects: LCSH: Women in the Catholic Church. |
Feminism—Religious aspects—Catholic Church.
Classification: LCC BX2347.8.W6 R83 2024 (print) | LCC BX2347.8.W6 (ebook) |
DDC 230/.2082—dc23/eng/20231222
LC record available at https://lccn.loc.gov/2023057304
LC ebook record available at https://lccn.loc.gov/2023057305

DOI: 10.1093/oso/9780197553145.001.0001

Printed by Integrated Books International, United States of America

Portions of the following chapters were previously published in the following journals or edited volumes:

Ch. 1 "Sloth," in *Naming Our Sins: How Recognizing the Seven Deadly Vices Can Renew the Sacrament of Reconciliation*, ed. David Cloutier and Jana Marguerite Bennett, (Washington, D.C.: Catholic University Press, 2019), 89–105.

Ch. 2 "#MeToo, #ChurchToo: A Catholic Social Ethics Response to Sexual Violence," *Journal of Catholic Social Thought* 16.2 (2019): 1–18.

Ch. 4 "Sex, Gender, and Revolution: Where Was Theology?," *Annual of College Theology Society* 64 (2018): 63–83.

Ch. 7 "Masculinity and Sexual Abuse in the Church," *Concilium* (2020/2): 118–127.

Ch. 9 "The Conscience of a Catholic Feminist Educator," in *Conscience and Catholic Education*, ed., David DeCosse and Kevin Baxter (Maryknoll, NY: Orbis, 2022), 198–211.

Contents

Acknowledgments	vii
Introduction	1
Why This Question?	1
Is This Question Really Worth Asking?	5
Who Is This Book For?	8
Writing from the Margins and the Center	9
1. Authentically Human	11
Tensions: Becoming Myself or Being for Others?	12
Common Threads in Christian and Feminist Accounts of Sloth	18
Rethinking the Self: What Does It Mean to Be Authentic?	23
Solidarity and Freedom	25
2. Sex	31
Feminist Engagement and Catholic Silence	33
A Catholic Feminist Response	38
Work in the "Space Between"	44
3. Work	49
Whose Room? Which Balancing Act?	49
Tensions in Feminist and Catholic Thinking on Work	51
Today's Balancing Act: Always On	55
Overlapping Catholic and Feminist Ideals	60
A Catholic Feminist Response to the Antiwork Movement	65
4. Marriage	69
Unorthodox Thoughts on Marriage	69
Feminist Criticisms of Marriage	71
Catholic Visions of Marriage	77
Catholic Feminist Families	82
Fidelity Revisited	89

vi CONTENTS

5. Life   92
  Identity Politics   92
  Unresolvable Tensions   94
  Starting in a Different Place   99
  A Catholic Feminist Story   111

6. Gender   115
  The Gender Problem   115
  Three Claims We Could Agree Upon   119
  The Potential of Dialogue across Differences   134

7. Power   138
  Power as Problem: Ordination   140
  The Deeper Problem: Clericalism   146
  Empowered Catholic Women   152
  Saving Power   158

8. Prayer   163
  I Close My Eyes   163
  Facing the Problem   167
  And Yet: The Need for Prayer   175
  Being Authentic: Catholic Feminist Prayer Spaces   179
  Praying with Open Eyes   183

9. Belonging   187
  Standing in Your Truth   187
  Why Answering the Question Is Harder Now   188
  Conscience Wrestling   191
  Why Stay? Why Belong?   197
  From Purity to Conscious Belonging   201

Notes   207
Index   249

Acknowledgments

Although I have been officially working on this book only since 2016, I have been a feminist and Catholic for as long as I can remember and I have a lot of people to thank for that.

I had the privilege of taking "Black Women and Their Fiction" with bell hooks at Yale, "New Testament" with Elisabeth Schüssler Fiorenza at Harvard Divinity School, "Women in Ministry" with Francine Cardman at Weston School of Theology, and "Feminist Theory" with Barrie Thorne at the University of Southern California. Also at USC, I was part of a group of women doctoral students who met regularly to eat dinner, drink wine, and commiserate about patriarchy in the Christian tradition we were studying. The only woman professor in the Religion department, Shelia Briggs, was a reader for my dissertation on family in Catholic social thought. While at HDS, I took a course with Lisa Sowle Cahill over at Boston College and had an important conversation with her about being a woman—and a mother—and a Catholic theologian. She has always been a role model, and has graciously provided guidance from afar over the years. For all of these women, I am grateful.

I spent 19 wonderful years at St. Louis University, the first woman to be tenured in the department of Theological Studies. I am grateful to my former colleagues—especially Grant Kaplan, J. J. Mueller S. J., and Wayne Hellman O. F. M.—for their support, and am delighted to see a new generation of women—including Emily Dumler-Winckler, and Elizabeth Sweeny Block—moving into central roles. In my last year at SLU, thanks to Peter Martens, I taught a doctoral seminar in Feminist Theology for the first time.

viii ACKNOWLEDGMENTS

In that year, I also had a secondary appointment in Women and Gender Studies, which allowed me to find a second departmental home, teach cross-listed courses, and learn from faculty like Penny Weiss and Amanda Izzo who had expertise I needed to take on this project. Just as significant was my experience leading a weekly feminist reading group for an extraordinary group of seven women undergraduates who taught me, among other things, that Beyoncé's "Lemonade" was feminist theology too.

At JST, I followed in the footsteps of trailblazers like Sandra Schneiders I. H. M. and Mary Ann Donovan, S. C. I am blessed to count as colleagues many extraordinary women, including Gina Hens-Piazza, Mary McGann R. S. C.J., Kate Barush, and Léocadie Lushombo, I. T. I work with wonderful Jesuits, including Dean Agbonkhianmeghe Orobator, who support women's leadership and ministry in the church. I am grateful for my students, including my first doctoral student, the late Alfonso Suico, CSsR, who wrote a passionate dissertation on Filipina women, and the amazing women who study at JST. Thank you: Ellen Jewett, Barbara Anne Kozee, Tracy Schriders Smith, Anne Zehren, Alexandra Bishop, and, especially, Maddie LaForge, whose extraordinary research and editing skills played a crucial role in the construction of this book.

My thanks to Theo Calderara and all the people at Oxford University Press and to Jason King who helped find the courage to submit a proposal to Oxford in the first place. I am grateful for the research time and money I received from St. Louis University and Santa Clara University, and for participants of the New Wine, New Wineskins seminar who welcomed me to present chapters of this book at their summer gathering at Notre Dame in the summer of 2022.

I dedicate this book to the women of the Jesuit School of Theology, with gratitude for your prophetic witness, and hope for the church you love into being.

Introduction

Why This Question?

I was raised Catholic. At some point—I cannot remember precisely when—I came to consciously embrace the faith as my own. There was no moment when lightning struck. Instead, when I look back at my younger self, I see someone who felt God's presence, hungered for community, and wanted to live a good and meaningful life. In fact, at high school parties, I used to ask people, "What is the meaning of life?" I wasn't sure, but certainly, I thought, the life of Jesus was something all Christians should emulate. I saw models all around me. In my high school, run by the Sisters of the Holy Names, I stumbled upon dusty copies of lives of the saints and found inspiring stories that gave me a sense of possibility. I found similar inspiration in the strong sisters who taught and coached me and the committed Catholic adults I knew.[1]

None of this felt limited by gender. I grew up thinking girls could be whatever they wanted to be. In college, when I began to call myself a feminist, my faith only grew stronger. Though the exclusion of women from priesthood disturbed me, it was not as striking then as it is now. Yale University, which I entered in 1983, had only admitted its first coed class ten years earlier. Imperfect institutions were evolving, and the post–Vatican II church seemed to be one of those. I began to read theology and excitedly copied long passages into my journal and letters to friends. I saw little tension between the Catholic and feminist parts of myself.

When I began my academic career in the 1990s, US Catholic feminist theologians were an established force, anchoring a small but

Can You Be a Catholic and a Feminist?. Julie Hanlon Rubio, Oxford University Press.
© Oxford University Press 2024. DOI: 10.1093/oso/9780197553145.003.0001

2 CAN YOU BE A CATHOLIC AND A FEMINIST?

growing cohort of women studying theology, and giving hope to women active in Catholic life. Catholicism felt hospitable to people with unresolved questions and complicated identities. Regardless of the strictures of any particular parish—or even any particular pope—memories of mid-twentieth-century Catholic heroes like Flannery O'Connor, Oscar Romero, Thomas Merton, and Dorothy Day were still fresh. Strong women and men, single and married, religious and lay, drew together in the work of parish life and social justice. The question that forms the title of this book did not trouble me much. Of course one could be feminist and Catholic.

But over the nearly three decades that I have been a Catholic theologian, Catholic feminism has seemed to be slowly slipping away. For friends, family, students, and Catholics I encounter in parishes, universities, and conferences, embracing a Catholic feminist identity seems less possible. Some are drawn to the beauty and prophetic witness of a countercultural faith that makes secular feminism seem empty by comparison. For others, feminism (named or unnamed) is part of who they are, while Catholicism, despite their best efforts, has come to feel like a place they visit rather than an identity they can claim as their own.

Feminism, of course, is a controversial term. Feminists have long had to contend with misunderstanding and backlash and, as a result, even today many feminists feel the need to assure people that they are not man-haters or bra-burners.[2] Women of color have raised serious questions about feminism, criticizing its concern with issues central to white women's lives and its neglect of and complicity with racism. People who identify as queer wonder how feminism could possibly be relevant to their lives given its traditional assumptions about who counts as a woman. These concerns significantly deepen the Catholic feminist dilemma.

This book begins with straightforward definitions of both "feminist" and "Catholic." Those definitions are focused on belief and action. A feminist is someone who acknowledges the reality of sexism as one of many intersecting oppressions and commits to

INTRODUCTION   3

working for the flourishing of women and all humans. A Catholic is a person who holds to the essentials of Catholic faith and engages in Catholic practice in everyday life. With these terms defined at a very basic level, we can begin to explore the tensions between them and move toward a more complex understanding of what it might mean to claim both.

The fundamental question of this book is stated plainly in the title: Can you be a Catholic and a feminist? To expand on this a bit, you might ask: Is it possible, in the twenty-first-century United States, to reconcile—logically, morally, theologically—a Catholic identity and a feminist one? This question has only been around a short time. With a few exceptions, Catholics did not begin identifying as feminists until the rise of second-wave feminism in the 1960s. It was during this period that Catholic feminists first focused on answering the question in this book's title.[3] The answers they adopted are hallmarks of popular Catholic feminism: "It's my church and I'm not leaving," "Change will only happen if people like me stay," and "The church is much more than the teachings that trouble me."

Since then, Catholic feminists have largely moved away from this book's central question. Major feminist thinkers have focused on contributing to the development of Catholic theology, balancing critique with retrieval of forgotten parts of their tradition and reconstruction.[4] At the same time, a new generation of Catholic women serving in leadership roles are claiming feminist identity and Catholic identity with much less focus on the tensions identified by feminist theologians.[5] Social media accounts named "FemCatholic" and "Catholic Feminist" emphasize the compatibility of Catholicism and feminism and attract tens of thousands of followers. There have been few attempts to make a substantial Catholic feminist case in the twenty-first century, even though new challenges have certainly appeared. As a result, the answers first articulated in the early days of Catholic feminism are largely still the ones we hear today, even as they are uttered with increasing

4   CAN YOU BE A CATHOLIC AND A FEMINIST?

tentativeness by adherents, and challenged by the claims of Catholics emphasizing the compatibility of their faith with feminist convictions.

Yet anyone who embraces both Catholic and feminist identities faces daunting hurdles.

Beginning in 2017, the #MeToo and #ChurchToo movements came together to raise profound questions. Not for the first time, Catholic women confronted the sins of the priests, bishops, and the Vatican, as well as the flaws of the hierarchical structure that enabled abuse. Some stopped going to Mass or putting money in the collection basket. Suddenly the possibility of not being Catholic seemed all the more real. Previously satisfactory answers to the question, "Why stay?" no longer felt sufficient in the face of such egregious failures.[6]

Slow progress on women's leadership in the church has become even more difficult to accept given the gains women have made elsewhere. Women are senators, congressional representatives, Supreme Court judges, and vice president; world-class athletes, professors, writers, and artists; CEOs and spiritual gurus. How is it possible that the church fails to recognize the potential of women? How can it be that Catholic women are still fighting for speaking and voting rights at the Vatican? Progress inside the church in some areas has created both more fulfillment and more frustration. There are more women teaching Catholic theology, ministering in parishes, and running Catholic institutions than ever before. Catholic women in online forums ably break open the Scriptures and pray with large audiences. Yet a mostly male cast of preachers, writers, pastors, and leaders remains dominant. As women's involvement inside and outside the church grows, their limited leadership opportunities have become increasingly frustrating.

In addition, growing social acceptance of diverse sexual orientations and gender identities is leading to increasing discomfort with Catholic approaches to sex and gender. A newly energized movement for reproductive justice is raising questions about

Catholic teaching on abortion, especially now that *Roe v. Wade* has been overturned. Catholic teachings on marriage and family, and its traditional notions of work and home, seem at odds with emerging acceptance of a diversity of lifestyles. The discovery of rich spiritual resources in online communities during the Covid-19 pandemic has further displaced parishes from the center of Catholic life. With all of these new challenges, it is time for a renewed engagement with questions of whether one can be Catholic and feminist.

This book attempts a new synthesis, arguing that Catholic feminist identity is still possible, but only if (1) we frankly acknowledge tensions between Catholicism and feminism, (2) we go deep enough into Catholic and feminist traditions to see the gaps between them and all they hold in common, and (3) we cultivate an authentically feminist way of being Catholic.[7] In the chapters that follow, I explore tensions, map synergies, and highlight strategies of authentic belonging through a variety of lenses.

Is This Question Really Worth Asking?

While not all Catholics and not all feminists can bridge the divides between them, there is potential for synthesis because both traditions are more capacious than is often acknowledged.

Feminism is typically described in three waves. The first, dating roughly from the mid-nineteenth century to the early twentieth century, was focused on the right to vote. The second, largely in the 1960s and 1970s, centered on changes in the workplace and the home. And the third, dating from the 1990s to the present day, has broadened to include a global diversity of women and the intersection of gender with race, poverty, sexuality, ethnicity, disability, and religion.[8] Each wave has been broader than the one before.

Feminists can also be divided into types. In this book, I highlight four: liberal, claiming individual rights; socialist, improving intersecting unjust social conditions; postmodern, pointing toward

6 CAN YOU BE A CATHOLIC AND A FEMINIST?

diversity and emergent possibility in all things; and new orthodox, reaffirming tradition.[9] Aside from these general categories, Black, Latina, Asian, African, and other ethnic groups bring distinctive concerns to feminism. Because of the history of antiblack racism in the United States, I am particularly attentive to Black feminism. I engage with a variety of feminist types to show the complexity of feminism as a tradition and a movement, while searching for an authentic feminism that can accommodate Catholic identity and belonging.

Catholicism has a long history and a rich array of theological, spiritual, and ethical wisdom within which a broad array of people have been able to find a home. Though often characterized narrowly, or identified only with its most visible leaders and political stances, the Catholicism I lift up in this book includes culture, theology, ethics, prayer, the lives of holy men and women, and the practices of a variety of adherents who claim this faith as their own. Like Catholic feminist theologians before me, I mine the tradition broadly conceived, seeking a Catholicism with space for feminism.

Despite well-known tensions between Catholics and feminists, when viewed in their complexity, they have significant overlap in their visions of what it means to live a good life. Both reject an extreme individualism and see human beings as fundamentally relational. Both view the public and private spheres of life not as separate or unequal but as inherently valuable and inextricably linked. Both see clearly the violation of sexual violence and raise questions about a sexual landscape that privileges (male) pleasure over mutuality and intimacy. Both share a recognition of the significance of embodiment and a vision of humanity not bound to sexual stereotypes. Catholic and feminist writers attest to the significant experience of motherhood. Both feminists and Catholics tend to question market-driven conceptions of the good life, calling for work-life balance and flourishing for all. Some feminist visions of egalitarian marriage are not so different from contemporary Catholic theology on families. There are resources in both traditions for empowerment and for questioning conventional notions of power. Feminists and Catholics recognize the significance of ritual and the sacred. There is a great deal of common ground between these two unlikely allies.

Still, if tensions between Catholicism and feminism are not frankly acknowledged, authentic Catholic feminist identity will be unsustainable. Feminists have raised important questions about Catholic understandings of the human person that prize sacrificial love and understand pride as the greatest sin. Though Catholics now condemn sexual violence, feminists rightly point to a long history of silence and shed light on ideals of marriage and gender that have made women vulnerable. Contemporary feminists affirm a spectrum of gender identities and orientations, while traditional Catholic theology assumes a heteronormative framework and an "equal but different" theory of gender complementarity. Catholic opposition to abortion rights places the church at odds with the vast majority of secular feminists who see reproductive rights as nonnegotiable. While feminists celebrate women's public work, Catholics seem preoccupied with women's role in the private sphere. Some feminists today call for leaving traditional family structures behind, while Catholic teaching affirms the centrality of family to society. Catholic liturgy is still presided over by men, and male language for God remains the norm. The empowerment feminists seek for women seems to be off the table in the Catholic Church. Though Catholic thought offers a strong defense of conscience, feminists ask whether belonging to a sexist church constitutes an unconscionable compromise. These tensions create a gulf between feminist and Catholic identities that must be confronted.

Yet authentically feminist ways of being Catholic are there if you look. They can be found in the writings of Catholic theologians who have long wrestled with these questions. They are there in reclaimed liturgies and in the new spiritual spaces that Catholic feminists seek out, from music, to social media, to prayer groups. They are present in the lives of ordinary believers who participate in and reclaim

8 CAN YOU BE A CATHOLIC AND A FEMINIST?

ancient practices. In exploring the authentic belonging of Catholic feminists, this book seeks to map new currents and contribute to further efforts to reconcile Catholic and feminist identities.

Who Is This Book For?

As a Christian ethicist and theologian, I bring the fruits of my academic research on systematic and ethical questions to the project, but in this book, I am speaking primarily to lay and religious Catholic women and men rather than to theologians. Unlike other works of Catholic feminist thought, mine is not designed around theological categories, though theology plays a significant role in the book. Each chapter begins with a question from the real world: something I have heard in conversation in parishes, parks, or coffee shops or seen captured in popular novels or films. Each draws upon Catholic tradition and feminism in the United States, as well as sources in social science and religious studies that help me describe Catholic and feminist ideas and show how they are actually lived.

I write with the hope that the book will be read in universities, seminaries, schools of theology and ministry, as well as parishes and book groups. I hope it will also be picked up by feminists who stopped going to church a long time ago in frustration and by Catholics for whom feminism is new and even strange. I hope it will help Catholics for whom the Catholic feminist dilemma has long been a concern as well as those who have just begun to see the problem. The questions that animate this book may have once mattered only to a small proportion of those with connections to Catholicism. Today, feminism's concerns are much more broadly shared and the dilemma of dual identity continues to spread and deepen.

While recognizing the challenge of speaking to such a broad set of concerns, I bring to this project long years of reading, listening

INTRODUCTION 9

to, and befriending Catholics of many ideological perspectives, and seeking common ground.[10] This work includes teaching, but also public lectures at universities and churches, as well as workshops for university faculty and staff, priests, parish groups, and students struggling to have conversations across deep differences. I think of this book as a resource for the kinds of difficult conversations I often engage in with students, colleagues, family, and friends.

While the depth and difficulty of Catholic feminist tension differs across the range of issues I consider, each chapter of the book takes readers deeper by mining the resources of the feminist and Catholic tradition and practice, mapping overlapping concerns, engaging disagreements, and seeking creative ways forward. Each piece contributes to a Catholic feminist identity with potential to ground authentic belonging.

Writing from the Margins and the Center

I grew up in a Catholic family that, at first, attended a traditional parish. But, by the time I was nine, we had joined a group of families in a small Catholic community called "Spes Nova" (New Hope) that met for liturgy in our homes. That community gave me an experience of church beyond structures, hierarchy, and rules. Eucharist, food, protest, and community anchored our faith. I never thought of Mass as an obligation or worried that not going would endanger my soul. I do not identify with "Catholic guilt." Yet, on my first Sunday at college, I walked into the Catholic student center, joined the folk music group, and never looked back. Eventually, I made my way to divinity school, a doctoral degree in religion, marriage and parenting, a job teaching theology at a Jesuit university, and a vocation as a Catholic theologian.

Today, I teach a very diverse group of priests, sisters, brothers, and lay men and women at a school of theology and ministry in Berkeley, California. Formed both by my unorthodox childhood

10 CAN YOU BE A CATHOLIC AND A FEMINIST?

experience of Catholicism and my career inside the church, in a profession that few women in the history of Catholicism have ever entered, I stand near the center of things. In my daily life as a theologian, the tensions I unpack in this book are inescapable. Each day, as I walk into my classroom, read another theology book, make decisions in my office, or participate in the community liturgies in our school chapel, I am faced with the question of how to reconcile the Catholic and feminist parts of myself.

From this unusual vantage point, I offer this book as a companion for days of anger and hope, disappointment and communion, fatigue and renewal. I situate the Catholic feminism that sustains me within the broader landscape of Catholic feminist possibilities. Walking together, readers identifying with some combination of Catholicism and feminism may not end up in exactly the same place, but I hope each will come away more able to imagine authentic and complicated possibilities of Catholic feminist identity and belonging.

1

Authentically Human

What was probably the first essay in feminist theology was written by Valerie Saiving in 1960. At a time when there were hardly any women studying theology, she wrote, "I am a student of theology. I am also a woman." Saiving challenged the primacy of pride in the Christian account of sin and suggested that, for some people, especially women, too much selflessness was detrimental.[1] When I first read it, thirty years later, I saw through new eyes my aunts, my mom, and my grandmother, as well as many other women around me. Though the essay's generalizations about gender will rightly trouble the contemporary reader, it is still read today because Saiving identified what seemed to be a glaring tension between Christian and feminist understandings of what it means to be human. In exposing the limits of self-sacrifice and showing the necessity of self-affirmation, Saiving hit a nerve.

Though she sought to use her experience as a woman and studies of gender in other disciplines to strengthen the Christian tradition's account of being human, it was not entirely clear even then that feminism and Christianity could be reconciled on this question. Feminism is associated with freedom, choice, and empowerment, while self-sacrifice is central to the Christian life of discipleship. Some feminists have come to believe that religion must be left behind precisely because of the damaging effects of its rhetoric of self-denial. Some Christians find feminism unattractive because they believe it denies the value of giving up one's own desires for the sake of others.

The problem is even more salient in contemporary Catholic circles. Catholic teaching identifies total self-giving as the calling of

Can You Be a Catholic and a Feminist?. Julie Hanlon Rubio, Oxford University Press.
© Oxford University Press 2024. DOI: 10.1093/oso/9780197553145.003.0002

12 CAN YOU BE A CATHOLIC AND A FEMINIST?

all people of faith, but women are understood to naturally excel at giving themselves for others and are called to embrace this calling, especially, though not exclusively, within the family. Pope John Paul II named self-sacrifice as essential to women's "special genius," and subsequent popes have continued to use this language in the context of a theology of "complementarity" that stresses differences between men and women.[2] Women's exclusion from most ecclesial leadership roles seems to suggest that women's empowerment is irreconcilable with a Catholic understanding of gender.

The questions raised by Saiving are not limited to academic circles. Many women continue to struggle with the relative importance of self-sacrifice and freedom. In this chapter, I will highlight two stories that capture popular alternatives. But both feminism and Catholicism are more complicated than these stories. By going more deeply into each tradition and weaving them together, I try to construct an authentic Catholic feminist vision of being human that balances solidarity with freedom. The material in this chapter might seem abstract at points, but my hope is to show that understandings of what it means to be human lie at the heart of the tensions between Catholicism and feminism. Getting a balanced vision in place is crucial to working through the more practical questions I take up in the rest of the book.

Tensions: Becoming Myself or Being for Others?

Out of concern for the many women who struggle with a tendency to give too much of themselves away, popular feminism often centers the self. The phrase "You are enough," attributed to author Mandy Hale, and prominent in Instagram posts, Twitter hashtags, and self-help books, affirms women as worthy or "good enough."[3] This self-acceptance movement is a response to pervasive feelings of insufficiency and a widely shared sense that in order to be valuable, one must be constantly productive and self-giving. While not unique to women, its central place in women's public conversation indicates that many women experience a need for self-affirmation.

What I call "Eat-Pray-Love feminism," referencing Elizabeth Gilbert's best-selling book, goes further by privileging freedom, romance, and the embrace of a life beyond mere duty.[4] The smart, beautiful, witty Gilbert can be seen as an icon of this new strain of popular feminism. In her best-selling memoir, Gilbert tells the story of her quest to find new life after a difficult divorce. She travels alone, enjoys beauty and culinary delights in Italy, tries long days of meditation in an ashram in India, and, in Indonesia, has a love affair with a kind, handsome Brazilian man, whom she later marries (they subsequently divorces). After a year immersing herself in pleasure, devotion, and love, the trappings of "should" no longer restrain her. She ends the book free and happy. Her feminist story resonates because it suggests one need not adhere to a predetermined social script in order to be a good person.

The feminist movement in the United States has often been associated with women's quest for freedom, with good reason. In the 1963 bestseller *The Feminine Mystique*, Betty Friedan gave voice to the dissatisfaction of mostly white, middle-class, educated women caring for husbands, kids, and homes.[5] Because prevailing wisdom held that women should be fulfilled in lives spent in service to others, many women mistrusted their own feelings of meaninglessness and ignored desires for something more. Psychologists tried to help them adjust to their role, and women's magazines offered tips for avoiding depression. Friedan's alternative solution for fulfillment drew from prevailing secular psychological models that juxtaposed independence and career with dependence and caretaking. In feminist consciousness-raising groups, this call for a life of one's own resonated with millions of American women who were tired of hearing that being good humans meant giving up their aspirations for the sake of family.

14 CAN YOU BE A CATHOLIC AND A FEMINIST?

However, the feminist quest for space to nurture a sense of self goes back even further. In 1929, Virginia Woolf tried to answer the question of why so few women have been writers. For a woman "to have a room of her own, let alone a quiet or sound proof room, was out of the question," she wrote.[6] Occupied by the needs of others and told repeatedly of their lack of suitability for the creative arts, few women have had the experience of "freeing whole and entire the work that is in [them]" so that "the poetry flows from them," as it does for the best artists.[7] Similar themes appear in the writings of working-class feminists such as Tillie Olsen, who speaks of the silences that remain in history because women were so busy being "the angel[s] in the house" that they had no time for work of their own.[8]

Friedan and Woolf are often labeled liberal feminists due to their assertions of men's and women's common humanity and concern with equal rights. This is in contrast to radical feminists who stress women's uniqueness and want to overturn patriarchy full stop. But concern for self, growth, and fulfillment mark both kinds of feminists. Mary Daly, who began the 1960s as a reformist Catholic theologian, exited the decade a radical philosopher with her own language for talking about being—or, really, becoming.[9] Daly's existentialist concerns echoed liberal feminist Simone de Beauvoir's depictions of women's yearning for life beyond the confinements of gender.[10] Both liberal and radical feminists drew attention to women's desires to fashion lives of their choosing.

One can even hear echoes of liberal and radical thinkers in postmodernist feminists. These feminists share with liberal feminists a commitment to becoming versus being. Rejecting the idea that anything is "natural," postmodern feminists recommend instead an openness to future possibility. "Wisdom lies in the unexpected and the unanticipated," one says: "To recognize new forms of politics, social structures, and personhood, we really have to take some big leaps into the unknown."[11] Religious postmodernists emphasize the Christian tradition's diversity and development over its "origins" stories, like the Creation narratives in the book of Genesis. The emphasis is on human agency and responsibility. To be human is to respond to God's invitation to flourish, not to fit into a predetermined mold. One writes, "There is space for newness, for things to be other than they were destined to be in 'givenness' from the 'beginning of time.'"[12] This theology admits of no limits, for to privilege some ways of life over others would be to claim a certainty we do not possess. We cannot say anything definitively about *being* human; we can only lift up human *becoming*. In feminisms postmodern, radical, liberal, and popular, the open-ended quest to become one's true self is a dominant theme. Gilbert's quest for self-discovery with no determined endpoint stands in a tradition of feminist concerns for freedom that cannot be easily dismissed.

But is feminism really this open? Catholic author Colleen Carroll Campbell rejects contemporary feminism not because it is without limits, but because it seems not to value the choices women like her make to sacrifice for the sake of faith and family. In her book *My Sisters, the Saints: A Spiritual Memoir*, Campbell describes her encounter with feminism in college, where she says she learned that to be human is to be career-hungry, not sacrificing for husband or kids but striving for fame, wealth, and status.[13] Though taken in at first, she is soon tired, lonely, and miserable. Eventually she finds more compelling inspiration in the stories of women saints who embraced self-sacrifice. She leaves Washington, DC, and her job as a speechwriter for the president to return to St. Louis, care for her sick father, and marry the man she loves. Her Christlike "little way" is exemplified by pregnancy, as Campbell and her husband move through infertility, miscarriage, and difficult deliveries of their children. She writes, "Lying cruciform on the operating table with the doctor frantically cutting my baby out of my womb, I realized what day it was: September 14, The Triumph of the Cross."[14] Campbell sees selflessness as the core of being human for all Christians, no matter their vocation. For her, feminists who claim to be radically open implicitly reject life choices like hers, because privileging

16   CAN YOU BE A CATHOLIC AND A FEMINIST?

becoming without limits inevitably destabilizes obligations to parents, spouses, and children. Faced with that feminist-Catholic divide, she chooses Catholicism.

Campbell represents a "new orthodox" strain of contemporary Catholicism, but even mainstream Catholic piety is notable for its focus on self-sacrifice.[15] For the most part, it has yet to integrate the feminist critique made by Saiving more than sixty years ago. Believers are encouraged to "take up your cross," "seek not to be loved but to love," be "a man or woman for others," or "give without counting the cost."[16] This piety is not out of sync with much of contemporary Catholic theology, which places self-renunciation at the center of Christian life. This language is not necessarily gendered; everyone is called to sacrifice. This is an essential part of what it means to *be* human. Mainstream Catholic piety sends a message of self-denial that is very much at odds with important strains of contemporary feminist thought.

Not long ago, the Christian message of self-sacrifice was both more gendered and more extreme. In the mid-twentieth century, the theology of the "Eternal Woman," treated most comprehensively in a 1934 book by German scholar Gertrud von le Fort, was ubiquitous.[17] Le Fort stressed female attributes of surrender, sacrifice, and passivity, and wrote that the Catholic role model for women, Mary, is powerful precisely because she surrenders her power. Taking a cue from Mary, "Wheresoever woman is most profoundly herself, she is not as herself but as surrendered, and wherever she is surrendered, there she is also bride and mother."[18] This ideology was echoed in popular Catholic publications of the time, which few Catholic women would have been able to avoid. "Literally, woman was to forgo her own personality as part of her sacrifice for others. She was told to strive for 'silence of mouth, mind, and will' and that 'losing herself in other people' was her vocation; woman was desirous of diffusing herself into others. Her only self-expression was to be her sacrifice and suffering."[19]

Today's Catholic theology speaks less of surrender than total self-giving. Pope John Paul II centered this description of Christian life in the late twentieth century. In some ways it is very traditional. Christians have always been called to lose their lives in service to others (Matthew 16:25). But John Paul II used personalist philosophy to give life to the ancient call, adding romance and modern notions of human nature. For him, the fundamental vocation of all persons is to love.[20] Whether male or female, celibate or married, to be human is to value giving over receiving. But it is difficult to disentangle sacrifice and gender. In the late pope's writing on women, the "genius" identified as female is the talent for seeing others with the heart, treating others with compassion, and serving them.[21] Men are also called to generosity, but women are understood to naturally excel at it, and because their familial role is primary, even though they are also called to serve the world, their lives are inevitably more circumscribed by their commitments to others at home.

The controversy over Justice Amy Coney Barrett's nomination to the Supreme Court in 2020 can be better understood in light of these tensions between feminism and Catholicism, between being for oneself and being for others. Many feminists worried about Barrett because she is a politically conservative, Catholic mother of seven associated with a religious movement that seemed to uphold differentiated and sacrificial roles for women.[22] Clearly, this did not prevent Catholic women adherents from having powerful careers. The "Eternal Feminine" of the 1960s differs from today's new orthodox feminism. Barrett holds in tension traditional Catholic faith and substantial public commitments. Unlike Campbell, Barrett has not written about feminism. But I suspect they share a deep appreciation for the tradition's call to limit personal freedom and embrace sacrifice.[23] These stories suggest that being human comes with an obligation to be for others, and that worries feminists like Gilbert who instead center the quest to become a self.

18 CAN YOU BE A CATHOLIC AND A FEMINIST?

Common Threads in Christian and Feminist Accounts of Sloth

The tensions between becoming myself and being for others may seem to lead to two irreconcilable visions of being human, but both feminism and Christianity are capable of holding the two together. Christians are to love their neighbors *as* (not instead of) themselves (Mark 12:31), and feminists have long seen commitment to social change (not self-expression alone) as central to the movement. An exploration of Christian and feminist writing on the vice of "acedia," or sloth, will help illuminate common threads. Understanding sloth can help point us toward a way of being human that holds together Gilbert's becoming myself with Campbell's being for others.

Historically, the vice of sloth was often rendered as laziness, while productivity was lauded as a virtue.[24] Sometimes today, the vice is embraced. One famous feminist playwright once wrote a book on the vice of sloth in which she celebrated her own laziness. More recently, Jenny O'Dell has lifted up the importance of "doing nothing."[25] However, sloth is not simply doing nothing. It can also be what O'Dell decries—a constant state of unfocused hyper-productivity. Both idleness and busyness can be considered slothful because both are ways of avoiding the kind of focused work of which humans are capable.

The Christian tradition speaks about sloth not primarily as laziness or busyness but as a failure to love God and others. According to Christian philosopher Rebecca DeYoung, *both* laziness and busyness are problematic, not because they lead to low productivity but because they allow us to escape from engaging with the reality and meaning of human existence.[26] For Christians, productive work is not the answer to sloth, nor is it an end in itself. Being slothful is going through the motions in life without due consciousness of where we are going or what all of our activity is for. In contrast, virtue is consciously seeking God and surrendering to God's desires for one's life.

AUTHENTICALLY HUMAN 19

Christian accounts also see sloth in the failure to attend to one's spiritual core by seeking wisdom. Thomas Aquinas argues that everyone has a call to pursue wisdom and to avoid being overwhelmed by this work. Sloth, he says, is the lack of disciplined attention to "one's spiritual good." One overcomes this sin by perseverance, for "the more we think about spiritual goods, the more pleasing they become to us, and forthwith sloth dies away."[27] If disciplined focus on what is most important is key, not thinking about God is a serious problem. Thomas sees sloth not simply as a feeling but as "deliberate resistance" to doing a good thing.[28] It is problematic for two reasons. First, for Christians, human beings are fundamentally oriented toward their Creator. Recognition of being loved by God should lead to joy, not resistance. Second, we are commanded to rest in God on the Sabbath, but sluggishness can lead to avoidance of spiritual practice. The failure to turn our hearts and minds to the God who desires to be in relation with us is, for Thomas, slothful and a rejection of who we really are.

Contemporary Christian writers on sloth bring these dimensions together, emphasizing that because the love of God and love of others are inseparable, sloth has vertical and horizontal dimensions. Both lack of effort in religious practice and lack of effort in relating to other people are outward manifestations of the inner condition of avoiding God. Sloth is a vice "because it involves inner resistance and coldness toward one's spiritual calling or identity."[29] We resist loving God and we resist deeply loving and being deeply loved by others.

On the vertical sloth axis, instead of experiencing joy in closeness to God, we feel disinterest and desire to avoid spiritual depth. Professing belief does not necessarily guarantee ongoing transformation in response to God. This is hard work requiring vulnerability and a willingness to change. Because humans are wired for growth in holiness, without it, Christian authors claim, we are restless. Sloth is "resistance to the transformation that God's love works in us, and in particular the painful nature of the death of the

20 CAN YOU BE A CATHOLIC AND A FEMINIST?

old self—that is, our willingness to . . . be made new."[30] Clinging to the old self and its familiar habits feels more comfortable than surrendering to God. Some cling to restless activity and prefer not to think about questions of ultimate meaning. Others become overwhelmed and are prone to despair.

Avoiding the demanding nature of a relationship with God also has a horizontal axis—avoiding the demands of relationships with other people. Just as it is easier to avoid spending time in God's presence, it is also easier to avoid spending focused time with people you love. Sometimes fidelity to relationships necessitates change, but sloth's resistance to the work of conversion holds us back. Though it is tempting to believe that, when we meet "the One," marriage will be effortless, Catholic theologian Richard Gaillardetz argues that spouses need to embrace the "paschal" nature of marriage by dying to their old selves and becoming the persons their spouses need.[31] Gaillardetz insists, "You always marry the wrong person," and calls for working at marriage for a lifetime, by striving to be the person you need to be in your marriage.

For Christians, overcoming sloth means refusing to take the easy way out with God and other people. Sloth is not opposed to industriousness; it is opposed to love. To overcome sloth, we have to "face up to the sources of our own resistance to the demands of our relationship to God, rather than grasping at a way out or a ready diversion any time we start to feel stretched or uncomfortable."[32] The same is true for relationships with other people. Sloth in the contemporary Christian tradition means resisting the challenging demands of being in relationship with God and others. When sloth is a problem, a person lives the life of her choosing, but may lose touch with the transcendental and relational dimensions of her personhood. The Christian tradition calls believers to reject sloth and embrace the vulnerability of surrendering to relation with God and others, and it claims that fulfillment is found only in this sort of life.

It should be clear at this point that most feminists would push back against a path to avoid sloth involving radical surrender to God and to the demands of loved ones, without qualification. What I call "Eat Pray Love" feminism, exemplified by Gilbert, can prioritize personal well-being over obligations to God and others, substituting an approach to spirituality and friendship that asks for very little. When Gilbert falls for Felipe in Bali, their sexual synergy is central, they envision a life in multiple locations around the world requiring little sacrifice by either of them, and Gilbert's days of meditating in the ashram seem mostly irrelevant. Concern for others is manifest only in a fundraiser for a family Gilbert befriended in Bali. Otherwise, there is little reflection on the responsibilities that might accompany a life of privilege. However, most feminist thinkers do not dispute the importance of continual wisdom-seeking or commitments to loved ones involving sacrifice. They do stress the importance of self-regard and duties to others outside the family. The good life for feminists requires attention to self as well as to building a better society, and that means avoiding what might be seen as another kind of sloth: inattention to self and the work of becoming.

Second-wave feminism, set in motion by Betty Friedan's *Feminine Mystique*, disputed the self-sacrificial ideal of womanhood and encouraged both personal and political empowerment. Like their first-wave sisters, second-wave feminists were concerned with social welfare and advocated for women's roles beyond motherhood. Consciousness-raising groups helped women who had lost a sense of themselves apart from duties to family link self-empowerment with concern for others in social activism.[33]

Women of color (some embraced the feminist label and others did not) were often more concerned with racial and economic injustice than with sexism, but they also called out stereotypes of Black women as powerful enough to do it all that hindered them. Their struggles involved the complex intersection of race and gender, but they were not untouched by social norms demanding

22 CAN YOU BE A CATHOLIC AND A FEMINIST?

self-giving of women.[34] Some dreamed of a better life for women centered not on surrender but on empowerment and justice. In her 1978 essay "The Erotic as Power," feminist poet and essayist Audre Lorde argued that the same passion we associate with sex, romantic partners, children, and self-development could also feed art, work, and justice. She claimed that when people are in touch with their emotional core, "our acts against oppression become integral with self, motivated and empowered from within. In touch with the erotic, I become less willing to accept powerlessness, or those other states of being which are not native to me, such as resignation, despair, self-effacement, depression, self-denial."[35] For feminists, attending to one's own becoming was not slothful. This important internal work often led to struggles against oppressive social systems.

The feminist alternative remedy to sloth acknowledges what Saiving named as sins to which women are particularly prone— "triviality, distractibility, and diffuseness; lack of an organizing center, dependence on others for one's own self-definition . . . underdevelopment or negation of the self."[36] Feminists offered an alternative vision of the self and the good life based on an integrated vision of a person animated by love for self *and* others, both near and distant.

Second-wave feminist activists gave life to this vision by working against laws that limited women's choice of profession, financial independence, and bodily autonomy, as well as by fighting for better healthcare, day care, and wages that would allow women to flourish at work and at home.[37] Feminist ideals of the human person and the good life involved both personal seeking and participation in political movements aimed at better lives for all. The classic feminist statement, "The personal is political," embodies this. My personal decisions about everything from clothes to marriage to parenting are not only significant for me, but affect others. Personal choices are always shaped by social structures, and social structures are in turn shaped by individuals. Attending to individual lives is not trivial, but part of a broader social transformation. Given social norms pressing women to put aside their own desires, focus on the self is understood by feminists as necessary to virtue.

Naming self-love and the struggle for justice as aspects of authentic selfhood and the good life is essential to moving beyond Eat Pray Love feminism and an overly sacrificial Christian spirituality that can unwittingly encourage self-neglect. Feminists speak from experience of the problem of excessive sacrifice for others, and rightly worry that uncritical demands for self-giving can encourage acceptance of suffering. In the face of pervasive sexism, caution in the face of the language of surrender is appropriate. Yet if a quest for becoming devoid of vertical and horizontal dimensions is hollow, some focus on becoming is a necessary foundation for just relationships, personal and political.

In sum, the Christian tradition on sloth upholds the importance of sacrifice and grapples with the perils of not being willing to be stretched and changed for God and others. Feminism insists that developing one's self is essential to avoiding sloth and that loving others well requires work for social change. Both Gilbert's and Campbell's feminisms are insufficient, but a deep read of Catholic tradition and feminism yields more complexity. Being for others requires becoming oneself and vice versa.

Rethinking the Self: What Does It Mean to Be Authentic?

Thus far I have traced diverging and converging lines in feminist and Christian thinking on being for oneself and being for others. It seems important at this point to acknowledge a parallel conversation among philosophers that raises questions about terms such as "the self" and "authenticity" that I have been using with the assumption that we all know what we are talking about. Though I cannot do justice to these thinkers here, I want to suggest that the

24 CAN YOU BE A CATHOLIC AND A FEMINIST?

questions they raise map onto feminist conversations and can help us see the importance of authentic selfhood for the central question of this book.

Philosopher Charles Taylor's *Sources of the Self* and *Ethics of Authenticity* are major works on the history and use of these central concepts.[38] In the former, Taylor tells the story of how we came to think of the self as something to struggle for, of the growing need for modern people to be original or unique, not just like everyone else. He shows that through the Reformation, Renaissance, and Enlightenment, increasing focus was placed on the individual subject, and with that came rights and duties but also anxieties. The latter is the impetus behind Taylor's argument for a version of authenticity beyond mere selfishness that still upholds the value of being true to oneself. To be authentic, Taylor argues, does not mean to define oneself over against one's relationships or a transcendent purpose, but it does require attention to self and to the search for a meaningful life project.

Taylor contrasts his understanding of authenticity with a thinner subjectivism, or what we might call individualism. As he sees it, some popular conceptions of the self give excessive primacy to choice, suggesting that to choose for myself is to live authentically. Being true to oneself is key to modernity, and moderns rightly value responsibility, freedom, and even originality.[39] However, Taylor argues, the idea of authenticity demands some account of value. All choices are not equally good or important. Some choices are significant, and others might be at least problematic. Against all types of individualism without limits, Taylor seeks to give freedom its due while insisting on the possibility of meaningful moral choices and their opposites. "It may be important that my life be chosen . . . but unless some options are more significant than others, the very idea of self-choice falls into triviality and hence incoherence."[40] Choice alone cannot confer authenticity; only significant moral choices can do that.

Modernity, Taylor notes, also privileges relationships as key to identity and meaning. If this is so, he claims, relationships ought to be nontentative and noninstrumental.[41] Authenticity cannot mean using people or only committing to them as long as they serve my interests. Though this may sound unhelpfully countercultural, Taylor contends that modern poetry, beloved by so many, suggests that being true to oneself, and expressing one's deepest desires, can move a person to care for others.[42] We know that obligations to others to whom we are in relation do not contradict authenticity. A good, authentic life balances self-care with care for and by others who contribute to my life's meaning.

This complex understanding of authenticity is attractive, but theologian Andrew Prevot calls attention to the whiteness of Taylor's account. He wonders why Taylor does not attend to Black struggles. His question is, "How to be black and a self?"[43] Rejecting postmodernist solutions offering only endless possibilities, he presents as an alternative Sojourner Truth, who finds in God the source of her sense of self and her hope.[44] Truth's life's struggle for freedom for herself and others offers a model of an authentic Black self. Similarly, feminists seek an authentic self that can speak to the realities women's lives. They ask, "How to be female and a self?" And how can our account of self ground something other than a life of endless generosity *or* endless possibility? Prevot's turn to Truth hints at the potential of a Christian, feminist vision.

Solidarity and Freedom

I began this chapter with the questions of an early feminist theologian who dared to ask if the Christian propensity to identify sin with pride neglected women's struggles to become their own selves. She wanted to know if women could sin by being too selfless, whether they might be harmed when told repeatedly to be a person for others. While our ideas about gender are more complicated today, we can still hear Saiving's concerns in jokes about "Catholic guilt" and the popularity of the phrase "You are enough," especially in women's circles.

Does being Catholic entail accepting a view of being human that is fundamentally at odds with a contemporary feminist vision? I don't think so. I approached this problem by going more deeply into each tradition, considering feminism as becoming myself versus Christianity as being for others. I found common ground between the two traditions by looking at their approaches to sloth. Both are more complicated than popular debates allow. Philosophical treatments of selfhood moved us beyond binaries in which becoming an authentic self and being for others are always opposed toward authenticity. It seems possible that a Catholic feminist could hold together aspects of the two traditions that compel her. Holding them in tension might even allow for a more wholistic vision. What might this entail?

To answer Saiving, it is crucial to bring the feminist becoming myself into Christian conversation. Feminist consciousness complicates Christian discussions of being for others, of self-giving and surrender. There is no way to achieve authentic selfhood without acknowledging the reality of ongoing pressures for female sacrifice and the long history of denial of women's self-determining freedom, which is further deepened by racism and economic inequality. In an essay titled "This Is My Body," Theresa Delgado both upholds and questions the idea of self-giving for others.[45] Yes, as humans we are called into relationship, called to be like our God in three persons—a being-in-relation. But because this message is inevitably communicated in gendered ways, particularly but not only in Latino/a culture, Catholic women can be subjected to emotional or bodily harm. A culture of submission for women can be destructive. Respect for women's embodied selves has to be more explicit in Christian understandings of what it means to be human.

But the being for others piece is also crucial. Christian consciousness troubles uncritical feminist assertions of agency, choice, and

AUTHENTICALLY HUMAN 27

freedom that have a great deal of resonance today. The Christian tradition's understanding of self-in-relation to God and others means neither sacrifice nor obligation can be avoided. Feminist consciousness of how gendered and distorted these concepts can become is crucial, but some account of self-giving to God and others is necessary to the Christian tradition. Becoming myself and being for others belong together, and bringing Catholic and feminist views together gets us closer a balanced view.

Like self and others, becoming and being have to be balanced. A notion of human beings as creatures of a certain kind is central to Christian faith. Christianity grounds its anthropology (or its vision of what it means to be human) in the Creation narratives of Genesis, interpreted as affirming three central truths: (1) humanity is created by God in God's image (Genesis 1:26), free (Genesis 2:15–16), and good (Genesis 1:31); (2) humans are made for relationship, especially "one flesh" relationship (Genesis 2: 24) with shared responsibility for stewardship of the earth (Genesis 1:28); and (3) humans are plagued by sin from the beginning (Genesis 3). This is who we are, the criteria against which to measure any human project. Feminists have, for good reasons, rejected static notions of being, such as those limiting women's roles to the home or ascribing to women motherly qualities that not all women find in themselves. It has been important for feminists to stress the good work of becoming a self, as Woolf does when she claims a room of her own, as Lorde does when she connects with the erotic power within her, as Truth does when she strikes out on her own to become a savior for her people. Even as both traditions have within them more complicated views, each tradition brings something important to the quest for an authentic way to be and become a person.

If the being piece sounds worrisome, it need not be. Having some account of who humans are is necessary for ethics, as long as it does not say too much. Feminist ethicist Margaret Farley strikes the right balance in her "just love" sexual ethic. She argues that when we experience the concrete reality of the persons in our lives, we see that human beings are both free and relational. They deserve to have their freedom and their relationality respected. We know that it is wrong to force other people to submit to our will or to treat them as objects. With this account of what it means to be human, we can say something about sexual ethics. We can say that loving others justly means respecting their freedom by seeking their consent and doing no unjust harm to them. We can say that respecting their relationality requires norms of fidelity, equality, and mutuality.[46] Just, loving relationships are possible, if human freedom and relationality are respected. This is not a sexual ethic of total openness or a blueprint with answers for every situation. It is an ethic that sets certain limits appropriate to who humans are.

If becoming seems too open-ended, it need not be. In her prophetic book *Enfleshing Freedom: Body, Race, and Being*, M. Shawn Copeland showing how white Christians who claimed to believe in the dignity of human beings consistently and violently denied it in Black people through the eras of slavery, lynching, and Jim Crow.[47] Conversely, Black women and men provide prophetic witness to Christian beliefs about human beings in their resistance to slavery and the limitations placed upon them. They rejected the lies they were told and asserted their rights to be free, to love, to raise their children, and to worship their God. Humans made in God's image were made for love, freedom, and creativity. When Blacks fought for freedom, they were fighting for their right to become more than they were allowed to be when enslaved. In Copeland's powerful telling, to be a self is to claim agency and to be in relation to God and others near and far. Humans are made not for domination or complacency, but for the freedom to become somebody. It is not slothful to love one's self or to desire to live with authenticity a life of one's own. In fact, doing so can mean that more rather than less will be required of us.

But the freedom of becoming is always limited by the duty of solidarity in Catholic feminist thought. Solidarity entails commitment to God and other people, with a focus on the most vulnerable, without asking for excessive self-denial. In contemporary Catholic social thought, solidarity is a virtue that firmly grounds us in obligations to others. The virtue is one to which all Christians are called, though we live it out in different ways. Copeland notes that this principle of Catholic social thought is ritualized in Catholic sacramental practice. As Catholics participate in the Eucharist, taking in the body of Christ "nourishes, strengthens, and orders us as we make visible his body through a praxis of solidarity, which counters the disorder of this world."[48] We practice in the liturgy by gathering together in Christ, so that we can *be* the body of Christ in the world, taking up engaged, mindful, activity in the service of solidarity.

Finally, a feminist version of solidarity provides a remedy for sloth that is challenging but not overwhelming. It calls us out of complacency, but rather than feeling obliged to embrace endless generosity or possibility, we are called to a deeper understanding of what it means to be human in a broken world. To be sure, solidarity can lead to anxiety and perfectionism. Conscious of my connection to others and responsibility to participate in the healing of the world, I may construct endless to-do lists of service commitments, advocacy, and efforts to live more simply. However, bringing Christianity and feminism together offers a corrective to this tendency to obsessiveness by affirming the importance of self-regard. I am not called to do everything but to discern what God is calling me to contribute to the project of returning the world to wholeness. Each one of us can focus on how to use our particular gifts to heal the world's brokenness.

Approaching the world's suffering with Eat Pray Love feminism or an uncritical sacrificial version of Christian piety can be either evasive or overwhelming. A Catholic feminist can embrace instead a more complex affirmation of humans as made for freedom, relation, and solidarity that coheres with fundamental Christian claims about God and persons created in God's image. She can also embrace a more complex feminist acknowledgment of the human

30 CAN YOU BE A CATHOLIC AND A FEMINIST?

need for becoming that is inextricably tied to politics. From this authentic Catholic feminist place, it is possible to better love ourselves, those to whom we are attached, and those we may never know, whose suffering nonetheless presses us beyond distraction or despair to action.

2

Sex

In 2017 the #MeToo and #ChurchToo movements came together to raise profound questions for many, including Catholics. As millions of women joined together to protest against sexual violence, Catholic women noticed their church's silence, the seeming lack of concern about their bodies.[1] At the same time, they confronted the sins of priests, bishops, and popes. Excluding women from the hierarchy hardly seemed to be producing good results. Many women stopped going to Mass or putting money in the collection basket. Some even went on strike.[2] Suddenly the possibility of not being Catholic was beginning to seem plausible, even to many women who had been in the church all their lives. Staying in the face of egregious failures seemed unconscionable.

Feminists have been on the front lines of movements to end violence against women since the 1960s, and have offered a thorough analysis of the "rape culture" that enables the prevalence of sexual violence.[3] "Rape culture" is the idea that pervasive cultural values and beliefs about sex and gender, as well as accompanying practices and structures, enable rape. Rape is not an aberration, but an extension, of normative sex and gender scripts. I remember encountering this analysis when I showed up for the first day of a women's studies class in college, where clips of the film *Rape Culture* were played.[4] Though I considered myself progressive, the sweeping indictment of mainstream culture and the acknowledgment of pervasive sexual violence were overwhelming. I dropped the class. Though it deeply embarrasses me now, I also remember trying to understand what made some women vulnerable to violence. In hindsight, it seems obvious that I was evading my own vulnerability and the reality

Can You Be a Catholic and a Feminist?. Julie Hanlon Rubio, Oxford University Press.
© Oxford University Press 2024. DOI: 10.1093/oso/9780197553145.003.0003

32 CAN YOU BE A CATHOLIC AND A FEMINIST?

that fighting sexual violence required so much more than avoiding and punishing "bad guys." I didn't get it.

Catholics have often been silent on sexual violence, not getting it. Though rates of clerical abuse of minors have decreased significantly, the church has decades of clergy sexual abuse of minors and cover-up to answer for and still struggles to respond well to allegations of abuse.[5] Though Catholics now speak of sexual violence as sin, feminists rightly point to religious leaders and cultures that keep women from leaving violent relationships and prevent their healing.[6] If being a feminist means understanding how internalized and structural sexism enables violence, and the church resists structural reforms in its own house and in society, being a Catholic seems that much harder.

But some Catholics worry that feminist solutions to sexual violence fail to acknowledge the sacredness of sex and the negative impact of too much sexual freedom. For them, the sexual revolution is a factor not only in sexual abuse but in the much more pervasive "bad sex" influenced by pornography, objectification, and the idea that sex is best when no strings are attached. If being Catholic means holding some account of sex tied to human dignity and commitment, being a feminist seems that much more difficult.

A Catholic feminist may have something unique offer to the #MeToo movement precisely because she is able to hold Catholicism and feminism together. While rarely standing side by side in public witness against sexual violence, both feminists and Catholics have important ideas that can contribute to our understanding of why sexual violence remains so prevalent, how victim-survivors are harmed, and what work is necessary to dismantle violence-enabling structures. In this chapter, I will describe the divide between feminist and Catholic responses to #MeToo, map the overlap in feminist and Catholic analyses of sex, and offer suggestions for moving forward drawn from a synthesis of feminist and Catholic thought. I aim to show not only that it is possible to be a Catholic feminist working to dismantle rape culture, but that the

SEX 33

unique strengths of both traditions are crucial to making progress. In the case of sexual violence, knowing the depth of Catholicism and feminism and blending them together is both possible and necessary.

Feminist Engagement and Catholic Silence

When the *New York Times* broke the Harvey Weinstein story, attention to sexual violence skyrocketed and we entered a new cultural moment. Thanks to courageous women and their allies, a better conversation on sexual violence was beginning. The #MeToo movement, which was founded in 2006 by African American activist Tarana Burke, emerged as a social media phenomenon in 2017. Thanks to this movement, hundreds of powerful men who harassed women lost their jobs. Funds were provided to help victims of sexual harassment bring their cases to court, and there have been some small changes in state and federal employment law, as well as a rise in required employee sexual harassment training programs, which have a mixed success record.[7] The most significant contribution of the #MeToo movement was bringing about cultural change in the form of increasing support for victim-survivors who speak out and decreasing tolerance for perpetrators.[8]

The #MeToo movement has drawn attention not only to the most egregious cases of sexual violence but to the more ambiguous, but no less disturbing, accounts of "bad sex."[9] The published report of one woman's sexual encounter with popular TV star and author Aziz Ansari, published by Babe.net, exemplifies the blurriness.[10] According to the woman's account, she accompanied Ansari back to his apartment after a dinner date. She repeatedly tried to resist his sexual advances with verbal and nonverbal cues, to no avail. Both the crassness of his attempts at sexual intimacy (seemingly drawn from a pornography script) and the difficulty his date had in extricating herself despite her discomfort struck a chord with

34 CAN YOU BE A CATHOLIC AND A FEMINIST?

women readers. "#MeToo," they tweeted. This was not shocking; it was just a typical bad date. A fictional story published in the *New Yorker*, called "Cat Person," was similarly ambiguous and, according to readers, ordinary.[11] Like Ansari, the man in the story is not overtly cruel or forceful during their sexual encounter, yet the script he employs is high on dominance and low on intimacy, and the woman goes along in spite of her reservations. A few months after she breaks up with him, he sees her at a bar and sends a cruel text, punishing her for leaving him. The *New York Times* interviewed hundreds of college-aged women and found the same phrases over and over again, "I didn't want to hurt his feelings," "I thought I owed him," "I wanted to be nice."[12] Thousands of women saw their own experiences reflected in these accounts and connected them to the feminist, anti-sexual-violence movement.

Extending the fight against sexual violence to cases like these quickly provoked a backlash, too.[13] French women published a letter suggesting women should not worry so much if their boss "touched a knee," lest they lose hard-won sexual liberation. Some prominent men argued that the balance had shifted too far, hampering both dating and the right of the accused to a fair hearing. "Don't take this too far, now," these writers seemed to caution. There is nothing amiss that clear communication and consent cannot fix. This is about assault, not sex; law, not morality.

Feminists pushed back, arguing that sex shaped by male privilege and male-dominant scripts is inherently problematic. The lines between rape and rape-culture-infused ordinary "bad sex" are not at all clear, argued Jessica Valenti.[14] Sexism, sexual violence, and bad sex cannot be completely disentangled because sex, as feminists have long argued, is inseparable from gender and power. Though some radical feminists hold that, given rape culture, no heterosexual sex can be equal, most make the subtler point that the sexual landscape "is socially conditioned by violence and gendered expectations regarding women's availability and submission and men's correlative sexual domination."[15] Rape is not just about power; it is about sex, or the way sex has been socially constructed as domination and submission. This is the patriarchal landscape that feminists work to dismantle, though this agenda remains difficult without a more substantial account of sexual ethics.

Catholics have not been major players in the #MeToo movement. A comparison to other issues can be instructive. There is a long history of Catholic advocacy for immigrants, which is rooted in US Catholic immigrant identity. The witness of Scripture is understood to be unambiguous, and there is a long list of documentary evidence to draw upon. Catholic groups all over the world lobby on behalf of and care for immigrants and refugees. The US Catholic bishops have spoken unequivocally about the right to migrate and the duty of wealthy countries to welcome refugees.[16] They have traveled to the Mexican border to protest US family separation policies. Catholic presence at marches is substantial, and prayer vigils, pilgrimages, and teach-ins have been held at parishes across the country. Immigration is a justice issue with fundamental place in Catholic social thought and practice.

By contrast, despite threats to legal progress on sexual violence and a huge movement calling attention to its pervasiveness and harm, there has been little Catholic engagement with the #MeToo movement: no official action from the US bishops, no major statements from individual bishops, anemic official Catholic presence at public protests, scattered attention in the Catholic press, and silence in most Catholic organizations and parishes—not even a nod from Pope Francis.[17] To understand why, we need to consider Catholic thinking on justice, gender, and the clergy sexual abuse scandal.

The language of justice that is so central to Catholic social thought is less often applied to sex, gender, marriage, or family. Though Catholic social thought includes reflection on what society owes families and on the social responsibilities of families, relationships between family members are generally treated under the virtue of love, often rendered as total self-gift. Sexual relationships outside

36 CAN YOU BE A CATHOLIC AND A FEMINIST?

marriage are declared inherently unethical, but potential injustices within those relationships are rarely discussed. This framework makes ethical consideration of sexual violations difficult, and that may be why official Catholic spokespersons have had so very little to say about sexual violence.[18]

Historically, Catholics employed the language of spousal rights over the body of the other in marriage.[19] This framing, especially when mapped on to gendered expectations about who will be exercising rights over whom, can yield highly problematic conclusions. Though this language has largely disappeared, even in recent teaching, highly idealistic visions of intimate relationships crowd out attention to possible sexual injustice inside and outside of marriage. John Paul II's description of a conjugal love that "leads to forming one heart and one soul" is typical in leaving little room for seeing violence.[20] In 2014–2015 there was a meeting of the world's bishops on the topic of the family. Its final report acknowledges violence as one of many aspects of the cultural context of families today, but does not dwell on this reality or allow it to enter into its discussion of marital fidelity.[21] In his writing on families, Pope Francis speaks of how God's love "heals and transforms hardened hearts, leading them back to the beginning through the way of the cross" and recalls a beautiful line from Psalm 63, "My soul clings to you," without consciousness of how idealistic visions of unity and sacrifice can enable perpetrators and silence victims.[22]

Nonetheless, Pope Francis has moved the church forward. More than any other pope in history, he denounces the scourge of family violence. According to Francis, some marriages are not just imperfect but marked by "authoritarianism" and "domination."[23] Without losing a sense of the importance of intimacy, he begins to bring sex down from the overly idealized space to which John Paul II lifted it and acknowledges the messy and uneven process of self-gift. Even more significantly, he names sexual manipulation, submission, and violence as fundamental distortions that contradict the very nature

SEX 37

of marriage. One can infer that these acts are at odds with the virtue of justice, though this language is never employed.

Still, the treatment of gender in contemporary Catholic teaching is ambiguous, and this contributes to the church's ongoing failure to speak more prophetically about sexual violence as injustice. While the "women's rights" movement is celebrated and "growing reciprocity" between men and women is lauded, most documents continue to be marked by unnuanced assertions about gender difference, as well as uncritical claims about distinctive "feminine genius" and virtues, with little recognition that celebrating such virtues can make women vulnerable to violence.[24]

In part because of the way the church narrates gender difference, mercy, not justice, lies at the core even of recent Catholic thinking about sexual ethics. Mercy is to be the mark of the church's accompanying ministry to people in their personal lives. It provides the impetus for the church to deal compassionately with all "wounded" families, approaching them not with "dead stones but grace and light."[25] While this commitment to mercy is welcome, a neglect of injustice in and outside of marriage impedes the ability of the church to respond to victims of sexual violence.

And of course, the elephant in the room is the church's own sexual abuse scandal. The church's failures—in the abuse itself, in the cover-up, in its treatment of victims, and in the many ways it valued saving face over facing credible accusations—limit its ability to speak authentically now. Pope Francis's unwillingness to believe survivors in Chile, right in the middle of the #MeToo moment, was an egregious error that added to the perception that the church does not take the suffering of victims seriously. Though he eventually reversed his position, the damage to his credibility remains.[26] As the summer progressed, revelations about the former cardinal McCarrick of Washington, DC, emerged, showing a pattern of abuse of seminarians. Protests during the World Meeting of Families in Ireland drew attention to abuse by priests and sisters. The release of the *Pennsylvania Grand Jury Report* recounted

38 CAN YOU BE A CATHOLIC AND A FEMINIST?

stories of scores of victims and the gross mishandling of their cases in several dioceses in the state. More recently, a similar report from Illinois once again raised questions about transparency. Despite substantial efforts to raise awareness of the problem and protect children, it is hard to avoid the conclusion that the church is still catching up.[27] Limited by the clergy sexual abuse crisis, by lack of attention to sexual sins of injustice, and by dated analyses of gender, Catholics have not been major players in the movement to the end sexual violence, especially compared to feminists.

A Catholic Feminist Response

Despite its failures and limitations, Catholicism does have unique resources that can help us analyze and respond to sexual violence and can be utilized if the church is willing to look critically at its own internal issues. The Catholic ideal of human dignity, its understanding of social sin, and its insistence that solidarity is not primarily a feeling but a virtue are all strengths. Feminist thinkers have a more robust analysis of sexism and sexual violence. By reading the two side by side in order to correct for the limitations in both viewpoints, I will try to sketch a coherent and credible way for a Catholic feminist to think about and respond to sexual violence.

Catholic social thought begins with the dignity of the person and views violations of that dignity as matters of justice. In his most important social encyclical, *Centesimus annus*, John Paul II insists that Catholic social thought at its core is about care for the human person—the only creature "willed for its own sake."[28] In the last chapter of the document, John Paul quotes Leo XIII, author of the first social encyclical, who looked at 19th century factory workers and said that silence in the face of the systematic denial of their dignity would be unconscionable.[29] The analysis of work in 1891 is surprisingly resonant. Leo considers the argument that just wages are determined by "free consent," and thus if employers pay the amount agreed to, they have met the demands of justice. However he insists that this analysis is incomplete. Work is not simply an exchange of time for money. It is necessary and it is personal, because "the force which acts is bound up with the personality and is the exclusive property of him who acts."[30] Contractual justice is insufficient. Natural justice demands just wages for workers because they are human beings. "If through necessity or fear of a worse evil the workman accepts harder conditions because an employer or contractor will afford him no better, he is made the victim of force and injustice."[31] Paying unjust wages, Leo insists, "is a great crime which cries to the avenging anger of heaven."[32]

Just as Leo XIII protested human persons being mistreated in his time, so, John Paul II says, the church continues to do in every age, "walking together with the human race through history," [safeguarding] "the transcendence of the human person."[33] Today, when we listen to the experience of victims of sexual violence, we hear stories of crimes against human dignity that cry out for justice and about persons who need someone to walk with them. Some perpetrators fit popular ideas of what violence looks like: the movie producer Harvey Weinstein, who was found guilty of rape and sentenced to twenty-three years in prison; the wealthy patrons of big hotels who abuse the housekeepers made vulnerable by the location of their work; along with all of the other too familiar stories with clear lines of violation, extensive networks of enablers, violent threats to ensure silence, and pervasive shame on the part of victims.

No less troubling and even more pervasive are accounts of "bad sex." The Aziz Ansari story and the fictional "Cat Person" narrative referenced earlier align in attesting to women's shared sense of violation *even when* they were not forced or threatened. Despite having, theoretically, the freedom to flee, something kept these women and others in the room.[34] For some it is the need to keep a job, but many others describe a complex set of pressures to be nice, to go along, to not cause problems, to accept what is not desirable

40 CAN YOU BE A CATHOLIC AND A FEMINIST?

because they believe they had no right to expect anything more, because they had agreed by "necessity or fear" to the dominant sexual script.

These accounts are similar to those that dominate studies of hookup culture on college campuses. Feminist sociologist Lisa Wade's studies show that women and many men are overwhelmingly dissatisfied with the coercive force of normative hookup culture and the typical hookup script in which alcohol is used to overcome inhibitions and blur the lines of consent, romance is sidelined, and emotional intimacy is hoped for but rarely achieved. She describes the hard work students do to avoid emotional connection: leaving before morning, avoiding eye contact, not calling, pretending not to be interested in anything serious.[35] As feminist author and survivor Donna Freitas says, it is a contest to see "who can care the least."[36] Women and men both attest to the toll this takes on their self-worth and to the frustrations of desiring a real relationship but succumbing to hookup culture because it is the only real option.[37] In accounts of sexual assault and stories of "normal" sexual encounters on college campuses, distinguishing between violence and bad sex is complicated. The narrative is very similar—a centering of male power and privilege, a disconnect between physical and emotional intimacy, and an intentional division between body and spirit on behalf of both perpetrator and victim.

Viewed through a Catholic lens, both sexual assault and bad sex violate the dignity of the person. Both deny the reality of the person as body and spirit, passion and intellect, emotion and reason, whether formal consent is given or not. Perpetrators instrumentalize their victims, whether they use force or persuasion. Victim-survivors attempt to divide themselves to survive a violent act or endure an unwanted act in the hope of greater intimacy, or in order to avoid giving offense. Consent, feminist theorists note, is always complicated in the context of rape culture. When the unity of self is violated, feminist social scientists attest, suffering can be profound. In opposition to highly individualistic economic or sexual thought, Catholic social thought read in light of feminism affirms that with sex as with labor, via socially normative constructs and contracts, people are systemically objectified and harmed.

Violations of dignity in Catholic social thought are understood not simply as individual acts of injustice but as interconnected parts of the web of social sin. In a 1987 document on social concerns, John Paul II gave his most detailed description of social sin. Some worry that he did not go far enough because he so clearly links social sin to individual sinful acts. While imperfect, John Paul's account of personal and social sin includes important insights.[38] In the context of economic inequality, he highlights the huge advantages of higher-income countries over lower-income countries, and the resulting lack of opportunity to flourish that marks much of the world. Yet despite the fact that few specific actions of ordinary individuals can be directly linked to structural sin, he insists that everyone is responsible. Sinful systems rooted in the desires to "impos[e] one's will upon others" do not sustain themselves; those who cooperate with and benefit from the system are in fact its sustainers, and they are responsible.[39]

Feminist theologians have offered the most sustained and helpful social analysis of sexual violence as social sin, while not naming it as such. In an influential essay, ethicist Karen Lebacqz quotes from a letter to "Dear Abby," in which a woman asked if a man who "overpowered" a woman on a second date, after having consensual sex with her on a first date, could rightly be accused of rape.[40] Lebacqz highlights the woman's confusion about whether forced sex is rape or just sex. She unpacks the social construction of sexuality and argued that "because violence and sexuality are linked in the experiences of women, the search for loving heterosexual intimacy is for many women . . . an exercise in 'loving your enemy.'"[41] Lebacqz insists women must not lose themselves in a desire to please. Rather, they must be conscious of the social construction of sex and sexual desire in order to survive. For feminist theologians, not just rape or assault but much of ordinary sex

42 CAN YOU BE A CATHOLIC AND A FEMINIST?

involves domination and is sustained by a systemic sexism that Catholics would name as sinful.

Feminist theologians also argue that Christianity has played a role in sustaining unjust social structures linked to sexual violence. In her 1994 book, *Body, Sex, and Pleasure: Reconstructing Christian Sexual Ethics*, Christine Gudorf argues that, historically, Christians have not recognized "bodyright" because the body was seen as separate from the self.[42] She remembers that male headship included both conjugal rights and the right to physically discipline wives, and that it was only in the 1970s that marital rape was legally recognized. From rape to unwanted sexual touching in the workplace, all sexually violent acts should be understood as bodyright violations. All say, "You are not in control of your body; I am."[43] Christianity has to own its contribution to the social construct of sex that makes women more vulnerable to violence.

Radical feminists have long argued that the parallels between women's stories of sexual violence and their stories of "bad sex" are striking and are evidence of the structural problem. New orthodox Catholic feminists today also grasp what is at stake. Some connect the promiscuity brought about by the sexual revolution to violence. As they see it, in the new sexual landscape, the lines of consent are confusing, and men have internalized scripts of domination and act (intentionally or not) in ways that violate women's autonomy.[44] Women have internalized scripts of submission, and they find themselves keeping the peace at the expense of their authentic, embodied selves. When we see a sexual landscape in which young women are asking if they need to accept choking as part of an ordinary sexual encounter, perhaps it is time for "rethinking sex."[45]

The deeper one goes into the research on sexual violence, the clearer the case for the existence of a social structure that enables and incentivize sin becomes.[46] Feminist theology from Asia is particularly helpful in illuminating how sexual violations are forms of injustice rooted in sinful social structures. Gemma Cruz describes the plight of Filipina domestic workers who endure the physical and sexual abuse of male employers, which ranges from unwanted touching to making the domestic worker a "virtual sexual slave."[47] Sexual violence is but one part of an interlocking systemic problem of injustice. Due to inadequate economic opportunities in their home countries, many women seek work in distant wealthier countries. Families need domestic workers, and because women are assumed to be better suited to that work, they dominate the profession. Women leave behind husbands and children, enduring infidelity, guilt, and anxiety. Their commodification is apparent in the language their employers use to describe them, for example, "my Filipino[a]," which "inscribes[s] domestic work in women's bodies . . . [and] racializes[s] it."[48] The larger social structures of gendered migration, economic inequality, and sexism sustain sexual violence against women.

Similarly, Theresa Yih-Lan Tsou's analysis of sex workers in Taiwan provides an analysis of the social structures that make sex work necessary for women who lack power. Echoing Leo XIII, Tsou argues that most women "voluntarily *choose* this work [only] because there were not so many options open to them. . . . Rationalizing that the work is temporary helps them maintain a sense of integrity."[49] The sex work they do ranges from entertaining businessmen (e.g., pouring drinks, joking, and singing, all while naked or dressed in revealing clothes and submitting to unwanted touching) to having sex for money. In general, they are asked "to play a lower, weaker, feminine role in order to give men an inflated feeling of masculinity and a sense of brotherhood especially when it is necessary to connect opposing business partners."[50] This way of doing business cannot be separated from inequality in marriage and a lack of educational opportunities for women, which results in limited employment opportunities. Tsou shows that sex work is rooted in a system of structural injustice with many interconnecting parts.

Asian feminist theological analysis of sexual violence illuminates the US context with which I began. Sexual violence cannot be separated from ordinary sexual relationships or from social structures, not only in the Philippines or Thailand, but in Hollywood and Washington, DC, on college campuses, in hotel rooms and family homes. Race, gender, and inequality interlock, and the disturbing narrative of socially enabled division of body and spirit that results in objectification and violation is pervasive in every sphere. While some would argue that sexual assault and "bad sex" are *merely* issues of personal morality or sexual ethics, Catholic social sin language in conversation with feminism shows us the depth and complexity of the problem.

Work in the "Space Between"

I have argued that Catholics have failed to adequately address the problem of sexual violence because of weaknesses in their approach to gender and sex, and their failures in the clergy sex abuse crisis, while feminists, with their long record of deep concern for sexual violence, have contributed to changing norms, policies, and laws. But Catholic concepts of human dignity and social sin, when read in dialogue with feminist analysis, have the potential to illuminate the problem of sexual violence and point toward comprehensive solutions.

A final crucial piece to my argument is a claim that has been implicit so far: addressing the issue of sexual violence requires attention to culture and to the important work that can be accomplished in local communities. Neither a focus on personal virtue and vice nor a focus on politics is capable of providing a comprehensive analysis of what is going wrong or what needs to be done. Strategies in what I call the "space between" are crucial to understanding the problem, building common ground, and making progress.[51] This is where Catholic thought and some strains of feminism can be crucial.

Moving forward requires not just marches, lawsuits, and workplace training, but cultivation of solidarity, which I treated in chapter 1 as central to a Catholic feminist account of being human. John Paul II spoke of solidarity as the reality of "interdependence, sensed [or understood] as a system determining relationships in the contemporary world."[52] We are all inescapably connected. He asked privileged people to see how their lives connect to the lives of people who struggle, to understand how social structures shape destinies. Today Catholic social thought both affirms solidarity as interconnectedness and says that once one sees this reality, a positive duty to promote the human rights of others and accompany them emerges.[53] Political strategies to ensure women's safety from violence must be a part of embracing solidarity. Yet listening to the voices of victims of sexual violence shows the relevance not only of laws and policies but of narratives about the body and cultural practices that are inescapably tied to those narratives. Here both Catholics and feminists have wisdom to share.

For instance, Catholic ethicists rightly argue that because HIV-AIDS arises in contexts in which women lack adequate health care, access to contraception, education, and income, efforts on these political fronts constitute a more effective AIDS reduction plan than abstinence campaigns. Yet the late feminist scholar Melissa Browning, who did extensive ethnographic research in Tanzania, shows that when women themselves speak of what makes them vulnerable, they name inequality in marriage, infidelity, and cultural expectations about sex that limit married women's freedom and safety.[54] Work to reduce the spread of AIDS needs to include both political strategies and community-based accompaniment. As John Paul II wrote, solidarity requires "changes of mentality, behavior and structures."[55] This framing helps us move beyond a simplistic view of solidarity as a stance ("I'm in solidarity with you") to a more grounded and difficult view of solidarity as a virtue ("I'm walking with you").[56]

If this sounds like an abdication of political or personal responsibility, it might be better understood as an attempt to treat problems in their complexity. Civil rights lawyer Bryan Stevenson highlights

46   CAN YOU BE A CATHOLIC AND A FEMINIST?

the importance of invoking both legal and cultural strategies in the social struggle against racism in the criminal justice system. "The policy work is critically important," he said, "but it has to be married with narrative work that does work on the hearts and minds. It's just not enough to pass the law."[57] Changing narratives and practices, whether in relation to racism or sexual violence, is a crucial part of the process of social change. It is work that the Catholic tradition, with its complex understanding of human dignity, social sin, and solidarity, is well situated to address, especially if it listens to feminists who can illuminate structures and cultures that enable and incentivize sexual violence, and restrict those who seek to harm.

Catholics and feminists together have the potential to move the #MeToo movement forward, because both understand the importance of work in the "space between." After the necessary outing of perpetrators, improvements in the law, and required trainings, there is no obvious place for solidarity to go, unless the personal and the political are connected, unless we can work on dysfunctional narratives and practices at the level of culture, as both feminist and Catholics have done.

In chapter 1, I noted that Audre Lorde gave voice to a feminist personal-political ethic when she wrote about the erotic as a life force flowing through people, giving them energy, inspiring them to resist conformity, drawing them into intimacy and community. This vision of the erotic begins in joy but moves toward justice. Lorde writes, "Once we begin to feel deeply all the aspects of our lives, we begin to demand from ourselves and from our life-pursuits that they feel in accordance with that joy which we know ourselves to be capable of."[58]

Catholic ethicist Margaret Farley, I argued, develops a similar vision. Humans who can be seen as "embodied spirits" or "inspirited bodies," Farley says, not only deserve not to be harmed or acted upon without their consent.[59] They also deserve relationships that are mutual and equal, giving and receiving, honest and intimate, personally satisfying and overflowing with love and life. If this is what humans are, "Only a sexuality formed and shaped with love has the possibility for integration into the whole of human personality."[60] Only relationships that engage human persons in their full reality are fully just. And commitment to social justice requires attentiveness to structures that make this possible for everyone.

Audre Lorde and Margaret Farley both speak of a unified vision of a human being—body and spirit, personal and political, free and yet fully alive in relation. They both value desire and are suspicious of desires that are socially constructed in problematic ways. Like Leo XIII and John Paul II, Lorde and Farley want much more than sexual autonomy, consent, and contractual justice. They seek flourishing both for individuals and for the communities of which they are a part, and both thinkers connect flourishing to a transcendent power. Despite key differences, they implicitly affirm core insights of Catholic theology: that bodies matter, that sexual gestures express something of who we are, that persons are relational at their core, that relationships at their best are both bodily and spiritual, that "pretending not to care" is not the way to treat or to be a person.

Of course, Catholicism has a great distance to go. The #SilenceIsNotSpiritual movement takes churches to task for their failure to empower and listen to women who have suffered sexual violence, and asks for a commitment to stand by women and help them heal. I carried a sign to the 2017 Women's March in St. Louis that said "Catholic and Feminist / #MeToo, #ChurchToo" which drew mostly curious stares from those marching beside me. Looking around, I thought, "Well, they could be forgiven for thinking that Catholics were not showing up for this fight." Where were the Catholics? At the very least, few were visibly present.

Because a Catholic feminist response to sexual violence has potential to change things at a deep level, I want to maintain hope that a "space between" strategy might be advanced. But this kind of conversation will not be possible if Catholics refuse to talk about sexual violence and bad sex inside and outside of marriage

48 CAN YOU BE A CATHOLIC AND A FEMINIST?

as violations of justice. It will not be possible if Catholics refuse to admit that responding to the current crisis does not end with calling out "bad apples"—individual priests who engaged in abuse and the bishops who moved them around. We move forward only by acknowledging cultures and systems in which bad sex and violence flourished, and perpetrators who were passed around and promoted, and too many others who knew and turned away. Catholics have to commit to self-scrutiny and to seeking help from others to see clearly the depth of the problem that existed then and, despite progress, exists still.

The #MeToo movement to end sexual violence drew attention to a pervasive, complicated problem, but it had limited concrete effects. Still, it presents new opportunities: to talk about problematic social cultures in high schools, colleges, and workplaces; to discuss toxic forms of masculinity and femininity; to talk about sexual violence in relation to racism and inequality; to challenge narratives of sex as conquest or exchange. A Catholic feminist perspective could help more people envision sex that is not only freely consented to, but also just and loving. It could help reduce violence and bad sex, and promote not only just sex, but just love. While Catholics have thus far remained mostly silent, the tradition has resources for analyzing and responding to this problem. Through dialogue with feminism, Catholics can strengthen their ability to respond in solidarity and commit to the long, slow work of changing the deeply sexist and individualistic culture that shapes and cheapens sexual practice.

Catholic feminists who can hold their two traditions together, allowing each to challenge the other, might have an important role to play in this effort. Hopefully, with their help, the hashtag "#ChurchToo" can come to mean not only that the church acknowledges its complicity in sexual violence, but that Catholics are willing to be self-critical so that they can help shape a new conversation about sex.

3

Work

Whose Room? Which Balancing Act?

As I noted in chapter 1, Virginia Woolf famously said that a woman needs "a room of her own" in which to write. She lamented the lost potential of so many women in history who lacked a quiet space to work. Most people know that feminists have claimed the right to take jobs traditionally reserved for men and associate the women's movement with attempts to break professional glass ceilings. The image of the woman in a business suit with a baby in one hand and a briefcase in the other is an iconic representation of this type of feminism. It suggests the importance of striving for success and achievement as well as the necessity of leaving babies in the care of unseen others. It contrasts with the iconic image of a woman that often graces covers of Catholic magazines—a mother on her front porch surrounded by many children. If she works outside the home, it is part time; her briefcase remains out of sight, and she identifies first as a mom. The woman in the fancy suit and the high-heeled shoes is trying to find that elusive work-life balance as she drops her baby off at day care before running to her job. The woman with the children has her feet planted firmly on the ground. The Catholic feminist dilemma is often presented in these terms, with the implication that women must choose between the self-serving feminist balancing act or the sacrificial path of the Catholic mother.

But the tension between Catholicism and feminism on work-and-life balance is more complicated. If we pull back from the baby and the briefcase, we have to ask about the unseen others doing the child care, cooking, driving, and cleaning. Some feminists have done exactly this,

Can You Be a Catholic and a Feminist?. Julie Hanlon Rubio, Oxford University Press.
© Oxford University Press 2024. DOI: 10.1093/oso/9780197553145.003.0004

50 CAN YOU BE A CATHOLIC AND A FEMINIST?

drawing attention to unjust wages and working conditions women of color face and insisting on the right of working-class women to rear their own children, a right that has historically been denied them. Socialist feminists have been much more concerned with labor justice for the working poor than work-life balance for women executives trying to "lean in." A more diverse third-wave feminist movement seeks justice for domestic workers and other women caught in exploitative, low-paying jobs. Their iconic image might be a woman taking care of another family's kids while parenting by cell phone and longing for more time with her own children. Feminists have concerns about these work-family issues, and so do Catholics.

While the religious Right in the 1970s and 1980s challenged second-wave feminists, claiming that women should be home with kids and thus setting off the "mommy wars," today few Catholic thinkers worry about women working. New orthodox feminists often combine motherhood with work on their own terms rather than choosing between the two. In the era of John Paul II, Catholic teaching affirmed women's equal access to work, though still insisting that their work was marked by a "feminine genius,"[1] Today, Catholic teaching celebrates women's roles in public life and advocates for work-family balance policies that benefit working parents. Concern about women in the workforce has given way to promotion of women in Catholic and public institutions. Both Catholicism and feminism are more complex than popular images suggest.

The changing shape of family and work may allow us to see this problem anew. The idea of the nuclear family never accounted for the diversity of US households, but today it accounts for only 19 percent.[2] Working patterns, too, have always varied but, today, only about one in five married parents with children under eighteen living at home (29 percent of moms and 7 percent of dads) do not work outside the home.[3] Among unmarried mothers, 20 percent do not work outside the home. Many parents now consider part-time or remote work ideal, especially given the high cost of child care.[4]

As I write, there is some evidence of a "Great Resignation" led by workers who are not going back to their jobs even after

WORK 51

Covid-related government benefits have been cut and evictions are no longer on hold.[5] The pandemic that began in 2020 forced a huge experiment with the flextime that feminists and labor activists have advocated for decades and gave some a glimpse of life without work at the center. It sent parents home from work to care for children and attend to domestic labors? often while continuing their jobs.[6] Some parents could not wait for in-person work to return, but a significant percentage are hesitating. Some who did continue working in essential jobs like healthcare, manufacturing, and food service have quit. Several forces are contributing to the labor shortage, but many employees say they want more flexibility, and many employers are not offering it yet. At least some workers are reconsidering the place of work in their lives. The current reckoning with work-life balance seems to be happening up and down the economic ladder.

Moving beyond iconic contrasting images from the "mommy wars" of the 1990s and thin notions of Catholic and feminist accounts of work, I want to reconsider the place of work in women's lives. To that end, I explore different feminist and Catholic accounts of work, map the landscape of work today, and search for overlap between Catholic and feminist concerns. I argue that being a Catholic feminist means understanding why work matters and seeking work-life balance for all women—the woman in the business suit, the mom on the front porch, and the domestic worker in the family home. On this issue, once we see feminists and Catholics clearly, while remnants of the earlier tension remain, there is considerable common ground and plenty of room for collaboration.

Tensions in Feminist and Catholic Thinking on Work

In 1931, Pope Pius XI wrote in a document on marriage of "false teachers" who claimed that women should be able to work outside the home. "This, however," he said, "is not the true emancipation of women, nor that rational and exalted liberty which belongs to the

52   CAN YOU BE A CATHOLIC AND A FEMINIST?

noble office of a Christian woman and wife; it is rather the debasing of the womanly character and dignity of motherhood, and indeed of the whole family, as a result of which the husband suffers the loss of his wife, the children of their mother, and the home and the whole family of an ever watchful guardian." He decried "this false liberty and unnatural equality with the husband [that] is to the detriment of woman herself."[7] The church opposed both suffrage for women and women's work outside the home because of a view that women's nature made them suited to work of homemaking and childrearing.[8]

Feminists of the first wave did not agree. After the ratification of the Nineteen Amendment granting suffrage to women in 1920, the National Women's Party sought full legal equality for women via passage of the Equal Rights Amendment. Alice Paul, who founded the National Women's Party and drafted the ERA, exemplifies this liberal wing of the women's movement. With a PhD and three law degrees, "She believed deeply in removing barriers to women's individual achievement and allowing women the same freedoms as men."[9] Socialist feminists, in contrast, turned to labor activism to secure better wages and conditions for working-class women. Esther Peterson, a teacher and organizer of women in the garment industry, exemplifies this wing, with a loving, egalitarian marriage to a Presbyterian minister, four children, and a strong commitment to coalition-building.[10] Though coming from different parts of the women's movement, both Paul and Peterson were fighting for emancipation, which included justice in the workplace and the family. When their struggles are viewed alongside papal teaching from the early twentieth century, the divide between Catholicism and feminism on work is clear. Catholics decried desires for public work and equality with men that they saw as diminishing women and endangering the family, whereas feminists sought equal opportunities for professional women and justice for women laboring in homes, fields, and factories. Over the next one hundred years, those tensions continued, though the gap gradually narrowed.

Second-wave feminism's best-known figure, Betty Friedan, is remembered for seeking an escape from domesticity for the many middle-class (mostly white) women who languished at home due to the "feminine mystique"—a belief that women were suited for the role of housewife and would find fulfillment through it. She advocated for freedom to pursue one's own life plan. "Who knows what women can be when they are finally free to be themselves? . . . Who knows of the possibilities of love when men and women share not only children, home, and garden, . . . but the responsibilities and passions of the work that creates the human future and the full human knowledge of who they are?" she asked, equating identity, authenticity, and passion with public work and assuming such work would enhance marriage and family.

The feminist quest for fulfilling work outside the home challenged the primacy of family in women's lives. Sociologist Kathleen Gerson notes that the revolution that began in the 1960s resulted in the demise of the male breadwinner model, "more fluid marriages, less stable work careers, and profound shifts in mothers' ties to the workplace."[11] New choices emerged, along with new tensions. Feminists sought not only equal access to the workplace but also egalitarian marriages marked by shared work and parenting, though most women had to embrace ambiguous strategies as they waited for the promised equality at home.[12] Equal access to work was premised on changes in family and society that were only just beginning, and the goal of transforming home, work, and policy remains central to the feminist movement.

The push for change was controversial then but has become less so over time. In the 1960s, pushback came from conservative Catholic women like Phyllis Schlafly who insisted that women's primary role was in the home, as well as from others on the religious Right who saw in feminism and the sexual revolution a threat to their deepest values.[13] At the popular level, the narrative pushed by the religious Right—that feminists promised women they could "have it all" and ruined family life—took hold and,

54   CAN YOU BE A CATHOLIC AND A FEMINIST?

ironically, Friedan herself furthered this narrative in her book *The Second Stage*, about how feminism needed to attend to the family.[14] Today, new orthodox feminists continue this line of critique, pointing to pressures to succeed at all costs that they experience as deeply at odds with their desires to prioritize family caregiving.[15] These concerns are not uncommon. Many women find work valuable but are tired and desire more time with their loved ones. For too many, work is necessity, provision, and, all too often, exploitation.

Yet, conservative backlash in the 1980s and today often relies on an inadequate analysis of feminism. Feminist scholars correct this distorted picture, showing how feminists sought a parallel revolution in the home that was a long time coming and were concerned with working-class women, not just elites. Sociologist Joan Williams, for instance, notes the power of the pervasive "ideal worker" norm of the unencumbered male who was always able to stay late or come in early because there was no "spillover" between work and home in his life. When women are unable to meet this ideal, they often say something like "It just wasn't working," but Williams insists that this narrative of personal choice overlooks the structural and personal obstacles making work-life balance difficult.[16] To remedy this, feminists have sought changes in the home, the workplace, and in government policy. The history of feminist activism on labor issues includes not just attempts to open professions to women, but also fights for just wages, the Pregnancy Discrimination Act (1978), justice for homemakers who were often left without support after divorce or the death of a spouse, the Family and Medical Leave Act (1992), and the continued fight for paid family and sick leave, flextime, child care, welfare rights, retirement equity, and rights for domestic workers. This agenda is ambitious, and though feminists have not achieved everything they wanted, historians credit them with striving for "a new, more egalitarian and just ordering of family and work life."[17] Still, the most visible changes brought about by feminism are women's presence in the workplace and the lack of work-life balance so many desire. The feminist dream of fulfilling and balanced lives remains elusive.

Contemporary Catholic teaching on work is not completely at odds with what feminists want. "Thank you, *women who work!*" said John Paul II in his *Letter to Women* in 1995, seemingly with no irony, and without noting the huge gap between his affirmation and earlier Catholic teaching.[18] Women in the workplace, contemporary Catholic social teaching insists,[19] should have supports they need to care for their families. Yet the insistence that women's work will be qualitatively different from men's is evidence of some continuing tension.

Today's Balancing Act: Always On

Before attempting to find common ground between feminists and Catholics, I turn to an analysis of the nature of work today. I have already alluded to changes brought about by the pandemic, but even before Covid-19 work was changing. Although professional or knowledge workers and part-time or gig workers are usually considered separately, a pervasive "always on" work culture is common to both, so I analyze them together. My hope is that by focusing on actual working conditions today, the overlap between Catholicism and feminism will become even more visible.

What I call "always on" work culture characterizes the work environments of a majority of US workers, more than 30 percent of whom are "knowledge workers" and at least 36 percent of whom are gig workers.[20] "Always on" is a concept that comes from the tech world and refers to "systems that are *continuously available, plugged in,* or connected to power sources and networks. Always on may also refer to systems... that do not take breaks, but continue to hum along through all hours of the day and night. It most often refers to an internet connection that is *always accessible.*"[21] This phenomenon is operative in the broader culture in two dominant forms of

56   CAN YOU BE A CATHOLIC AND A FEMINIST?

work: gig work (in which workers are paid by the hour, typically with no guarantee or expectation of full-time work or benefits) and "knowledge work" (in which employees with formal training use knowledge to create products and services). Although these two groups are my focus, we might also include retail, hospitality, and other shift workers who are often expected to be available on short notice. In all of these areas, the expectation or requirement of being always on leads to excessive work and anxiety. As was evident during the pandemic, "always on" does not work when people are sick or have to care for loved ones. It has never worked for women or other caregivers, but Covid made visible the dysfunction of a system that has no plan for when caregiving conflicts with work. Always-on culture assumes not just that workers will be "at" work much of the time but that they will be "on" even when they are else-where, "always accessible," "available," or "plugged in." This holds for both knowledge workers and gig workers, though the latter's situation is far more precarious and unjust.

Always-on work culture is marked by limited autonomy and illu-sory flexibility. The modern workplace theoretically frees both sets of workers to complete their work on their own time but in reality works best for those at the top, the most secure professionals and gig workers who do not need the income they earn for ordinary living expenses. Still, even the most privileged groups experience pressure to be "available," "operational," "plugged in," "accessible," or "connected to a network." Neither kind of job was supposed to be this way. Yet workers across the board report feeling less free. Even though their days look very different from factory workers of the Fordist era with whom we associate a controlled workplace, fewer workers today are finding freedom or fulfillment.[22]

Instead, workers experience anxiety because they are never fin-ished with work. For gig workers trying to string together enough jobs to pay their rent, it can feel like any free time should be spent looking for work. For knowledge workers, digital communica-tion has taken over the workday. As Cal Newport shows in *A*

World without Email, workers are reporting that they experience a constant pressure to be "on."[23] The average business person today checks email every six minutes. Ride share drivers constantly check platforms for potential jobs. We are not made for this environment, says Newport. When people contact us, we feel obligated to respond, but the scale of email we receive makes this an impossible task.[24] Workplace norms exacerbate the problem, but social pressure also plays a role, leading to a constant nagging sense that we owe people something.

Limited autonomy and illusory flexibility shape always-on work culture and are associated with dissatisfaction. Newport, links dissatisfaction with the lack of "deep work"—work to which one gives full attention and applies specialized skills, work that enables "flow."[25] Scholars of gig work often focus on more concrete problems, such as declining wages and workplace protection, but they, too, speak of disillusionment with broken promises of the sharing economy—the loss of desired authenticity, community, and the feeling of helping other people. Read together, these analysts of work identify a crisis that is both economic and spiritual.

Newport argues that the arrival of email changed the way we work just as the Industrial Revolution did. To be sure, Newport is concerned about how constant communication diminishes productivity. He repeatedly promises that structuring work differently will benefit individuals and workplaces. Knowledge workers typically send and receive over a hundred emails a day. Newport shows that not only is this volume of asynchronous back-and-forth messaging highly inefficient, but that trying to keep up with it makes for a fragmented workday during which everyone feels busy but no one gets a lot of work done. The asynchronous structure of email forces knowledge workers to be always on, constantly diverting attention away from deep work to manage electronic communication.[26] This way of working is so embedded that most of us cannot imagine an alternative.

58   CAN YOU BE A CATHOLIC AND A FEMINIST?

But the current "ecology" of work is not conducive to human happiness. Newport's own survey data found knowledge workers feeling anxious, frustrated, and isolated because they are "under siege by obligations" that never seem to end.[27] Interestingly, Newport, whose father was a religious studies professor, identifies this as a problem of "the human soul."[28] He does not unpack this term but, throughout the book, he finds that despite freedom in how to organize their workday, knowledge workers are unhappy. Newport argues that knowledge workers are not able to work deeply because of poorly designed workflow processes. In a better-organized workplace, they would experience greater autonomy. They would be more satisfied because they would have time to focus on deep work. Fulfilling work is desirable and possible, Newport claims, even if it is mostly elusive for knowledge workers today.

If knowledge workers have a soul problem at work, gig workers are often enmeshed in the kind of soul-crushing work they sought to avoid. Sociologist Juliet Schor details the promises of the sharing economy that attracted many of the gig workers she studied: more personal autonomy, less bureaucracy, "'sharing' with strangers," work that felt like "helping other people," a way of earning money that was "something I really believed in."[29] The sharing economy has its roots in the 1960s counterculture and originally combined faith in technology with egalitarian and communitarian impulses. By the 1980s, it had been co-opted by neoliberalism. Companies moved from global outsourcing to broader use of part-time workers, and in the first decade of this century, Uber-like platforms began to multiply, creating even more precarious and disconnected workers.

Corporations relied on idealized rhetoric promising economic, social, and environmental benefits, as well as humble "origins stories," to attract workers. Workers embraced this new alternative. As one Task Rabbit worker said, "I can be that nice girl, and be myself, and not be, like, Trader Joes fake nice."[30] But instead of the promised flexibility, autonomy, connection, and sense of purpose, most gig workers found precarity, low wages, intensive monitoring, and pressure to stay tied to a platform. Sociologist Alexandrea Ravenelle's in-depth interviews with gig workers on four platforms present a grim view of the gig worker experience.[31]

A key factor in the lives of gig workers is dependency. Schor finds that less than one-quarter are "platform dependent," about one-third are earning "supplemental" income, while a majority are "inbetween."[32] Those earning supplemental income are more selective and more satisfied. But dependent workers who earn poverty wages, lack autonomy and flexibility, and have to worry more about losing their jobs are, unsurprisingly, less satisfied overall. Similarly, Ravanelle finds that gig work for those who are dependent on it is theoretically flexible, but it never ends. While they are not reporting to supervisors, they are always being observed. Fear of being let go leads many to give up leisure time in order to be constantly on the platforms. Connection has proved to be as illusory as autonomy; instead, no contact is the norm and workers feel isolated and stuck.

High-end gig workers, Ravenelle acknowledges, are exceptions ("Success Stories") who have more flexibility and control over when and how much they work. But those who considered gig work their "dream job" were a minority who had skills and capital that most gig workers lack.[33] For them, gig work was a choice, rather than a last resort, and their resources enabled them to be discerning, regardless of how platforms and algorithms tried to shape their choices. Because they did not have to be always on, they found gig work satisfying, but they are the minority, and even they are susceptible to perceived need to be constantly productive. Though Schor is more optimistic, she concurs that conditions are worsening.[34]

Gig workers and knowledge workers share idealism about what work could be and disappointment with the reality of always-on structure of work that leaves them feeling anxious, isolated, and constrained. Social scientists usually describe the situation using words like "precarity" and "dissatisfaction." Only occasionally does the vocabulary shift to "authenticity," "belonging," or "the soul."

60 CAN YOU BE A CATHOLIC AND A FEMINIST?

Catholic and feminist thinkers, both of whom have a long history of grappling with these kinds of issues, can better illuminate the problem of work and point the way forward.

Overlapping Catholic and Feminist Ideals

If work today can be described as uniquely demanding in its claims on both male and female workers, as it expects them to be always on, Catholics and feminists have wisdom to offer. Both see work as not simply a means to a paycheck or fulfillment but as having inherent value tied to human flourishing. They value ordinary labor in the workplace and the home, and advocate limits on work. Unlike "antiwork" scholars and activists, they advocate for the rights of workers while holding that work is more than a means to an end.

In 1981, John Paul II continued traditional Catholic affirmation of a living wage and the rights of workers. But he also offered a theology of work that stresses its inherent value. He calls work "a key, probably the essential key, to the whole social question" and emphasizes that the person called to self-realization is "the subject of work."[35] The focus on self-realization is key as, apart from just wages, people want to know that they are in some important sense working for themselves. The pope's theological valuing of work is not simply idealistic or individualistic; he recognizes the toil that work has always involved and claims that it is valuable.[36] Through work, we become cocreators and cohealers with God. Some critics worry that this spiritual emphasis downplays the pervasive reality of dehumanizing labor.[37] It differs from most Catholic social teaching on labor, which emphasizes just wages and working conditions. Yet concern for the "end" of persons and their spiritual development is also part of Catholic social thought.

Is it misguided to seek meaning in work? Studies of those who are unemployed or underemployed suggest the inherent value of work, complementing accounts of distress in always-on workers for whom stress crowds out meaning. Studies of the unemployed and underemployed show that feelings of worthlessness and depression are common.[38] If workers choose underemployment in order to secure other benefits, they tend to experience greater satisfaction, but if they are forced into it, the reverse is true. Being underemployed can lead to an acceptance of decreasing job satisfaction, lower expectations, and declining overall life satisfaction.[39] Like always-on employment, unemployment and underemployment have emotional and spiritual dimensions that go far beyond the loss of a paycheck.

Catholic theology provides a lens through which to understand why unemployment and underemployment have negative effects. In Catholic social thought, all persons have inherent dignity and worth that cannot be taken away. Persons also have a right and duty of participation, or contributing to society, which is fulfilled in part by work. The dissatisfaction of the unemployed and underemployed makes sense in part because an essential form of participation is being denied. Catholic social thought "recognize[s] that the principle value of human work is . . . that it is done by a human person [and] that employment is the principal means by which one participates in the economy; and that one's social world is created through work."[40] Work provides much more than sustenance. It is a means by which persons act in accord with their social nature.

Work is important for Catholics because it enables persons to be subjects, using their gifts to contribute to the common good and, ultimately, God's project of healing the world.[41] Moreso than Newport, Catholics are comfortable talking about the soul. In light of Catholic teaching, always-on employment is problematic because human beings need and deserve work that is appropriate for persons with souls and destinies beyond this world. In Catholic social thought, work is meaningful because it is one important way human beings use their gifts and talents for the good of this world and in collaboration with God.

62 CAN YOU BE A CATHOLIC AND A FEMINIST?

This admittedly lofty Catholic vision of work applies to even the most ordinary of labors. John Paul II, who was involved in the Solidarity labor movement in Poland in the 1980s, was certainly not unaware of unjust labor conditions. Catholicism decries the exploitation of workers and recognizes that far too often toil destroys subjectivity and crowds out hope.[42] However it also has a sacramental worldview that allows even the most ordinary tasks in and outside of the home to be seen as vehicles of grace, for, as ethicist Christine Firer Hinze puts it, "As embodied, reflective, spiritual beings, we are enmeshed simultaneously in the deep and the daily. . . . Always present, this depth is available for notice by the rightly attuned eye, ear, mind, and heart."[43]

Yet, despite this strong sense of work's value and potential to connect with "the deep," Catholic thought has always recognized the need to limit work. Because human beings have a destiny beyond this world, "Justice demands that . . . religion and the good of [a person's] soul must be kept in mind."[44] Traditionally, rest was seen as necessary so workers would have time to fulfill their religious and familial obligations. A family wage was a means to empower the working poor in a world of inequality not only so that their material needs would be met but also so that they had time "to cultivate their abilities and aspirations, and to participate in just, enlivening social relationships."[45] Today we might say that because workers are persons who are embodied, social, and spiritual, they need a mix of work and rest like that which is attributed to God in the Creation story (Genesis 2:2–4) and given as a commandment to Israel (Exodus 20:8–11). As human beings move toward ultimate rest in God, knowledge of their ultimate end should shape sensibilities about good work. Rest helps us to remember that we are made for work that engages our subjectivity and allows us to contribute to the common good.

I noted at the outset that feminism is best known for advocacy of upper- and middle-class women's right to work, and associated with claims that women can "have it all," but in reality, the feminist vison of work is much broader. Its fundamental tenets cohere with Catholic theology in seeing work as more than a means to a paycheck or personal fulfillment.

Feminists have spoken eloquently of the inherent value of work. Second-wave feminists may be faulted for undervaluing work in the home and failing to see the drudgery of the labor their working-class sisters did, but they did not have an instrumental view of work. Some called attention to an emptiness born of isolation and to the superficiality of focusing so much energy on food and housekeeping. Others spoke movingly of their artistic vocations thwarted by mindless work and family obligation. In the language of Catholic theology, they attest to work's subjective dimension and its connection to human flourishing.

Feminists have been particularly attentive to lifting up the inherent value of work outside the home to counter the idea that women would somehow be diminished by engaging in it. Ethicist Carole Coston notes that lay Catholic feminist educators and religious sisters see their work as self-expression, participation, and contribution to the common good.[46] Today, these ideas are common among new orthodox feminists as well. One Catholic lawyer and mother of six describes her work as a calling.[47] She feels supported by the Catholic teaching that work is a way of using one's gifts to serve God. Though she admits to sometimes dreaming of abandoning her career to homeschool her children, she concludes that she can live a Catholic life of faith and service without quitting her job. Though not unaware of the harsh reality of work for many people, feminists retain idealism about what work should be. One meditates on the well-known passage from Proverbs 31 that praises the virtue of a woman who works, noting that today many women are forced into work they would not choose, many men work too much, and many women struggle with underdevelopment. Still, there is value in viewing work in light of Catholic understandings of Creation, human relationality, and the right and duty of participation.

64   CAN YOU BE A CATHOLIC AND A FEMINIST?

Feminists, like Catholics, uphold the value of ordinary labor, including care work that takes place in and outside the home. Black feminists draw attention to the complexity of Black mothers' labor. On the one hand, they show how domestic work under slavery created an egalitarian, caring space as an antidote to the harsh workdays of Black men and women. This was not private domesticity, but the hard work of care for the sake of loved ones and "the race."[48] While concurring with the import of Black women's work in the home, Patricia Hill Collins cautions that uncritical focus on "the invincible strength and genius of the Black mother . . . can be as bogus as [focus on the image] of the happy slave."[49] The reality is that their central role as workers involves both oppression and empowerment. It gives them status as mothers but comes at a cost. Black feminists value the ordinary labor of Black people without looking away from the social context of oppression in which it takes place. The context of domestic labor today, ordinary work done primarily by women of color, is similar. Feminist scholars today draw attention to the work of caregivers, especially those forced to leave their own families behind to provide care far away from home. Like Collins, they criticize the social context that makes such choices necessary, the inequality inscribed in caregiving relationships, and the abuse endured by too many caregivers.[50] Yet they also recognizes the value of care women provide for their own children and the children of others.

Feminists have sought to challenge the idea that homemaking or women's work is frivolous. They have shown how the often-invisible work of gift-giving, card-making, and hosting family gatherings that women do connects people within and across family and community.[51] Today we might include the many women who do this work for others, for instance via apps like Task Rabbit and Thumbtack. Family in Catholic social thought is not simply a private institution, and feminists who show the social import of seemingly mundane private tasks similarly value domestic labor.

Finally, like Catholics, feminists call for limits to work and fight for the rights of workers. Some critics continue to see mainstream feminism as holding an individualistic anthropology with little room for duties rooted in interdependence.[52] However, feminists have long advocated for limits on working hours, a living wage, and family-friendly policies that would enable women and men to fulfill their caregiving responsibilities. Contemporary feminists talk about self-care as virtue and critique structures and ideals that leave women feeling depleted. Work for feminists is not an idol but one part of a good life.

Both Catholics and feminists recognize work's tie to sustenance and advocate for the rights of workers and limits on work on that basis, but both also see work as something more. Feminists who stress the desire for work as expression and advocate for just labor policies ought not present a threat to Catholics. Their advocacy affirms the basic Catholic insight that all people have the right to good work and a balanced life.

A Catholic Feminist Response to the Antiwork Movement

The overlap between Catholics and feminists that I have presented thus far is promising, but it is being challenged by prominent antiwork feminists today whose vision arguably does conflict with fundamental Catholic claims about the inherent value of work and, indirectly, the transcendent and social nature of the human person called to work for the common good and cooperate with God. Antiwork thinkers have come to greater prominence with the rise of always-on work. I close this chapter by briefly engaging their claims and sketching an alternative, Catholic feminist view.

In her widely read book *Work Won't Love You Back*, journalist Sarah Jaffe details the exploitation of workers in a variety of industries tied to the distinctively modern myth that you should

66 CAN YOU BE A CATHOLIC AND A FEMINIST?

love your work. In a passionate manifesto of a final chapter, she urges readers to love people, not work, and to look for meaning elsewhere. She pokes holes in a range of ideas people have used to find meaning in work (e.g., vocation, calling, passion, suffering for a cause, care, and family). Along the way, she shows how modern constructions of work and family are tied together. Siding with care feminists, she claims that love belongs in private, where we find connections that matter and people who will, unlike work, love us back. If our imaginations are enlarged and our needs are covered by universal basic income, she says, we will have time to care for ourselves and the people we love, and we can still "create beautiful things together in a world beyond work."[53] When more people than ever before are enduring or walking away from always-on work, Jaffe's critique is difficult to dismiss. A recent essay by a university lecturer exemplifies the new thinking, as she concludes that the myth of loving your job is being used to justify unjust pay and working conditions, and she is coming to believe that she should focus on loving her family, not her job.[54]

The feminist antiwork critique is not without merit. The notion of "labor of love" has always been more dangerous for women whose work has not been taken seriously because it is understood as coming from love, whether in their own home or the homes of others, and, increasingly this notion of love is becoming central to the "ideal worker" in every sphere, leading to exploitation.[55] Work can stifle personal freedom and limit human becoming. Loving work can be dangerous.

However, for Catholics and arguably for feminists, an antiwork vision is inadequate. In many ways, it reinscribes the very divisions between the personal and the political that feminists and Catholics critique. Feminists and Catholics reject the idea that love does not belong at work, just as they reject the claim that families should not be marked by justice. Though simplistic ideas of companies as "families" are offensive, Catholics and feminists do see family ties as extending beyond blood and home. Because we have responsibilities to people to whom we are not close, work is more than "a way to connect"; it is a means to connect one's energy and talents to the world's needs.[56] Yes, not all work is worthy of love and family responsibilities of workers must be honored, but, ultimately, love and work belong together.

To be clear, Catholic thought has never claimed that work is the *only* way persons have worth or is the only important thing in life. It has always given due weight to family, leisure, religion, and civic life along with work. Its principle of solidarity lies behind Catholic involvement in labor movements and support for just wages and work policies. Its principle of subsidiarity affirms a thick, complex view of society within which institutions (e.g., workplaces, community organizations, churches and other places of worship, families) are all good places for love. Love, for Catholics, is not just passion. It is willing the good of the other, and it does not apply only to the people we know best. Pope Benedict XVI argued that "authentically human social relationships of friendship, solidarity and reciprocity can also be conducted within economic activity, and not only outside it or 'after' it."[57] We can experience true solidarity on a factory floor, in a day care center, or on a committee. The private realm is not meant to be the source of all meaning. Family, like other spheres of life, is complicated by conflicting motivations and sin. There is no zone where love is unproblematic nor where it is inappropriate.

In a postpandemic world, the problem of work is that it asks too much. No one wants to be always on, and the fact that we ask the most vulnerable among us to do so without a living wage or affordable child care or sick days is fundamentally unjust. It can be tempting to ignore the injustice, propose personal strategies for balance, or dismiss work altogether. In this context, creative embrace of a Catholic feminist identity is a possible and necessary alternative. Old conflicts about women and work have all but evaporated. Lingering differences pale in significance in the face of larger challenges.

68 CAN YOU BE A CATHOLIC AND A FEMINIST?

A Catholic feminist can respond to the current situation not by ignoring injustice or giving up on work, but by giving work its due. Work is one place where we can bring our whole selves, provide and receive care, seek belonging, pursue the common good, and cooperate with God. Family, of course, is another. Elsewhere, I have used the concept of "dual vocation" to capture the experience of being pulled, called, and obligated in both realms.[58] Twenty years ago, I was a young mother of three toddlers and a new professor. "Dual vocation" captured my own experience as I moved back and forth between the playground and the classroom. In the midst of the "mommy wars," I found confirmation of the importance of work and family in the writings of feminists and Catholic theologians. Two decades earlier, as a Girl Scout, I often enacted a different story of work and family on the stage at summer camp. In the late 1970s, a commercial for the perfume Enjoli was popular. Because it captured the ethos of feminism in the eyes of some of its supporters and many of its critics, it is still analyzed in feminist texts today. The woman in the commercial looks a lot like the iconic woman with the briefcase, but she exudes confidence in her ability to master the balancing act: "I can bring home the bacon, fry it up in a pan, and never let you forget you're a man, 'cause I'm a woman. Enjoli." It's a fun song and captures something important about feminist calls for freedom and empowerment. But if this were all feminism had to offer, I would have as little confidence in its ability to speak to present challenges as I do in early twentieth-century Catholic dismissals of women's work. Thankfully, both traditions are more complicated and profound, making Catholic feminist identity a little easier and underlining the need for Catholics and feminists to come together in support of work-life balance for all workers today.

4

Marriage

Unorthodox Thoughts on Marriage

Unorthodox, a popular television miniseries that aired in 2020, portrays a young woman's escape from her marriage and her tight-knit, very religious extended family. Esty's life in an ultra-Orthodox Jewish community is marked by an unhappy arranged marriage and limitations linked to her gender. The ritual bathing she does before her wedding seems to signal a loss of identity, and sex between her and her husband brings pain and distance rather than pleasure and bonding. By contrast, when Esty walks into the sea and sheds her wig as she prepares to leave her family behind, it reads as a secular baptism into a new, authentic life. Later, her distressed husband travels to find her, cuts off his curls, and begs her to return. But, though she has been in her new home of Berlin for only a short time, Etsy already has new friends and a new romance. She tells her husband that it is too late.

According to a reviewer, the series depicts the complexity of Esty's decision and treats her community with compassion, so that "we get the reasons Esty runs; what we also get is her grief over it."[1] Yet, aside from some positive portrays of extended family gatherings, the series shows little curiosity about what Esty's family finds compelling about their life. At best, there is an understanding that some people need family and religion to sustain them in the confusing modern world. Esty's quest is presented as far more interesting and relatable. She seeks freedom from the limits placed on her by her family and religious community. She embraces her new identity as a young single woman in a cosmopolitan urban setting,

Can You Be a Catholic and a Feminist?. Julie Hanlon Rubio, Oxford University Press.
© Oxford University Press 2024. DOI: 10.1093/oso/9780197553145.003.0005

70   CAN YOU BE A CATHOLIC AND A FEMINIST?

where friends are chosen family, the arts provide transcendence, the cafe is a sacred space, and freedom leads to happiness. The series gives no indication that the initial euphoria could fade, leaving the young moderns empty. Esty may grieve what she has left behind, but viewers know she cannot return to New York, or Hasidism, or her marriage. To be her authentic self, she must be free from ties that bind, free to embrace a life that is actually fulfilling.

Esty's story is a typical modern narrative of finding freedom by leaving an oppressive religion. Like Tara Westover's *Educated: A Memoir* and Margaret Atwood's *The Handmaid's Tale*, it portrays religion, gender, and family ties as inextricably linked in webs of subjugation—which, of course, they sometimes are. But if, just decades ago, women's "departure narratives" out of marriage and religion were countercultural, today the reverse may be true.[2] Mainstream culture celebrates these narrative themes, including some we discussed in chapter 1—becoming oneself instead of losing oneself in service of others, having the courage to be different or original—but also breaking unhealthy attachments, finding passion outside traditional institutions, and embracing life's messiness.[3]

These cultural developments largely followed a path laid out by important strains of feminism, which claimed freedom for women from oppressive family structures. Truly horrifying circumstances have led feminists to seek freedom from sexual, gendered, and relational norms that have been used to harm, constrain, and judge women for centuries. Feminists rightly worked to change these harmful norms and structures. As I argued in chapter 1, Catholicism also values freedom as essential to an authentic human life and is committed to challenging structures that undermine human dignity. Yet, given the centrality of marital fidelity in Catholicism, some kinds of feminist distancing from marriage and family pose a difficult challenge for the Catholic. The pain of women locked in abusive or miserable marriages—the suffering that drives the desire for exits and alternatives—has to be taken seriously by Christians

MARRIAGE 71

who believe that human beings were created to be free and in loving relationships. Too often, this suffering has been ignored or interpreted as a cross women have to carry. Yet Catholicism's commitment to lifelong marriage as the locus for sex, love, and children, and its celebration of vowed religious life, stand in undeniable tension with a feminism that gives undue weight to liberty and agency.

Can Catholicism and feminism be reconciled on the question of marriage? To find out, first I contrast reformist feminist concerns about the harms of traditional marriage with radical feminist questions about whether any particular form of relationship is natural, given, or universal. Next, I describe contemporary Catholic thinking about marriage that tends in a reformist direction. To close the gap between the two, I draw on both second-wave Catholic feminists in marriage partnerships of mutual fidelity and single exemplars of the same era. In the contemporary context, I argue, the harder question to answer is not "Why go?" but "Why stay?" Married and single feminists who model steadfast and outward-facing love provide a credible response and offer an important alternative to a culture that needs narratives of fidelity to balance departure stories.

Feminist Criticisms of Marriage

From the earliest days of the movement, feminists criticized sex and marriage as they experienced them and imagined better versions of what sex and marriage could be. Charlotte Perkins Gilman's famous story, "The Yellow Wallpaper" (1892), illustrates central concerns of first-wave feminism.[4] The woman in Gilman's story, a new mother, is confined to her room and told she is weak and in need of rest. Her husband, a physician, insists that she not return to work. Her efforts to escape confinement go nowhere, and as the story progresses, she begins to visualize the peeling wallpaper as a moving, frightening trap. In the story, marriage, corrupted by gender roles, stereotypes,

72 CAN YOU BE A CATHOLIC AND A FEMINIST?

and power differentials, *is* the wallpaper—a source of women's oppression.

I vividly remember reading Gilman in high school and sympathizing with her plight. I had yellow, checked wallpaper in my room that I had always hated. Looking at it and wishing it were gone, I could sympathize with Gilman's story of the entrapped woman. But though I knew marriage had a checkered history and saw few marriages that struck me as models for my own life, I had confidence that something better was possible. Despite her famous story Gilman, too, believed that, ideally, "marriage should be a partnership of equals."[5] Other early feminist leaders called out men who drank away their wages; they advocated for women and children through moral reform movements for temperance, against slavery, and on behalf of prostitutes. The struggle for suffrage was linked to a broader call for women's rights with regard to marriage and divorce. Despite their concerns, most feminists nevertheless retained their belief in marriage as an ideal, though some, like Susan B. Anthony and Sarah Grimke, who were more convinced of marriage's inherent limitations, chose not to marry.

Other early feminists made similar critiques but put forth alternative visions of marriage. A century before Gilman, Mary Wollstonecraft wrote in *A Vindication of the Rights of Woman* (1792) that marriage should be a friendship marked by "equality, free choice, reason, mutual esteem and profound concern for one another's moral character."[6] Wollstonecraft thought that the highly gendered kind of romance she knew was incompatible with both marital friendship and good parenting. Instead, she prioritized stability and mutual affection, because the ideal—a union of eros and friendship—was nearly impossible to attain.[7] Similarly, early feminists who advocated for more equality in family law did so in order "to free wives from dissolute husbands not in any sense to win more sexual freedom for themselves."[8] A reformist position that challenged divorce laws, restrictive gender roles, domestic violence, and laws restricting women's financial independence, while upholding the ideal of marriage as friendship, was the dominant position in the early feminist movement.

Black feminists of the first and second waves also affirmed the value of marriage despite racist barriers that limited their freedom. Sojourner Truth and Harriet Tubman advocated for racial equality and challenged gender stereotypes via the lives they led. Nonetheless, both married, and neither mounted a serious critique of marriage. The endurance of enslaved people who married at great personal risk, maintained commitments despite forced separation and sexual violence, and searched for lost spouses and children for years after emancipation, is invoked by Black feminists as evidence that marriage mattered to Black people who embraced it. As historian Tera Hunter writes, "Despite the terror that slavery spawned and no matter how much it altered and disfigured black marriages, it did not and could not annihilate them."[9]

Yet, even as they uphold the ideal, Black feminists call attention to the many ways Black women have been disadvantaged by marriage. In her classic 1991 book *Black Feminist Thought*, Patricia Hill Collins notes the restrictions on love endured by slaves and the abuse and infidelity endured by Black women.[10] Sociologists reviewing years of Black feminist thought conclude that racial oppression makes Black marriage harder to sustain. Black marriages can be more "egalitarian, empowering, and pioneering" than white marriages.[11] Yet marriage rates are lower, divorce rates are higher, and women's satisfaction rates are lower in Black communities. Black women continue to affirm marriage as an ideal but are increasingly reluctant to marry unless they find partners who can provide the respect and stability they seek.[12] Yet Black feminists have also been critical of white feminists who overlook how crucial it is for Black women and men to remain united. As Fannie Lou Hamer said, marriage has meant both "love and trouble" to Black women.[13]

New orthodox feminists embrace a reformist vision of marriage with a countercultural zeal. Like some women of color who reject

74 CAN YOU BE A CATHOLIC AND A FEMINIST?

white feminist agendas, they stand in tension with the mainstream of the movement, sometimes proudly choosing early marriage and large families and placing motherhood at the center of their identities. They see themselves as defying cultural norms that question their marital investment and their tightly knit religious communities. They boldly reject gender norms that would leave them out of the workplace while insisting that feminism means supporting marriage and family, something they see mainstream feminism failing to prioritize. As Leah Libresco Sargeant, founder of the substack *Other Feminisms* argues, "The world must remake itself to be hospitable to women, not the other way around. That means valuing interdependence and vulnerability, rather than idealizing autonomy."[14]

In every stage, and across liberal, socialist, and new orthodox types, feminists have attempted to strengthen marriage and remove structures impeding family flourishing. They can all be considered reformist. In contrast, radical feminists have mounted critiques that lead them beyond marriage. Philosopher Simone de Beauvoir grew up Catholic and mourned the way women gave themselves up for love with an intensity that could only be understood as religious. A convert to atheism, she maintained an open relationship with Jean Paul Sartre for over fifty years, which freed her for intimate relationships with other men and women. She avoided the trap of most women for whom, she said, "to love is to relinquish everything for the benefit of a master."[15] Beauvoir thought that love too often became a source of identity, transcendence, and even salvation for women. She worried that women chose to love instead of taking responsibility for their own lives, hoping marriage would provide the sense of purpose they lack. Beauvoir rejected this model and advocated relationships founded in mutuality in which both spouses retained some measure of independence.

In the early feminist movement, some "free love" feminists shared Beauvoir's pessimism about marriage, but they were a distinct minority. Emma Goldman, a socialist feminist who saw free

MARRIAGE   75

love as essential to revolution, was "a fierce critic of the institution of marriage," and fellow socialists Pauline Newman and Frieda Miller, among others, had a "Boston marriage," living together as partners.[16] Radicals were often marginalized as the mainstream feminist movement was dominated by religious feminists for whom marriage and family were sacred, socialists who prioritized labor rights, and others who did not want countercultural positions on sex and marriage to derail broader goals of suffrage, property rights, and access to employment. Still, radical questions about marriage were a part of feminism from the beginning.

In the second wave, as the sexual revolution gained traction, radical critiques spread. Catherine McKinnon developed a theory of sexual violence that saw a continuum between ordinary sex and rape—as long as men retained power over women, there could be no true consent.[17] Some feminists came to think that, given the depth of sexism, equal relationships between men and women were impossible, so they turned to friendships and romantic partnerships with women. Coming to see gender as a social construct distinguished from biological sex led some to deeper feminist analysis of all that was previously assumed to be natural, including marriage and family. Still, some radical critics of the sexual revolution were skeptical that male-defined sexual freedom was truly revolutionary for women.

Poet Adrienne Rich, like other radical feminists, contrasted the oppression of motherhood as an institution with the complexity of her own experience. She illustrates the latter with beautifully remembered moments from a summer with her sons when her husband was absent and she and her boys "lived like castaways on some island of mothers and children. . . . This is what living with children could be—without school hours, fixed routines, naps, the conflict of being both mother and wife with no room for being, simply, myself."[18] Rich's groundbreaking essay "Compulsory Heterosexuality" extends her critique beyond motherhood to marriage.[19] She seeks to free women from the normativity of marriage by questioning the

76 CAN YOU BE A CATHOLIC AND A FEMINIST?

assumption that most women are heterosexual, revealing the invisibility of lesbian existence, and uncovering the power of heterosexuality as an institution. She encourages women to consider how their assumptions about love have been socially constructed. After the death of her husband, Rich found a partner in fellow writer Michelle Cliff. Radical feminists like Rich pushed beyond marriage reform to free love, lesbian partnerships, and ways of living and loving that released women from constraints they saw as inherent to the institution of marriage.

Though first- and second-wave feminists raised significant questions about marriage and saw clearly the ways it was corrupted by patriarchy and white supremacy, most continued to believe that committed relationships, whether recognized as marriages or not, were ideal. Apart from the minority of free love advocates, most sought to clear away the sexist and racist trappings of marriage and parenthood, to free women and men for relationships that were deeper and more satisfying. However, many postmodern and queer theorists today question the assumptions that held together this largely reformist feminist vision.

Queer theorists generally reject the idea that anything is "given" or "natural" for human beings. Jack Halberstam's manifesto, *Gaga Feminism: Sex, Gender, and the End of Normal*, moves beyond reform to "improvisation, customization, and innovation."[20] Embracing fluidity and variation in gender and relationships, rather than limiting ourselves to "the oppressive ideology" of marriage, we should, he says, seek "alternative intimacies" in various shapes and forms.[21] Gender theorist Judith Butler has similarly characterized same-sex marriage as an "unacceptably conservative" goal because it privileges marriage above other possibilities.[22] Within her ethical framework, it makes little sense to argue for certain relational configurations over others because there is no definitive understanding of what it means to be human to anchor relationships by giving them a particular shape, form, or end.

Queer theorists lift up the positive in alternatives to marriage. Saidiya Hartman's *Wayward Lives, Beautiful Experiments* highlights transgressive practices of Black women in the early twentieth century, showing that "young black women were radical thinkers who tirelessly imagined other ways to live and never failed to consider how the world might be otherwise."[23] Hartman's depiction highlights women's efforts to live freely that were shut down by people who could not see the beauty of their experiments. She writes, "Those who dared to refuse the gender norms and social conventions of sexual propriety—monogamy, heterosexuality, and marriage—or failed to abide the script of female respectability were targeted . . . [for their] practices of intimacy and affection."[24] Some contemporary Black queer thinkers claim that since Black family life has always been diverse, fluidity is crucial to Black family ethics today.[25] We cannot, they argue, allow fixed notions about family to coerce people into relational forms they do not desire. Queer theorists place few limits on relationships, stressing possibility, creativity, and openness to change. The new postmodern emphasis on fluidity and variation now competes with the reformist vison of marriage that was previously central, widening the gap between Catholics and feminists.

Catholic Visions of Marriage

Feminist critics often link Christianity to traditional marriage, pointing to its biblical roots (Genesis 1–3; Ephesian 5: 21–33) and sexist shape. There is certainly some basis for this critique. In an encyclical from the 1930s, Pope Pius XII calls feminists "false teachers" who wrongly advocate equality in place of just hierarchy, encouraging women to abandon their rightful role in the home. More recently, Christians have championed "family values" and opposed reforms sought by feminists (e.g., no-fault divorce, birth control, sexual liberation, and marriage equality).[26] But Christian

78   CAN YOU BE A CATHOLIC AND A FEMINIST?

thinking about marriage is complex and has developed over time in conversation with culture, moving from patriarchal and duty-focused to egalitarian and rooted in love.

Likewise, a lot has changed in Catholic teaching on marriage since the time of Pius XII. It is impossible to offer a full treatment of Catholic theology on marriage and family in this space, so I will focus on four essential themes: (1) marriage as an "intimate partnership of life and love"; (2) marriage as fruitful; (3) marriage as rooted in a lifelong promise of fidelity; (4) marriage as one way to live as a Christian. Each of these themes can cohere with feminist concerns, though tensions will certainly remain.

The phrase "intimate partnership of life and love" comes from the Vatican II document *Gaudium et spes*, "The Church and the Modern World." In the twentieth century, the Catholic Church developed a greater appreciation of love in marriage.[27] Incredibly to us, theologians previously argued that love was not necessary for a legitimate marriage. But now the mutual gift of self is viewed as essential. Understanding marriage as rooted in love between spouses has allowed for a deeper appreciation of the unitive purpose of sex. While Saint Augustine saw sex as justified by procreation, John Paul II writes movingly of the passionate life of couples as analogous to the Eucharist for, in both, one could achieve intimacy with God.[28] The new characterization of marriage as partnership is also significant, as it indicates the church's willingness to move beyond a primarily hierarchical understanding of marriage to a mostly egalitarian one.

To be sure, a theology of complementarity, which assumes heterosexuality and some essential gender differences, still marks all of contemporary Catholic theology, but only rarely does it shape ideals about activity in marriage. Contemporary teaching includes no division of labor between husbands and wives. Men are no longer called to headship over women, machismo is criticized, and Christ's example of sacrificial service is what men should emulate.[29] The vast majority of Catholic theology on marriage is addressed to both spouses without differentiation. Both are called to self-giving love, openness to life, service to society, and the work of making their home a hospitable space of prayer and community.[30]

Still, despite progression toward equal partnership, vestiges of complementarity in Christian theology remain problematic, as they rely on gender stereotypes and fail to account for the diversity of ways in which two individuals can complement each other. In addition, it is not clear that embrace of intimate partnership takes seriously the place of sex in marriage. Though theology has progressed, often the view of marriage Catholics encounter on retreats, in homilies, and in marriage preparation classes remains stubbornly stuck in the past. While Catholic theology has become more positive about intimacy and more egalitarian, a gap remains.

Contemporary Catholic theology also has a broader view of what makes marriage "fruitful." Marriage for Catholics has never been just a way for two people to come together to have babies. It is a vocation to a life in which two people orient themselves to serving others. The Catholic tradition does not limit fruitfulness to the physical. Couples experiencing infertility can marry, as can couples whose fertile years are past. Infertility is not a just cause for annulment, which means it does not signal the illegitimacy of a marriage. In the Catholic wedding liturgy, couples have always promised to be open to children. However, the liturgy now suggests that the mission of their marriage is broader.[31] Blessings during the wedding rite speak not only of future children, but of extended families, home, and the church. Marriage, as Karl Rahner, SJ, wrote, "is not the act in which two individuals come together to form a 'we,' a relationship in which they set themselves apart from the 'all' and close themselves against this. Rather it is the act in which a 'we' is constituted which opens itself lovingly precisely to the ALL."[32]

Recent papal teaching furthers this expansive vision. John Paul II used the term "spiritual fruitfulness" to describe how couples who could not have biological children might produce fruits other than children, and insisted that a married couple's obligations did

80 CAN YOU BE A CATHOLIC AND A FEMINIST?

not end with their children. They were also called to serve society via hospitality and political action.[33] Pope Francis speaks movingly of a couple walking hand in hand looking outward and of the home as "a hub for integrating persons."[34] Marriage in Catholic social thought is not simply private but public, an essential part of the common good. This means that just as couples have a duty to reach out, families have rights, and society owes them conditions that make possible their flourishing.

Reformist feminists might find common ground with Catholics in this broader vision. Still, questions about where this leaves same-sex couples remain, as do questions about whether it is even possible to say what marriage must be for everyone. What if a couple does not want this kind of life? Can they decide for themselves what they want their marriage to be about? Is there sufficient social support for this ambitious project? Given the limitations of much the church has said in the past, universal claims about family remain troubling.

Contemporary Catholic marriage theology is also controversial because of its commitment to an ambitious fidelity. Rather than backing away from lifelong commitment, today's vows take the traditional "to death do us part" one step further by asking spouses to promise to "love and honor" each other "all the days of [their] lives." Though occasionally secular vows incorporate some wiggle room, the vast majority of people who marry still promise to stay married for life. Even knowing divorce by statistics and experience, they dare to hope that their love will carry them through good times and bad, sickness and health, abundance and poverty, so that the person they love now will be the one with whom they will grow old. Echoing this widely shared desire, contemporary Catholics see staying married not as a duty but as an essential aspect of love that by its nature points toward forever.

The difficulties of fidelity are real. Contemporary Catholic theology encourages people to do the work necessary to keep a relationship strong over time. Rejecting the cultural convention

MARRIAGE   81

of finding "the one," Catholics embrace the idea that marriage binds two people together and gives them the stability and grace they need. Still, there is a recognition that some situations (e.g., abuse, addiction, abandonment) will make divorce and separation necessary. Annulments opening a path to remarriage have become easier in recent years. Pope Francis has insisted on compassionate inclusion of those whose marriages do not last, repeating again and again, "No one can be condemned forever."[35] His is a more merciful fidelity. Yet the ambitious ideal remains.

Even for some reformists, Catholic idealization of lifelong fidelity does not make enough room for diverse circumstances. Given the history of women forced by economics or custom to stay in violent or unhappy marriages, many feminists would want greater acknowledgment of the necessity of divorce and recognition of the possibility of finding new life in remarriage (without an annulment) or singleness. For these feminists, because marriage has historically been limiting and harmful, at the very least there has to be more room for exceptions.

Perhaps the least-known aspect of contemporary Catholic theology is that marriage is not for everyone, nor is family limited by blood. In some ways, this teaching is ancient. The primary family for Christians has always been the church, or the community of brothers and sisters in Christ, living and dead, and by extension all of humankind.[36] Marriage is *one way* Christians have lived as disciples of Christ, not the only way. Single life and vowed religious life have been equally important in the history of Christianity. In the Gospels, apart from Mary and Joseph, there are very few examples of married couples with children.[37] Rather, Jesus gathers a diverse community of people with and without partners and children. In prophetic "hard sayings," Jesus raises profound questions about duties to family and asks followers to place their commitment to God before all other obligations, including those arising from family ties.

82 CAN YOU BE A CATHOLIC AND A FEMINIST?

Most Catholics are familiar with what this looks like for religious sisters, priests, monks, and mystics, but, until recently, less consideration was given to what it means for everyone else. A new generation of married theologians have found this aspect of Catholic theology to be refreshingly countercultural.[38] In the Catholic tradition, they note, family ties that bind go beyond blood not only for single saints, but for everyone. Pope Francis often talks about the earth as "our common home," the "human family," and the need to love beyond artificially imposed boundaries.[39] The importance of family bonds is acknowledged, but so too is the challenge to be open to how God might call believers to spread their love beyond the confines of home.

In this aspect of contemporary theology, there is great potential for common ground. A vision with room for a variety of singles and married people all called to a more expansive love could be attractive to feminists who value inclusivity and a diversity of possible life paths. Along with more egalitarianism, broader conceptions of fruitfulness, and a more ambitious and merciful fidelity, it has the potential to open up liberating paths for Catholic feminists, if some of the remaining tension can be resolved.

Catholic Feminist Families

In the last two sections, I contrasted the views of reformist and radical feminists and showed how contemporary Catholic theology on marriage answers many reformist criticisms while resisting some of the more radical moves beyond marriage. Catholic feminist thinkers illuminate how Catholic theology could further evolve in a reformist direction. Below I organize their contributions around two lingering questions: "Can Christian marriage be mutual?" and "Can Catholic theology transcend sex negativity?" In Catholic feminists, I find a coherent account of marriage in theory and practice, a synthesis of Catholic feminist wisdom on love and fidelity that responds to important feminist concerns.

MARRIAGE 83

Can Christian marriage be mutual? Catholic feminists have long thought so, though they were not unaware of the challenges they faced. In a retrospective essay in *America* magazine in 2013, Catholic intellectual Sidney Callahan wrote on the fiftieth anniversary of Betty Friedan's *The Feminine Mystique*:

> Was it really that bad? the young may ask. Yes, it was. In the 1950s my father, who told me I was intelligent enough to be a doctor, also warned, "Don't be too smart or no one will marry you." Women were not welcome in graduate and professional schools, and the glass ceiling was universally in place. Married women could hardly aspire to combine work and family. Women were considered too different from men to expect fulfillment in anything other than marriage, children and the domestic arts.[40]

Yet despite her agreement with Friedan's critique of the cult of domesticity and limitations on women's professional advancement, Callahan pushed back against Friedan's disdain for religion and marriage on the lecture circuit and with books like *Beyond Birth Control: The Christian Experience of Sex*. Callahan's disagreement with second-wave feminism on marriage and religion was typical of Catholic feminists of the era. She recalls that Friedan called her "an Aunt Tom" for supporting "motherhood, marriage, religious vocations and love's free gift of service" and admits that she was critical of Friedan's seeming unwillingness to balance children's needs with women's quest for identity.[41] Callahan insisted that her faith in God, who could be addressed as "Mother," Christ, in whom "there is no male or female," and a tradition alive with saints who "transcend their gender differences" grounded her feminism. For this mother of seven, married for sixty-five years to ethicist Daniel Callahan (with whom she engaged in spirited public argument) the connections between Christianity and social justice were clear, and so was the compatibility of feminism with marriage, sacrifice, and childrearing.

84 CAN YOU BE A CATHOLIC AND A FEMINIST?

For Catholic feminists in the 1960s, marriage needed to be reformed through dialogue with the radical roots of the Christian tradition. Historian Mary Henold notes, "The earliest Catholic feminist writers believed the church contained within it the seeds of liberation," and that included its teaching on marriage and family.[42] While some participated in consciousness-raising groups, early Catholic feminists were primarily inspired by Vatican II and lay movements of the 1930s to 1960s that gave single and married women the chance to take leaderships roles and participate in discussions about church reform.[43] The Grail, the Catholic Worker, and the Friendship House movements were all part of the Catholic revival of the early twentieth century. By the 1960s Grailville was established as a center to which women came for Christian formation.[44] It provided opportunities for women to train for lay missionary work abroad, service careers, and religious education jobs. Catholic feminists were formed by groups like these both to take on new roles and to challenge prevailing cultural norms about family.

In the 1960s, their main target was the "Eternal Woman," a ubiquitous concept popularized by German scholar Gertrud von le Fort, whom we met in chapter 1. Le Fort lifted up virtues she understood as essential to Catholic womanhood—surrender, sacrifice, and passivity. She saw Mary as exemplifying these virtues and wrote that Mary "exercises power only by surrendering it."[45] To be a woman, for her, is not to find oneself but to surrender oneself; this is what being a good Catholic wife and mother was all about.[46] This complementarian ideology was echoed in popular Catholic publications of the time. The powerful image of a sacrificial, silent, suffering woman had a hold even among progressive Catholics.

Catholic feminists of the 1960s rejected this model of womanhood while maintaining commitments to intimacy, fidelity, and mutuality in marriage. The Marriage Encounter movement, founded in 1962 in Spain, was a significant progressive force in the lives of ordinary Catholics. It influenced hundreds of thousands via weekend retreats that encouraged couples in the practice of

MARRIAGE 85

daily writing, reading, and listening. Fr. Chuck Gallagher, who popularized the movement in the United States, insisted on the revolutionary nature of married love. In Marriage Encounter, "Couples are willing to face the shallowness of their marriages and family relationships and to seek a better way to live."[47] The deeper intimacy they attain enables them to move beyond more common quests for possessions and power, the very "things that lead to war, poverty and alienation" and instead find "a sense of mission."[48] Married couples who led retreats all over the country believed that greater intimacy was a step toward healing the world.

Optimism regarding marriage can also be seen in the Christian Family Movement led by Pat and Patty Crowley.[49] Attractive mainly to middle-class professional Catholics, it would claim over one hundred thousand members by 1970. One of its radical features was having women and men meet together to talk about serious topics. A study guide from the time is titled *The Family in Revolution* and addresses racism, busing, and affordable housing. By gathering couples in mixed groups and focusing outward, CFM effectively downplayed gender roles. While most of the cake and coffee recommended for meetings was likely prepared by women, the general orientation of the group was away from the surrendering Eternal Woman and toward mutual partnership. Progressive Catholic couples were at the forefront of lay movements in the 1960s. They gave witness to the power of two people committed to each other and to using their partnership as a foundation to better the world around them.

This combination of questioning rigid gender roles yet seeking equality and intimacy in marriage is just as evident in the words of ordinary women interviewed by Sally Cunneen in her 1968 book *Sex: Female, Religion: Catholic* as it is in the writings of theologians and intellectuals. The same women who were frustrated by the pervasiveness of talk about the submissiveness of Mary and the archetypal Eternal Woman were deeply interested in renewed attention to "a theology of love and marriage" with an orientation toward

86 CAN YOU BE A CATHOLIC AND A FEMINIST?

working for a more just society.[50] In this respect, they differed from radical secular feminists for whom marriage was irredeemably linked to women's lower status as "the second sex."

Today, Catholic feminist theologians continue the work of pressing for deeper mutuality in marriage and parenting. They link this ideal with advocacy for the practical supports that make mutuality more possible. Policies like paid family leave, just wages, affordable child care, universal healthcare, and laws protecting women and children from domestic violence are in line with contemporary Catholic social thought and provide necessary scaffolding for strong, mutual, justice-seeking relationships. Mutuality, it seems, is possible in Catholic marriage. But what about sex?

Here, too, Catholic feminists of the 1960s were trailblazers, in their own way. These women did not, for the most part, embrace the sexual revolution, but they did begin to rethink sex. There is little evidence of interest among theologians or ordinary Catholics in the sort of sexual freedom championed by some second-wave feminists. Still, for middle-class Catholics, secular and religious books on intimacy in marriage were important. I remember noticing the presence of some of these on the bookshelves of my own parents in the 1970s. Andrew Greeley was the best-selling apostle of the sexual marriage, with titles such as *Sexual Intimacy: Love and Play* (1973). *The Virtue of Sex: Pleasure and Holiness in Marriage* (1966), written by lay theologian José de Vinck and endorsed by Thomas Merton, was also widely read. De Vinck moves away from a restrictive pre-Vatican II theology to a more positive ethic of sexuality by engaging poetry, literature, and experience. Defending the value of sexual passion in remarkably ungendered prose, he concludes, "Let us love with sweet madness and enjoy it in full; let us love with art and ardor, with imagination and fire," not limited by prudishness but by an orientation to lasting love.[51] The seemingly excessive idealization of marital sex was a necessary and popular corrective in its time.

Catholic feminists who did pay attention to the sexual revolution were not convinced that it was freeing for everyone. Radical feminist Mary Daly saw calls for sexual freedom as thinly veiled assertions of male privilege. She writes, "Female becoming is *not* the so-called sexual revolution. The latter has in fact been one more extension of the politics of rape, a New Morality of false liberation foisted upon women, who have been told to be free to be what women have always been, sex objects."[52] The majority of Catholics focused on sexual liberation *within* marriage rather than outside it. Even the more liberal among them were more interested in claiming freedom for intimacy than in trying to disentangle sex and commitment. Prominent Catholic progressives of the time included several longtime married couples (e.g., Sidney and Daniel Callahan, Sally and Joe Cuneen, Pat and Patty Crowley, Frank Sheed and Maisie Ward), as well as singles like Thomas Merton, Dorothy Day, Daniel Berrigan, and Flannery O'Connor, who were, for the most part, celibate.[53] Catholic heroes from this era did not question vows of fidelity, but they were not sex-negative either. They looked for freedom around the edges of commitment without seeking to free sex from all constraint.

One might say that for Catholic feminists of the 1960s, sex may not always be "grave matter" (as they had been taught in Catechism class), but it matters. Sally Cunneen describes how the women she interviewed mourned the anti-body, legalistic sexual theology they had been taught, yet yearned to understand the depth and meaning of sex. "We are coming to really accept the Incarnate God," said one married woman.[54] Sidney Callahan was typical in forging a way between the sexual revolution and theological treatises that make sexual love so exalted and mysterious that it seems completely unrelated to blood-and-flesh human beings.[55] She locates the gravity of sexual matter in the couple's lasting sexual relationship, which will involve joy, pleasure, sorrow, seriousness, and play over time. For Catholic feminists, sex mattered, not for procreation or pleasure

88 CAN YOU BE A CATHOLIC AND A FEMINIST?

alone but because of its power as a passionate practice sustaining couples through the joys and challenges of their lives.

Since the 1960s, Catholic feminist thinking has moved to the academy, where many more female lay theologians, married and single, are at work to bring sex positivity to a Catholic thinking about marriage.[56] These theologians have the necessary training to bring feminist theory together with developments in Catholic theology. They have continued to integrate experience with traditional sources. The feminists are more conscious of the ways gender-based violence shapes sex in and outside of marriage and thus of the need to integrate justice into sexual ethics. They are also more attentive to the need to reclaim sexual pleasure as a good related to intimacy. Most contemporary feminist thinking on marriage and family also includes LGBTQ Catholics. Same-sex marriage is broadly accepted as a legitimate development, a way to claim the goods of mutuality, fidelity, and fruitfulness for a couples who complement each other in a variety of ways. Of course, it is not yet accepted in official Catholic teaching.[57] But feminist theologians strive to speak more inclusively to the diversity of Catholic families.[58] The project of Catholic feminist revisioning of sex and marriage continues along reformist lines and speaks more credibly about both mutuality and intimacy.

New orthodox feminists, who are primarily indebted to first-wave feminists rather than their second-wave sisters, are distinct among contemporary Catholic feminists in their advocacy of mutuality rooted in sexual difference and sex positivity tethered to very traditional ethical norms.[59] Like reformists, they are critical of a lack of social support for families. But they contend that feminism lost its way when it encountered the sexual revolution and aim to recover its more conservative roots. While respecting these concerns, I have argued instead that, historically, free love and related trajectories have been on the margins of the feminist movement, which challenged patriarchy but valued egalitarian marriage. Since the 1960s more feminists have raised radical questions about

MARRIAGE 89

sex, gender, and family. While these questions are difficult to reconcile with Catholicism, for the most part, mainstream Catholic feminism continues the feminist reformist project, providing a unique space for creative revisioning of committed sex and egalitarian, justice-seeking marriages, while honoring the unique contributions of single people, including vowed religious.

Fidelity Revisited

I began this chapter with an analysis of the popular TV miniseries *Unorthodox*, which I argued is representative of contemporary cultural sensibilities, especially the view of religious communities and their sex and marriage norms as at odds with authentic self-expression and relationships. I argued that serious concerns about marriage underlying the popularity of this narrative have been central to the feminist movement, but that a Catholic vision and practice of marriage that integrates the best of feminist critique presents a compelling contrast.

Historian Stephanie Coontz, at the end of her definitive history of marriage, argues that while today marriage has greater potential to be satisfying than ever before, limits of any kind have become impossible to maintain because we value fulfillment so highly, and thus, "We can never reinstate marriage as the primary source of commitment and caregiving in the modern world."[60] We are finding it more difficult to anchor the quest for freedom and the remaking of the self. Becoming has won out over being. Both thick visions of the good and limitations on adult desire seem problematic because we are so much more conscious of the suffering the old rules have caused. And given the history, we are much more skeptical of ideals and norms, especially when it comes to marriage. This is why departure narratives remain so compelling.

Where does this leave a Catholic feminist? Real-life models of outward-facing mutual love brought forward in this chapter

90 CAN YOU BE A CATHOLIC AND A FEMINIST?

suggest a way forward. So does a Catholic feminist vision of marriage that brings together deep respect for intimacy and mutuality, an insistence that relational energy flow outward to society, and a more ambitious and merciful fidelity. Catholic feminists embrace Jesus's hard questions about overvaluing family ties by encouraging strong ties across a diversity of single and partnered households. This strain of Catholic thought has some resonances with early and midcentury liberal feminism, as well as socialist feminism, and engages some aspects of postmodern feminist critique as it continues the reformist project. It insists on both freedom *from* oppressive structures and freedom *for* flourishing. Authenticity, for Catholic feminists, is rooted in the idea that humans are made for relationship. Fidelity and solidarity can lead to deeper fulfillment but require accepting some limits.

Importantly, this vision makes room for a more diverse set of families, all of whom, as Pope Francis says, "can become a light in the darkness of the world."[61] It acknowledges that not all marriages will make it (nor should they), and offers compassion rather than judgment to those whose commitments must end. Lifelong love and fidelity are, in this view, goods worth seeking. The vision of flourishing in committed partnership remains, as do the powerful witnesses both single and married who show us what is possible. Along with models from the 1960s, there are many ordinary couples today who witness to mutual love, hospitality, and commitment to a better world.[62] And there are also singles who can love radically precisely because they are not committed to just one person. These icons of the possible inspire Catholic feminists today to claim the egalitarian practices of love and fidelity their feminist foremothers could only imagine.

Perhaps, with these visions in mind, we can reimagine how *Unorthodox* might have ended differently. With mercy and a commitment to an ambitious fidelity, Esty might accept her husband's apology when he comes to find her. They might then walk the streets of the city all night long, talking through their failures, disappointments, hopes, and dreams. Perhaps they might even decide to take up the admittedly daunting project of forging an intimate, egalitarian partnership. The eclectic mix of singles and coupled households that Esty had begun to know could be invited to become something more—a interdependent community of family and friends who would promise to be there for this couple in good times and bad. Perhaps there would be room, too, for the God who continues to invite all people into ever deeper mutual relation and calls them to turn that love outward into the world.

5

Life

Identity Politics

On January 21, 2017, women in cities around the world marched in protest the day after the inauguration of President Donald Trump.[1] Accounts of why women marched vary, but many were stunned by the demeaning way the president spoke about women and by the many credible accusations of sexual assault against him. They worried about how violence against women would be treated during his tenure and chanted, "Women's rights are human rights." As many groups joined in, the agenda broadened to include workers' rights, healthcare, migrant rights, environmental justice, and, in response to the efforts of women of color, racial justice.

But when New Wave Feminists, a group of young women who identified as pro-life and feminist, applied to join the march in Washington, DC, their request was denied.[2] Planned Parenthood and NARAL Pro-Choice America were major sponsors of the event. The idea that a pro-life group would join the Women's March was unimaginable. The organizers included abortion access in their "unity principles" and declared the march itself to be pro-choice. Knowing this, most women who identified as pro-life stayed home. Their views on abortion led them to believe that they did not belong at Women's March. The controversy over New Wave Feminists was brief. Unlike the conflict over racism, this conflict is not remembered in most reports of the event, the largest march in US history. Many on both sides would likely agree with the division the organizers insisted upon. The march was for feminists, not

Can You Be a Catholic and a Feminist?. Julie Hanlon Rubio, Oxford University Press.
© Oxford University Press 2024. DOI: 10.1093/oso/9780197553145.003.0006

pro-lifers. New Wave Feminists knew they were doing something radical by asserting their desire to hold these identities together.

The divide on abortion has once again taken center stage. In June 2022, the Supreme Court declared in *Dobbs v. Jackson Women's Health Organization* that abortion access was no longer a constitutional right. More than twenty states have since moved to protect abortion rights, while over half have banned or restricted abortion. Most feminists are distraught about the loss of abortion rights. They are outraged because women have lost the right to make decisions about their own bodies, because vulnerable women (especially women of color) will be left without legal options, and because women's health will be at risk. They argue that criminalizing abortion does not reduce its frequency. It just makes it more dangerous.

By contrast, pro-life supporters, including many Catholics, are taking in the reality that something they have long sought has finally come to pass. They rejoice that they are the #ProLifeGeneration that ended a national commitment to legalized abortion. Some argue for increased social and government support to help women carry unplanned pregnancies to term, but their opposition to the use of abortion as a solution to unplanned pregnancy remains.

In this chapter, I unpack the tensions between Catholics and feminists on abortion, knowing that for those who struggle to maintain Catholic feminist identity, these tensions are often internal. In an earlier book, I reflected on the politics of abortion.[3] While political challenges continue, here I am more concerned with how to think about abortion as a Catholic and a feminist. I turn to women's experiences of pregnancy, pregnancy loss, and birth, and use those stories as a foundation to construct a Catholic feminist approach to prenatal life. Despite differences in these stories, values of agency, relationality, and concern for the most vulnerable can be perceived at the heart of both feminism and Catholicism.

Admittedly, abortion presents a difficult case for this book's project. In the last three chapters, on sex, work, and marriage, I found that seeing the complexity of Catholic and feminist views

94 CAN YOU BE A CATHOLIC AND A FEMINIST?

allowed common ground to emerge and set the stage for dialogue, authentic identity, synergy and collaboration. In this chapter and the following two, because the challenge of reconciling Catholicism and feminism is more difficult, new strategies become necessary. In this chapter, because dialogue has so often proven fruitless or harmful, I place stories at the center. My hope is that compassionate listening will open reflective space that has previously been unavailable to those seeking to hold their Catholic and feminist commitments together. The common values I find animating feminist and Catholic stories cannot resolve all tension, but they can provide a foundation for an authentic Catholic feminist stance that honors women's lives and the lives they carry.

Unresolvable Tensions

Though popular accounts sometimes characterize Catholic opposition to abortion as recent, the belief that abortion is unethical has a long history in the Catholic Church.[4] Yet before abortion was legalized via *Roe v. Wade* in 1973, abortion was not nearly as central to Catholic culture. When the law changed and rates climbed, Catholics joined with Evangelicals to defend the lives of the unborn.[5] The most visible aspects of Catholic advocacy include lobbying efforts of the US bishops, statements by some local bishops and parish priests that a Catholic must not vote for a pro-choice candidate, and denial of communion to some pro-choice Catholic politicians.[6] The movement also extends to protest; collections of diapers, clothes, and food; concern for adoption and fostering of children; and support for pregnant women.[7] Catholics—especially those who are formed by Catholic institutions—often grow up thinking of being pro-life as an essential part of being Catholic, though their personal and political views are diverse.

Abortion holds a unique space in Catholic culture, but it exists within a broader set of commitments. The late cardinal Joseph

Bernadin of Chicago coined the phrase "consistent ethic of life" and used the image of a seamless garment to connect abortion to poverty and war.[8] John Paul II linked abortion to the death penalty and euthanasia. Catholic social teaching ties together opposition to abortion, poverty, the unjust treatment of immigrants, and, more recently, racism and environmental destruction.[9] Catholic hospitals, schools, and nonprofit agencies manifest a consistent ethic of life by providing care for a broad spectrum of vulnerable people.

When Pope Francis links abortion to the "throwaway culture," he stands in this tradition, even as he tries to find a new balance by talking more about poverty, migration, and climate change.[10] Catholic pro-life identity is being stretched under Francis. Consistency, in concern for the many lives cut short due to human action or inaction, has become even more important. Compassion and support for women faced with difficult pregnancies coexists with respect for the life of the fetus. There is an obligation, as some current advocates say, to #LoveThemBoth.

Still, abortion continues to receive more attention than other life issues, as is evident from Catholic voting guides and the US bishops' website.[11] Abortion is treated differently in part because Catholic moral teaching holds that it is never just to directly target innocent life.[12] Killing in other circumstances, such as in a just war or self-defense, may be licit. Phenomena such as disease, climate disaster, and poverty that lead to the deaths of innocents despite our best intentions or because of what we fail to do differ from "intrinsically evil" acts such as abortion, the bombing of population centers, or murder, which are always wrong.

Still, Catholic tradition does not require that all intrinsic evils must be illegal. There is no movement to outlaw lying or adultery, which are understood as intrinsic evils. Today's contraception fights are more about preserving space for those whose views place them outside of public consensus than on limiting access for everyone. The tradition allows that reasonable people can differ on policy

96 CAN YOU BE A CATHOLIC AND A FEMINIST?

directed to curb evils that undeniably lead to loss of life, such as poverty or climate change, but holds that the law ought not tolerate the direct killing of innocents, so limiting the legality of abortion has long been a central goal.[13] Even so, there is room for prudential judgment when this goal is not achievable, partial efforts can be permissible, and compromise may be required in the face of limited consensus.

Catholic tradition is unwavering on the humanity and right to life of the developing embryo or fetus. This stance is based both on faith (Psalms 139:13–14) and reason. Scientists can identify the genotype of the embryo as human, and by the week 8, a primitive heart, circulatory system, and brain emerge, along with the beginnings of facial features, and by week 12, fingers, toes, ears, and genitals.[14] The Catholic tradition argues for the personhood of the fetus despite its vulnerability, dependence, and early stage of development. The countercultural claim of equal dignity for persons at all stages of life is central to Catholicism.

Being pro-choice has played a similarly central role in feminist identity, especially since the 1960s. Early feminists concerned with equal rights for women soon realized that without control over whether and when to have children, the rights to suffrage, education, and the professions were limited. Planned Parenthood founder Margaret Sanger and early socialist feminists worked for access to birth control and abortion in the 1930s because they wanted women to be able to plan their families.[15] Radical and liberal feminists of the second wave decried men's control of women's bodies through law.[16] In 1967, the Comstock Law was overturned, allowing married women to obtain birth control even without their husbands' approval, and in 1973 the right to abortion followed. Similar victories were won by women across the globe, and where this right remains elusive, feminists are still fighting for it.

Yet despite the centrality of abortion in contemporary feminism, nearly all first-wave feminists opposed abortion, and they blamed men for causing the desperation that sometimes led to it. They

LIFE 97

fought instead for "voluntary motherhood," or women's right to limit pregnancy in marriage via abstinence.[17] As feminist historians point out, early feminists assumed that all women were naturally oriented toward motherhood and virtue.[18] These feminists worried about growing individualism. They called out capitalists *and* radical feminists, both of whom they saw as threatening family and community. Pro-life feminists today claim to carry on the legacy of the first wave, though not without controversy.

But for nearly all other feminists today, birth control and abortion are essential to women's autonomy. Embryos and fetuses are understood as potential rather than actual persons with claims on others. Trusting women to make decisions about their bodies rather than trusting their partners, parents, or government to decide for them is thus imperative.[19] Feminist historians have demonstrated the extent to which women have not had freedom over their own bodies—whether in marriage or outside it—and showed how women of color have had far less control than white women. Given that history, opposition to a pro-choice stance is understood as opposition to women's autonomy and bodily integrity. Abortion rights have become nearly impossible to separate from feminism.

However, in 1986, a little over a decade after *Roe*, Catholic psychologist Sidney Callahan published "A Case for Prolife Feminism" in *Commonweal*, a lay Catholic magazine. Callahan carved out a space for progressive Catholics who were sympathetic to feminism, but opposed to abortion.[20] She challenged central tenets of the pro-choice position, arguing that a pro-life view was a better way to respect women, balance values of autonomy and sacrifice for others, and recognize the humanity of the unborn child. Callahan was much more interested in providing support for pregnant women than in legally restricting abortion rights. However, she argued that when *Roe* legalized abortion, it also made abortion the default choice for women with unwanted pregnancies. Even women who may have wanted to carry their babies to term felt pressure not to inflict the costs of pregnancy on their families or communities.

98 CAN YOU BE A CATHOLIC AND A FEMINIST?

Moreover, access to abortion made government support for pregnant women that much harder to attain, Callahan argued.

In her piece, Callahan alluded to first-wave feminists who, in her reading, opposed abortion because they thought that feminism could not be authentic if it sought to secure women's liberation at the expense of the lives of vulnerable unborn children. Though Callahan embraced gender equality, she shared with early feminists a belief in gendered differences in approaches to sexuality and family. Abortion was a way to make it easier for men to have what many wanted—sex without commitment. Though she did not explicitly draw upon Catholic teaching, she easily might have, since she stressed the inherent dignity of the fetus and a moral duty of care that transcends choice. Yet, in drawing attention to difficult situations women faced due to structural sexism and by calling for social support for women and their children, she was also attempting to work within a feminist framework.

In recent years, Callahan's synthesis has become more difficult to sustain. Pro-choice advocates have become more comfortable with abortion and less willing to characterize it as a difficult moral choice. In 2020, the Democratic Party platform no longer included the goal of making abortion "safe, legal, and rare."[21] Advocates characterize abortion not as tragic necessity but as healthcare. Limitations on choice rooted in concern for fetal life or the diversity of US public opinion were no longer on the table. The "Shout Your Abortion" movement gained traction, as women refused to be shamed for something many saw as either morally necessary or uncomplicated.[22] Even as abortion rates continued to decline, support for choice was coalescing.

At the same time, the movement for reproductive justice, which began in 1994, has increased its reach by challenging the focus of the mostly white feminist dialogue around abortion that preceded it.[23] Insisting on securing the right to have or not have children, movement leaders brought to public consciousness the long history of women of color who have been denied those rights. In slavery they were forced to be sexual partners, breeders, and mothers to their masters' children, and after slavery, they experienced sexual violence and bodily harm at work and at home, underwent forced sterilization, endured racism in healthcare, and were often unable to parent their own children.[24] Today's advocates seek a society where contraception, abortion, sex education, prenatal care, healthcare, and child care are available to all. This movement, like the contemporary pro-choice movement, does not hold that a fetus has rights to be balanced with women's rights.[25] It is gaining adherents after *Dobbs*, as many experience a world without abortion access for the first time. Feminist support for abortion rights as a dimension of justice for women has perhaps never been stronger.

On the other side, the pro-life movement has become a less hospitable space for feminists. The mainstream pro-life movement's choice to throw its unwavering support to President Trump was, for many, a fatal moral compromise.[26] Many moderate and liberal Catholics who previously might have felt comfortable on the edges of the movement were alienated by its extremism, especially as the movement's fiercest advocates seem uninterested in promoting a consistent ethic of life. Many of those who did follow the president are convinced it was worth it, as the Supreme Court is in their hands and *Roe* has fallen. The lines first drawn in the 1970s have hardened, so that those who disagree rarely engage, and all of this makes Catholic feminism seem all but impossible.

Starting in a Different Place

In the face of such strong divisions between feminists and Catholics, instead of attempting a synthesis of claims as Callahan did, I turn to narratives of pregnancy, pregnancy loss, and birth. In doing so I attempt to take seriously Catholic concerns about the humanity of unborn children and feminist commitments to women's bodily autonomy. As in earlier chapters, I also look for a more complex

100 CAN YOU BE A CATHOLIC AND A FEMINIST?

picture of both Catholicism and feminism. In women's stories of carrying life, mourning loss, and giving birth, in the stories women tell about life and death, I find just enough unifying threads to stretch across a difficult divide.

In utilizing women's experience, I acknowledge with Susan Bigelow Reynolds that "feminist theology operates at the complicated intersection of celebration and suspicion of the role of distinctly female bodily experiences, especially those surrounding fertility and reproduction, in dynamics of knowing and theological insight."[27] Feminists both insist that moral knowledge can be gained by attending to women's distinctive experiences *and* worry about collapsing differences among women and overidentifying women with experiences that are particular to them. I try to analyze women's experience with this complexity in mind.

Thinking about agency in pregnancy has been central to the feminist movement because this most intimate of women's experiences has rarely been in women's hands. The history of medicine is one of male family members and doctors controlling access to birth control, pregnancy care, and the birthing process itself. Women's voices were rarely taken seriously.[28] Women's agency in the birthing process was rarely recognized. Women of color were forced into pregnancy, bearing children conceived by sexual violence and becoming surrogates for women who could not bear children. They have also been sterilized against their will and shamed for having children while unmarried or receiving public assistance. The feminist cry, "My body, my choice," is linked to an insistence that women should be in charge of their pregnant bodies. And yet, studies of pregnant women show that, even today, "Women's own embodied knowledge about labour progress and fetal wellbeing [is] disregarded in favour of care provider's clinical assessments."[29] In their families and intimate relationships, at a time when their vulnerability necessitates more care, pregnant women often face mistreatment and abuse.[30] Others still exert control over their bodies.

LIFE   101

The second-wave feminists behind the best-selling book *Our Bodies, Ourselves* wanted women to have more knowledge, so that, "freed . . . from the constant, energy-draining anxiety about becoming pregnant," they would be better parents and would have "a larger life space to work in."[31] This was the era of natural childbirth, when feminists raised critical questions about birth control, pregnancy, and the birthing process. Yet this work to increase agency was never separate from a concern from relationality. These feminists carried on the early work of feminists like Margaret Sanger, who saw in birth control a path for a woman to "understand the cravings and soul needs of herself" and become a better lover and mother.[32] Themes of agency and relationality would mark feminism for the next century—women deserve the freedom to choose to have sex or not and to decide whether and when to become mothers. Because they knew too many stories of forced motherhood, early feminists saw reproductive choice as crucial to their freedom. Feminists in the mid-twentieth century gave women information about their bodies and empowered women to embrace pregnancy and motherhood in their own way.

In the post-*Dobbs* era, agency in family planning remains a central concern of feminists, who worry that the right to contraception might suffer the same fate as the right to abortion, but women's narratives around family planning show a concern for relationality as well. Contraception is now widely available and accepted. Yet while teen sex and pregnancy have declined, birth control usage is much less consistent for poorer and less-educated women who are less worried about potential motherhood than women with more privilege.[33] Qualitative studies on young poor mothers show that pregnancy, even in difficult circumstances, is sometimes embraced as a source of hope. Harvard researchers report that, while they may dream the same dreams of their more affluent peers, poor women's circumstances sometimes push them to "grab eagerly at the surest source of accomplishment within their reach: becoming a mother."[34] These stories suggest that relational concerns are

102 CAN YOU BE A CATHOLIC AND A FEMINIST?

central. Support for pregnancy in less than ideal conditions is at least as pressing as worries about agency, especially for the most vulnerable women.

For Catholics, relationality is a more significant concern than agency, but agency is not completely neglected. Traditional Catholic narratives relating to family planning emphasize procreation and intimacy as equally significant purposes of sex, which belongs, ideally, in marriage. Before the advent of natural family planning (NFP) in the 1980s, Catholic couples had only the much less effective "rhythm method," and stories from these times tend to confirm feminist worries about the negative effects of fear of involuntary pregnancy.[35] One frustrated Catholic in a large survey spoke for many, saying, "Rhythm leads to self-seeking, promotes excess in infertile times and strain in fertile times."[36] However, contemporary stories from Catholic women using the much more effective, newer methods that give them more agency are considerably more positive. In a previous analysis of existing studies, I found the overwhelming majority of users saying that NFP promotes self-giving, greater sexual pleasure, mutuality, and spiritual intimacy. Women in particular have become vocal advocates of NFP as a practice that strengthens both marriage relationships and faith.[37] While in the last two decades greater honesty about the struggles of the method has emerged, most narratives are marked by a profound appreciation for sex as tied to intimacy and new life.

Yet Catholics are not of one mind. Catholic women who use artificial birth control attest that contraception can enable rather than impede the love and intimacy that their tradition sees as the heart of sexuality, while facilitating responsible parenthood, which is also key. The goods affirmed by Catholics using contraception parallel to those I found in the NFP literature. Catholic ethicist Emily Reimer Barry's ethnographic work on married couples living with HIV-AIDS similarly shows women and men juggling concerns about intimacy, health, and children, aided by contraception.[38] Catholic theologians have for decades utilized these experiences as

LIFE 103

an important source for their assessment of the legitimate place of contraception in a loving, life-giving marriage.

Though diverse, these family planning narratives all emphasize a complicated mix of agency and relationality. For both feminists and Catholics, desires to plan a family and exert some control over one's future coexist with deep concerns for relationships—for sexual intimacy, pregnancy, and the ability to care for children already in their home.

Pregnancy narratives are also complex. The vast majority of women in the United States experience pregnancy at some point in their lives, and though many are bearing children later, 86 percent will become mothers by age forty-four, a higher percentage than in previous decades.[39] Amid tremendous variation, there are also commonalities in how pregnancy is experienced.

Second-wave feminists celebrated the experience of pregnancy and attested to the toll it takes on women. In a foundational feminist text on motherhood, Adriene Rich characterizes herself as "allergic to pregnancy" and writes movingly of how childbearing impeded her vocation as a writer.[40] She tells the story of a woman who took her children's lives in desperation and expects it will resonate, at some level, for women who know the stresses of caring for children. Yet she also depicts her intense love for her sons. Her criticism is of the institution of motherhood (especially the isolation and the heavily idealized gendered expectations that put pressure on women and limit their agency); the relational experience is something she values and longs to free from social constraints.

Pregnant teen mothers' narratives reveal a similar tension between experience and institution, agency and relationality. A case in point is a digital storytelling project created by two researchers to show the lived experience of young mothers.[41] In giving teens the tools to tell their own stories, researchers sought to honor the knowledge pregnant teens gained and to question social disapproval of their choices. "Angela," a Puerto Rican teen, faced rejection by her family and left home. Angela's dreams of her future

104 CAN YOU BE A CATHOLIC AND A FEMINIST?

daughter are complicated by a premature birth, but she portrays herself as resilient and ready to sacrifice: "I cried, but of joy. I knew I'd never leave her alone, not for one minute. She was everything I had. She was the only thing that kept me alive."[42] Another mom, Zemora, resists the stigmatizing narratives of a second teen pregnancy, speaking not of shame or failure but of her concern "with finding enough love in her heart and strength in her body for both of her children."[43] In the face of considerable hardship, these teen moms articulate their desire and capacity to sacrifice for their kids. While feminist scholars voice legitimate worries that women have internalized social norms of mothering as all-consuming, feminist social scientists argue for paying attention to the embodied knowledge of women that is often ignored by the medical establishment.[44] Those narratives show concern for both agency and relationality.

Traditional Catholic narratives prize relationality over agency, but a broader view of the tradition shows that agency is also a concern. In pregnancy, the late John Paul II writes, a woman's body stretches to make room for another, enfleshing the human vocation of self-giving.[45] Though the late pope romanticizes the significance of pregnancy, his description of the experience coheres with what many women themselves attest. Feminist theologians follow the lead of feminist social scientists who attend to women's embodied knowledge by reflecting on their own experiences of pregnancy. They also go a step further, arguing that experiences of pregnancy and nursing are a neglected source of theological wisdom. Methodist theologian Bonnie Miller-McLemore writes about how knowing that a nursing mother's milk can let down when she hears a crying infant who is not her own gives us an embodied example of human connection to and compassion for others.[46] Orthodox theologian Carrie Frost shows how maternal wisdom is captured in Christian iconography depicting the pregnant Mary and Elizabeth.[47] New orthodox feminist Colleen Carroll Campbell speaks from within that tradition of long struggles with infertility and of her joy when pregnancy finally arrived.[48] These are not monolithic accounts of suppressed agency. Rather they show that many women find in pregnancy the powerful connection and selfless giving they seek.

Though it is important not to sentimentalize the experience of pregnancy, common themes emerge, if not universally or immediately, then with time. Dorothy Day tells of how being pregnant with her daughter Tamar brought her "blissful joy" and led to her decision to leave her beloved partner Forster, who refused to marry her.[49] Pregnancy as a single mother with few resources was a liminal time in Day's life during which she walked the beach in Staten Island, became convinced that there must be a God, and began to pray. While those around her found religion to be an unacceptable compromise of their freedom, for Day, "The very fact that we were begetting a child made me have a sense that we were made in the image and likeness of God, co-creators with him. Because I was grateful for love, I was grateful for life."[50]

In women's pregnancy narratives, Catholic and feminist, despite very real differences in circumstances, commonalities emerge: accounts of being stretched and changed by the experience of carrying another life; of fear and anxiety about taking responsibility for this new life; of gratitude, hope, and joy. These themes expand upon those I have already identified—agency and relationality. Fear and anxiety can lead to a sense of constrained agency; the experience of being stretched can deepen a commitment to relationality; gratitude, hope, and joy can sometimes outweigh fear, even in difficult situations. While women's experiences of planning for motherhood and being pregnant do not always match, they do have common threads. Experiences of prenatal loss provide further evidence of common ground, though not without complications.

About 65 percent of known pregnancies result in live births, while 15–20 percent end in miscarriage and another 18 percent end in abortion.[51] Yet most often, we talk about women's experience of miscarriage or stillborn births separately from abortion, if we talk about either one. The overlap between the experiences is rarely

106 CAN YOU BE A CATHOLIC AND A FEMINIST?

recognized. Sometimes when an embryo or fetus has died, women have a dilation and curettage procedure, which is also utilized in abortions of viable pregnancies. In both miscarriage and abortion, women can (though do not always) experience pain, shame, isolation, and depression. In 2021, New Zealand became the first country to offer paid leave following a miscarriage no matter the age of the fetus, in belated recognition of the trauma many experience, though it did not offer similar benefits following abortion.[52] There is little public acknowledgment of abortion-related trauma. In theology, as in public discourse, "The abortion debate has moved far from real women's lives into an ethereal realm."[53] Even Catholics and feminists who should share strong concern for prenatal loss rarely engage women's experiences.

In the Catholic Church, women may baptize and bury babies they lose in miscarriage, though there are no particular blessings for either one and no rituals at all for a woman who has had an abortion.[54] These experiences of loss are rarely considered together in Catholic life or theology. But as feminist theologians seek "to grapple with the embodied, broken, and nonidealized dimensions of contemporary motherhood," it is important to include the full range of experiences of prenatal loss.[55] This means hearing not only stories of miscarriage and stillborn births, but also abortion stories. All experiences of prenatal loss deserve a hearing.

Feminist accounts of women's experiences of abortion show a range of emotions and moral assessment. Some women perceive that abortion was the only possible choice given their life situation, whether single or partnered, with or without children. The #ShoutYourAbortion campaign includes few stories of regret. One woman writes that though abortion was a difficult choice, it was still the right thing to do. She wants "a child of mine to be born into a life better than what I go through" and declares, "As the mother, I get to decide if it will be so."[56] In another story collection, a woman describes her choice to abort two of the three fetuses she was carrying in a matter-of-fact way, saying, "I could form remorse and

LIFE   107

guilt to go along with knowing that decision was the best, but what is remorse going to get me?"[57] Women confirm in their narratives the complex reasons the Guttmacher Institute finds for abortion (e.g., obligations to others, financial concerns, and relational instability), and only rarely speak of regret.[58] Reading abortion accounts in feminist spaces in light of the long-established data from Guttmacher suggests that most abortions are viewed by women as necessary even if the choice is difficult. And sometimes the choice is not difficult at all.

As I have shown elsewhere, stories from crisis pregnancy centers are surprisingly similar, though they are interpreted differently by pro-life advocates, including Catholics.[59] In these narratives, women tell of a lack of support, pressure from family, and the need to stay in school or work environments that do not accommodate pregnancy or parenting. Where pro-choice advocates see difficult but necessary choices made with relational concerns in mind and little regret, pro-life advocates see failures of family and community to support women who would rather not turn to abortion. Reporting from Elizabeth Dias of the *New York Times* on crisis pregnancy centers confirms the pressures women experience and highlights the desires of many women in less than ideal circumstances to have their babies. One formerly incarcerated woman told her that God "blessed me with another chance of being a mom, and I did not want to mess this up."[60] For those who do not find this support and end up having abortions, shame, regret, and depression can result, though they are far from universal.

While Catholics tell stories of abortion as constrained choice and tragic loss, feminists lift up stories showing the relative ease with which women make necessary decisions to have abortions and move on with their lives. How do we reconcile these different stories? Are there really common threads here? Stories of difficult miscarriages and abortions as well as unplanned but welcome pregnancies sit uneasily with feminist accounts of relatively easy abortions. This is perhaps why they are often not voiced. But

108 CAN YOU BE A CATHOLIC AND A FEMINIST?

attending to them provides a new way to think about these conflicting narratives. One physician who experienced prenatal loss writes that, given her context, she was "ashamed to admit how angry I was in the days following the miscarriage. Angry that the breast tenderness and morning sickness, which once provided secret reassurance of the life growing inside of me, lingered and became cruel reminders of the pregnancy that no longer would be. Angry that 1 week later, I was still grieving."[61] She wasn't supposed to be this upset by a miscarriage, yet she was. Some claim that the trauma of miscarriage is related to the loss of a hoped-for future. But this physician seems to suggest that more is going on. When women speak of prenatal loss, many are speaking of the loss of a child. On September 2, 2021, Catholic philosopher Jennifer Frey posted on Twitter that she had "buried a human fetus that I named Felix . . . who had a human face, perfectly formed limbs, an umbilical cord growing out of its belly button, and ten fingers and ten toes." Later, she posted photos of her family at the burial. Support poured in from hundreds of followers, many recalling their own experiences of loss. Another academic posted, "Seven years ago I sat in a hospital as the doctor uttered those words, 'I'm sorry there's no heartbeat.' Today I start my PhD in stillbirth/preterm research at that same hospital because a mother's love never dies. #ForAurora." There were over fifty-five thousand "likes." A former student, a birth doula and writer, who suffered an ectopic pregnancy in fall 2022 named her daughter Miriam and had for her a Catholic burial and a tombstone reading, "Before I formed you in the womb, I knew you." Though their suffering is too often minimized in well-meaning assurances about the future, women's experiences of miscarriage raise questions about feminist abortion stories that fail to acknowledge the gravity of prenatal loss.

Catholic feminist theologian Susan Reynolds perhaps best captures the shape of this loss. First, it is traumatic for most: "A significant percentage of women experience miscarriage and stillbirth as a psychologically traumatic event, and many exhibit symptoms of post-traumatic stress disorder in the aftermath of their loss."[62] Second, trauma is linked not to loss of a future hope but to loss of a child: "Numerous studies suggest that most women, including those who have had early miscarriages, understand their loss as the loss of a baby," even if to do so is confusing given questions about how to mourn, whether to name or bury the baby, whom to tell, and how to talk about the child now and in the future.[63] Third, the woman is not separate from the loss. In pregnancy, she carried a child; with pregnancy loss, in Bigelow's memorable and heart-breaking image, her womb becomes a tomb for the child who has died and, after removal, an empty tomb:

> The pregnant woman becomes a communion of persons, one making room and one dwelling. When her child dies, the communion of her body does not cease. Her body . . . takes the death of her child into itself. Among her organs and bones, she contains death. Her womb becomes a tomb, and yet she remains, somehow, alive.[64]

Reynolds's account helps us see common threads in feminist and Catholic stories of abortion and narratives of miscarriage and stillborn babies. Most women who tell their abortion stories as nontragic or tragic but necessary tend not to mourn their unborn child, but others, like those who miscarry, do. For some, the fetus is more potential than actual, human but not a person. For others, the fetus was "dwelling" in their womb and, when it dies, as Reynolds's reading of the literature attests, "The communion of her body does not cease." Perhaps all types of prenatal loss have this loss of communion in common, whether a child was wanted or unwanted, whether loss is chosen or not, even if not all are ready to mourn the losses their bodies have sustained. Taking experience seriously, we can see in feminist narratives concern with constraints on agency that lead women to feel they have no choice, along with the relational concerns of women who long for the children they

110 CAN YOU BE A CATHOLIC AND A FEMINIST?

bear to have a better life than the one they have. In Catholic spaces, relational care for the unborn child lost to abortion is prominent, while concern for agency needs attention. But looking at accounts of women who speak or write about miscarriage helps balance this picture, as they show women claiming agency in insisting that their experiences be taken seriously and developing ritual practices that allow them to mourn the losses they and their families have sustained. Though it is easy to characterize the tension between Catholic and feminist stories as freedom versus relationship, considering a full range of prenatal losses helps make common values more visible.

After walking through stories of pregnancy and prenatal loss, I end this section with brief attention to narratives of birthing in Catholic and feminist writing. While second-wave feminists raised questions about medicalization of birth and urged women to embrace natural births, today's feminists stress that women need not embrace any particular kind of birth experience. Even though feminists continue to question romanticization, they also celebrate the unique and powerful experience of birth. The beautiful feminist birth story "I Was There in the Room" was a late addition to Eve Ensler's feminist play *The Vagina Monologues*.[65] Ensler describes being present as her daughter gives birth. She writes in vivid detail about the changing shape and colors of vagina as it is stretched to make room for the baby, as it becomes "an operatic mouth" that sings a new human being into the world. She expresses deep appreciation of the vagina, which can "change its shape to let us in," "expand to let us out," and "ache for us and stretch for us, die for us and bleed and bleed us into this difficult, wondrous world." Though Ensler does not write from a religious perspective, she uses words like "sacred" and "awe" to tell her birth story, words that Catholic writers also use. Carroll's birth story similarly highlights the stretching, the blood, and the pain.[66] Ensler describes the body as "mutilated," and for Carroll, this physical sacrifice can only be seen through the lens of the cross. The pain becomes sacred as it

LIFE 111

connects her with the God who brings new life into being through death. The power of birthing is acknowledged in both.

Interestingly, Day's story of her daughter Tamar's birth, published in 1928 and shared around the world, is much less religious. She describes the pain, "Where before there had been waves, now there were tidal waves. Earthquake and fire swept my body," but is most effusive about the ether, on account of which she "floated dreamily and luxuriously on a sea without waves" while others completed the work of childbirth. Once she awakes, Day is enamored of her new child ("Nothing will interfere with her grace") as well as with her "flat stomach," and she ends with simple contentment, "Everyone is complacent, everybody is satisfied, everybody is happy." It is only in looking back on her experience years later as she writes her autobiography that the spiritual import of the experience emerges for her.[67] This soon to be Catholic saint is not so different from her feminist sisters.

In women's experiences of pregnancy, prenatal loss, and birth, there is an undeniable diversity. The universalizing tendencies of both feminist and Catholic discourses are tempered by the complexity of many stories. Yet if we read these experiences side by side, common threads emerge. Imagining these women gathered in one room, talking about experiences of family planning, becoming pregnant, and losing the lives growing within their bodies, I have to believe they would find shared values animating their stories that would enable them to see each other as allies and have compassion for each other, despite their differences.

A Catholic Feminist Story

This chapter began with an account of how central the issue of abortion is to Catholic feminist identities and an exploration of the tensions that make differences difficult to resolve. I walked through accounts of women's experiences of family

112 CAN YOU BE A CATHOLIC AND A FEMINIST?

planning, pregnancy, miscarriage, abortion, and birthing. In these experiences, three main common threads emerged. A drive for *agency* is evident in the fight for access to birth control and the countercultural insistence on NFP, in resistance to totalizing institutions and constraints, in assertions of control over pregnancy, abortion, and birthing. A deep concern for *relationality* is evident in stories of pregnancy and birthing as opportunities to love even in imperfect situations; in pain-filled accounts of prenatal loss; and in narratives speaking to the pressures and responsibilities that make inducing such loss thinkable and regret impossible to hold. Relationality animates the commitment to provide support for pregnant women in crisis and lies behind the agonizing choices women make around abortion, as well as the embodied understanding of prenatal loss as tragic.

Seeing common threads of agency and relationality does not necessarily get us closer to a political resolution. It does not dissolve the tension between bodily integrity that is more central to feminism and the dignity of unborn children that is more central to Catholicism. In this chapter, due to the depth of tension between Catholic and feminist claims, I offer a narration of family planning, pregnancy, prenatal loss, and birth, and attempt to read conflicting voices into conversation. My hope is that listening will allow for mutual recognition.

But what about a third value to which I alluded at the outset—concern for the vulnerable? Does it get us any further? For feminists and Catholics, it seems to be the key value pushing them to one side or the other. *Concern for the most vulnerable* can be seen in movements for reproductive justice and crisis pregnancy centers that advocate for women and their families, in poor women's decisions to prioritize hope and attempt to raise children who come unexpectedly, in the stories of women who mourn the loss of their unborn children no matter how young, and in the stories of women who felt compelled to choose abortion for the sake of their families. Concern for the vulnerable is present in all of these stories.

LIFE 113

Claiming the value does not solve the problem, but seeing it at work still matters.

Being a Catholic feminist means not only recognizing common values pushing people in different directions, but seeing double vulnerability as inescapable in abortion. Abortion is so difficult because the vulnerability of unborn children stands in tension with the vulnerability of women who carry them. Ethically, abortion can be complicated, especially in the earliest stages of pregnancy when the status of the fetus is more contested and in cases of pregnancies endangering women's life or health. What seems clearer is that a Catholic feminist cannot see abortion as separate from pregnancy, miscarriage, or birth. She cannot see a woman in crisis pregnancy as anything but caught in a tragic dilemma involving two vulnerable human lives. An authentic response must involve caring for them both, with attention to women's agency and their relational commitments.

I will end with one last story. Cornelia Connelly, the nineteenth-century founder of the Sisters of the Holy Child of Jesus, was a mother before she became a sister. Connelly lost four of her children in tragic deaths. She saw her own vulnerability as a mother as inextricably linked to the vulnerability of her children, and to the vulnerability of "that Divine child enclosed for nine months in the womb of his creature, born in a stable, . . . a humbled God."[68] Not long before she died, she exclaimed, "In this flesh I see my God!"[69] The vulnerability of pregnancy, birth, and child loss revealed to her the vulnerability of God made flesh and helped her to know the presence of God with her through all of her earthly pain.

Telling a Catholic feminist story about pregnancy, prenatal loss, and birth means acknowledging the central Christian narrative of the Incarnate God who comes as a vulnerable child through the body of a courageous and vulnerable woman, and accepting the tension this view inevitably creates. Neither a simple pro-choice or a simple pro-life position makes sense within this framework. In the child in the womb and the mother who carries life within

114   CAN YOU BE A CATHOLIC AND A FEMINIST?

her, Catholics see the face of God. To tell the story another way, both mother and fetus have inherent worth and make claims on us. Both agency and relationality matter. From this vantage point, Catholicism falls short when it places undue emphasis on abortion, fails to take women's agency seriously, and offers too little support for women experiencing crisis pregnancies. From this same vantage point, feminism falls short when it fails to adequately value the lives of unborn children, women's unrealized desires for pregnancy, and widespread pain following prenatal loss. For Catholic feminists, authenticity lies in valuing both lives in their vulnerability.

To take vulnerability seriously, one need not carry a sign to the Women's March or the March for Life. Reasonable people can differ on political solutions. As we are beginning to see even more clearly after *Dobbs*, restrictive laws may not be helpful in stopping most abortions, because women are able to travel to neighboring states where abortion is legal or obtain "abortion pills" for use at home via telemedicine.[70] Healthcare workers need sufficient room to provide adequate miscarriage care, or else women's health and lives can be endangered. Supporting women and children (e.g., via reduced cost or free prenatal care, birth, family leave, child care, etc.) may be a more effective way to reduce the demand for abortion, yet it cannot address all of the circumstances that make pregnancy difficult. The politics of abortion are irreducibly complicated. The argument of this chapter is that authenticity for Catholic feminists can be found by listening to each other's stories, making the pain of vulnerable others—mother and child—our own, and continuing the Christian story by accompanying them.

6

Gender

The Gender Problem

Does the Catholic Church have a gender problem? When Catholic schools fire employees who identify as LGBTQ, students ask, "Why does the church hate gay people?" It is incomprehensible to them that the church could deny marriage to couples in love or label people "intrinsically disordered" because of their sexual orientation. They have grown up with legal same-sex marriage and rapidly increasing acceptance of LGBTQ persons and relationships. Why isn't love enough, they wonder? Why does the church have a problem with gender? When young couples take classes to prepare for a Catholic wedding, in some dioceses they will be confronted with what seems to be a different gender problem. They will hear a celebration of differences between men and women that are understood as natural and even "ontological," or existing at a deep level. Claims about how these differences ought to shape their marriage often seem overly prescriptive and at odds with their experience. They wonder, why doesn't the church get it?

These experiences of disconnect are related. In both cases, Catholics are alienated by what seem to be failures to consider individuals in their uniqueness and acknowledge important ways in which they seek to live out their faith. Instead, the church insists on drawing gendered lines that exclude, restrict, and overlook goodness. Both kinds of line-drawing are rooted in a theology of complementarity, or the idea that God created men and women as unique, different, and for relationship with each other. In the first section of this book, through deeper engagement with Catholic and

Can You Be a Catholic and a Feminist?. Julie Hanlon Rubio, Oxford University Press.
© Oxford University Press 2024. DOI: 10.1093/oso/9780197553145.003.0007

116 CAN YOU BE A CATHOLIC AND A FEMINIST?

feminist traditions, I was able to find common ground and synergy. In this chapter, as with the chapter on abortion, the work of cultivating authentic Catholic identity becomes more difficult as we go deeper, and authenticity will require a different strategy.

Just how wide is the gap between Catholic and feminist views on gender? When Pope Francis comments on "gender ideology," the gender gap seems very deep. He has compared gender theory to "a nuclear bomb" because of its potential to destroy the natural order and insisted that it is "a great enemy of marriage today," a form of "ideological colonization" by which the global North tries to impose its views on the global South. He has suggested that gender transition is "a new sin," for with it, "The image of God is being annihilated."[1] Most of his commentary on gender theory is from interviews rather than official documents, but these comments, along with the release of the first Vatican document on gender theory during his pontificate, have been disappointing to many Catholics who want to recognize and honor a diversity of gender identities.[2]

Another group, including some identifying as Catholic feminists, find the Catholic insistence on sexual difference to be a compelling alternative to emerging cultural trends.[3] While affirming a multiplicity of roles for men and women, new orthodox feminists argue that new understandings of gender identity deny Catholic teaching on the unity of body and spirit. Yet even they worry about gender stereotypes that can be very strong in traditional Catholic subcultures. Others, while not as certain, are confused by the new conversation and seek to be compassionate rather than judgmental as they navigate new ways of thinking about gender.

What is gender? As recently as the early 1900s most people assumed a basic congruence between biological sex (male and female) and the personality traits and behaviors of men and women. Sex was understood in binary terms and was thought to be easy to determine except in rare cases. Most everyone was assumed to be heterosexual. Though there was room for diversity within the binary, discrimination on the basis of sex could be criticized, and assumptions about characteristics were not consistent across cultural lines, the sexual binary was largely taken for granted.

In the mid-twentieth century, with the rise of second-wave feminism, both Catholics and feminists came to see more separation between sex and what was now being called gender.[4] Feminist texts typically began with this basic distinction and explained how gender (meaning characteristic traits and roles), unlike sex, was culturally constructed. Debates between essentialism (the idea that some gender traits are fundamental to men and women) and constructivism (which stresses the role of culture in shaping gender) continued among feminists. They were thinking through the complex interplay among distinctive experiences (e.g., menstruation, pregnancy, nursing), diverse expressions, and powerful social forces. Catholics debated, too, even as Catholic magisterial teaching tended toward the essentialist side. In the 1990s. John Paul II distinguished sex from gender while amplifying the distinctiveness of femininity. He broadened Catholic ideas about what women could do and asserted that women's "special genius" was needed both at home and in the world.[5] Catholic feminist theologians argued for equality between men and women and more access for women to diverse roles in society, family, and church.[6] Jesus's inclusion of women, along with the promised overcoming of gender in Galatians 3:28, and the significant roles of women in the early church recovered by biblical scholars, gave these thinkers hope that their tradition carried within it the seeds of a feminist future where biology need not be destiny.

But the rise of gender and sexuality studies in the 1990s raised further questions about the sex/gender distinction for feminists.[7] If sex was more ambiguous than previously thought, feminist use of the category "woman" could unintentionally marginalize those identifying outside the binary. Perhaps feminism should advocate not for women only, but for women-identified persons. As third-wave feminism became more global and intersectional, feminist

118 CAN YOU BE A CATHOLIC AND A FEMINIST?

claims about "women's experience" became more fraught. With so much cultural and racial diversity, how could there be one universal experience? Many identifying as gender queer or trans saw gender differently—as linked to but not determined by the body, culturally shaped, *and* personally felt.

In the face of these changing views of sex and gender, in the first decade of the twenty-first century Catholic magisterial theology found it necessary to mount a more robust defense of essentialism, widening the Catholic feminist divide.[8] Catholic feminist theologians, still primarily focused on justice for women, considered the import of exceptions to the sexual binary. But even they held onto male/female sexual difference rooted in the body, with a broad space for diversity in gender expression.[9] Some ventured thoughts on how intersex and trans people could be part of the diversity of God's Creation.[10] However, the distinction between sex as a mostly stable category and gender as related to sex but culturally shaped remained, placing Catholics in tension with the more radical, postmodern strains of contemporary feminism.

Given the movements in feminism and in the broader culture, Catholic views can appear to be lacking in compassion and out of touch. Simple distinctions that seemed accurate only a few decades ago no longer suffice. Catholics need to think more deeply about sex and gender. Like Darwin in the nineteenth century, gender theorists raise fundamental questions about who humans are—questions that cannot be ignored, especially by those seeking an authentic way to be Catholic and feminist. But the Catholic tradition remains an important source of wisdom about what it means to be human. Gender is one the most difficult issues for someone wanting to be Catholic and feminist. In the last chapter, given the depth of the current disconnect, I focused on finding shared values by listening to diverse stories. In this chapter, I suggest a different strategy often employed in difficult dialogues: focusing on what we can agree upon.

GENDER 119

Three Claims We Could Agree Upon

Dialogue between Catholics and contemporary feminists could be framed as wholly oppositional. Finding a way to reconcile Catholicism and feminism on gender requires a focus on what is held in common and commitment to ongoing dialogue. To that end, in this chapter, I map three claims feminists and Catholics might agree upon: (1) sex and gender are not the same, (2) experience must be critically and compassionately engaged, (3) gender is important but not of ultimate significance. To be sure, these claims will not get us to full agreement or easy synthesis. Catholic theology offers significant challenges to feminism, and feminism likewise challenges Catholicism. A gap between the two cannot be denied. Yet by affirming what is held in common and allowing each to challenge the other, a Catholic feminist approach to gender is possible, and this means that Catholic feminist identity is possible, too.

Sex and Gender Are Not the Same

The Catholic tradition assumes the existence of a sexual binary of male and female, but it recognizes that sex and gender, though related, are not identical. Catholic teaching links gender complementarity to sexual difference.[11] That is, differently sexed bodies are understood to shape gender or how men and women live and move in the world. Yet, today, despite the insistence on some gender differences, rarely is gender tied to hierarchy or to specific roles, save those roles reserved for the ordained, which will be addressed in chapter 7.[12] In *Amoris laetitia*, Pope Francis writes that sex and gender cannot be completely separated because "we are creatures, and not omnipotent."[13] Some things about maleness and femaleness are, he argues, part of the Creator's design that we discern in our bodies. Pope Francis rejects the idea of male superiority and acknowledges the "excesses of patriarchal cultures that considered

120 CAN YOU BE A CATHOLIC AND A FEMINIST?

women inferior."[14] While assuming sex (male and female) as given in the body, Francis accepts that gender (masculine and feminine expression) is at least partially culturally shaped, sometimes in deeply problematic ways. In this, he is in line with contemporary social science. For instance, studies show that girls experience much greater pressures to be thin and sexy and are much more vulnerable to sexual violence.[15] Recent research on boys and men describes the "manbox" of gendered expectations limiting male flourishing and a growing crisis of underachievement among boys and men.[16] By calling out "rigid categories" that limit people, Francis signals that overly confining gender scripts are incompatible with Christian understandings of human dignity.[17]

Feminist gender theorists also differentiate between sex and gender but go much further. Judith Butler famously argued that gender is constituted by "the stylized repetition of acts through time," or culturally specific performance.[18] A woman or man does not live and move in a vacuum. Rather, she or he walks into a gender identity as an actor walks onto a stage. A script is waiting for the person, as are props, a director, a voice coach, and a costume designer. Each actor interprets an existing role in his or her own way, but "The gendered body acts its part in a culturally restricted corporeal space and enacts interpretations within the confines of already existing directives."[19] For Butler, gender is not simply a set of characteristics or an expression of sex. Though persons are assigned a sex of male or female at birth, "This construct called 'sex' is as culturally constructed as gender."[20] Sex is not given but is always read through the lens of gender and is always an interpretation. Each person performs gender within social confines that can be punitive to those who stray too far from the binary, but there is freedom to be claimed, for gender is "an identity tenuously constituted in time, instituted in an exterior space," "neither fatally determined nor fully artificial and arbitrary."[21]

Butler's understanding of the social construction of gender, widely influential among gender theorists, contains essential

GENDER 121

insights that Catholics also affirm, if the distinction between sex and gender is maintained. Despite Pope Francis's frequent references to the "feminine genius" of women (including female theologians, who, he famously and unfortunately said, are "the strawberry on the cake"), the Christian tradition calls both men and women to compassion for others, assuming both are capable of being Christlike.[22] Yet Catholic teaching consistently affirms the existence of sexual difference with some link to gender. Embodiment as male and female is understood as making some difference in how individuals live and move in the world. As feminist ethicist Lisa Sowle Cahill argues, "Surely women's diffuse and receptive sexuality, cyclic reproductive capacity, and deeply connective relation to their children both born and unborn, contribute to women's sense of self."[23] Importantly, though sex matters for Catholics, it is but one of many factors in the makeup of human beings, who are much more alike than different in their qualities and capacities. Francis celebrates the "growing reciprocity" between men and women in families and affirms women's contributions to public life and their rightful access to power.[24] Growing acceptance of women in a range of ministerial, teaching, and leadership roles in Catholic institutions suggests the slowly diminishing influence of narrow cultural constructions of gender, and, while the sexual binary remains in place, its import for women's and men's roles, apart from those requiring ordination, is waning.

Despite this common ground between Catholics and feminists, recent scholarship on people who identify as intersex or trans raises questions about sex and gender that Catholics have not yet adequately answered. The term "trans" can be used to cover a broad range of persons, including "individuals who feel trapped in the 'wrong' sexed physical body or whose gender identification does not 'match' with a biological sex," as well as persons who see themselves as beyond gender, gender fluid, or nonbinary.[25] Because there is no one agreed-upon method and due to a paucity of data, estimates of the percentage of babies born with some kind of ambiguous sex

122 CAN YOU BE A CATHOLIC AND A FEMINIST?

(DSD, disorders or diversity of sex development) vary widely.[26] For the very small percentage for whom sex characteristics do not line up (intersex), it was previously thought that doctors could easily decide on the necessary intervention to resolve the issue, but today it is not so clear.[27] For people identifying as trans or nonbinary, the mismatch is primarily between body and internal sense of self. The percentage of adults identifying beyond the male-female binary is perhaps 0.5 percent of the adult population and 1.5 percent of youth ages thirteen to seventeen.[28] There is a lot scientists still do not understand about the relationship between sex characteristics and gender. These ambiguities, along with advances in gender theory, are the basis for the new focus on gender as an identity.

There have been a variety of responses from feminist thinkers. Postmodern feminists, like Butler, argue that sex, like gender, is socially constructed. Some liberal feminists see sex as a more stable category that should be retained because sexual embodiment shapes the way people experience the world, though not wholly determining their gender expression.[29] This sense undergirds the claim that women's presence (in texts, classrooms, leadership roles, etc.) matters, as it assumes that those born with female bodies bring something distinct into male-dominated spaces. If sex and gender are disentangled, activism on behalf of women becomes more complicated. "Strategic essentialist" feminists argue for retaining sex as a category even if it is in part constructed. Others adopt an inclusive approach that groups all persons identifying as women together by recognizing the oppression experienced by cisgender and trans women alike.

Thus far, few Catholic theologians have taken account of the changing gender landscape. Yet younger scholars are beginning to argue that Catholics need not fear thinking through these new developments. Ethicist Katie Walker Grimes claims that there is a fundamental affinity between the Catholic tradition of natural law and Butler's gender theory. Both pursue reason via observation and therefore appreciate the importance of " 'being willing, in the name of the human, to allow the human to become something other than what it is traditionally assumed to be.'"[30] There is, in principle, according to Grimes, a way to broaden notions of sex and gender.

But the capacity of a tradition wedded to the idea of male and female created in God's image to accommodate this expansion is still uncertain. The Creation narratives in Genesis 1–3 have a foundational place in the Catholic tradition as truth-telling myths. Biblical scholarship in the 1980s and 1990s raised important questions about the historical context and current relevance of most biblical texts used to condemn same-sex sexual activity, but most Catholic scholars held onto to an understanding of men and women as creatures who are made for each other. To affirm same-sex marriage was a significant move that could only be justified by acknowledging biblical writers' limited knowledge of sexual orientation, an increasing awareness of the social construction of gender differences previously thought to be central to marriage, and widespread experience of the faithful goodness of same-sex relationships.[31] To include same-sex couples was to add to the original story, leaning on the broader themes in the narrative of the social nature of humans and the call to committed, fruitful, loving partnership. Questions about further expanding the story to include intersex, nonbinary, and trans persons are just beginning.

For now, despite differences, Catholics and feminists can agree that sex (identified at birth) and gender (as lived out) are related but not identical; culture, biology, and personal agency all contribute to gender; some cultural ideas about gender are destructive; and new scientific findings deserve a hearing even if they cannot tell us everything we need to know. Within Catholicism, the ambiguity of sex (apart from intersex conditions) and gender understood as an identity are not yet widely accepted. Even still, Catholics and feminists can both welcome and respect people whose experience challenges traditional norms, listen to their stories, and practice humility in the face of new questions about gender. They can agree to challenge gender norms that constrain women and men, while affirming that sexual embodiment matters.

What does this mean for the ordinary Catholic feminist? The couple taking marriage preparation classes and the young adults who want the lives and loves of their LGBTQ friends, relatives, and selves to be valued are both concerned about gender. A full reconciliation may not be possible. However, the contemporary Catholic tradition makes room for a distinction between sex and gender that can help a conscientious Catholic feminist question overly prescriptive gender scripts and value the loving commitments of a diversity of people. With compassion, she can remain open to learning new things and considering how her living tradition might respond.

Experience Must Be Critically and Compassionately Engaged

Arguments about gender can sometimes turn on the crucial importance given to experience. Some argue that if Catholic tradition points in one direction, and experience points in the other, the tradition wins and experience loses. But the Catholic tradition does not exclude experience. It approaches experience with generosity and insists that it must be considered in dialogue with other sources of wisdom. Catholic ethics on sex and gender can rightly be called a "theology of the body." The term is usually associated with John Paul II's collected homilies on the topic from 1979 to 1984 and their subsequent popularization.[32] This theology attracts fervent fans and equally passionate critics. Yet the essential insights of this theology (though not all of its specific claims) are arguably central to the Catholic tradition: (1) experience is a source of wisdom, and (2) our understanding of what experience teaches is fallible, grows over time, and cannot be accepted uncritically. Catholics and feminists might find agreement on this complex understanding of the importance of experience in relation to gender.

The goodness of the body that many people sense is an essential part of Catholic theology and ethics. Theologically, the doctrines of Creation, Incarnation, and Resurrection all affirm the goodness of the body. We are created with bodies, God was incarnated in a human body, and bodies will somehow be part of our existence in the life to come. Through reflecting on our bodily experience, we can, Catholic theologians argue, gain wisdom about what life is for. We can discern that we are made not to live alone but in relation to God and other people.[33] If in and through embodied relationships, in loving and being loved, many people find their most profound experiences of grace, we can affirm relationality as essential to a good life. Catholic beliefs that human beings are created in God's image and that bodies are good lead them to believe that they can learn from bodily experience something of God's desires for their lives. Experience contributes to Catholic beliefs that humans are created for relationship with God and other people.

And yet, even if bodily experience is a source of wisdom, the history of the tradition itself reveals the limits of experiential knowing. Experience, it seems, does not tell us everything we need to know. What we think we know by experience sometimes does not reflect the fullness of truth. For instance, Scripture contains many more stories about kings, bridegrooms, and fathers than about queens, brides, and mothers. If images of God come from reflecting on experience, Christians have reflected more about how men's experiences reflect something of God and help us think about who God is.[34] This omission is a failure to see the fullness of God and the richness of human experience.

Key developments in Christian ethics have come from feminist theologians critically thinking about embodied female experience. As I noted in chapter 1, Valerie Saiving argued from women's experience that sin can manifest not only as pride but also as a failure to develop one's potential.[35] Feminist scholarship has followed Saiving, lifting up virtues of appropriate self-care, self-love, and vocational growth that have often been left out of moral

126 CAN YOU BE A CATHOLIC AND A FEMINIST?

teaching. Feminist theologians have engaged issues in women's experience that previously received little attention, including pregnancy, nursing, and menstruation, as well as the plight of domestic workers, rape as a weapon of war, and the exploitation of women in pornography and sex trafficking.[36] Women's voices brought to theology new perspectives, questions, and ways of thinking about God and Christian discipleship. In the field of moral theology, before the entrance of women into the field, the question of women's dress as a source of temptation for men received more attention than sexual violence or childrearing.[37]

The basic insight—that bodily experience can offer wisdom about God and the moral life—was right, but it needed to be developed over time. Theologian Cristina Traina challenged John Paul II's claim that experience confirms the immorality of contraceptive sex, which is, he said, fundamentally selfish. Drawing on her own experience, Traina claimed that married sex is no less self-giving when aided by contraception, which enables couples to give themselves to each other without worrying about unplanned pregnancy.[38] Taking seriously the pope's claim, "We have nothing to fear from experience," Traina reflects on experience but critically examines how interpretations of experience might be flawed and in need of correction. Her theology of married sexuality is in tune with the countercultural papal ideal of self-giving but informed by the everyday reality of married life in which self-gift has many facets.

We can also see the failures of Catholic tradition's reasoned reflection on experience by considering racism. Theologians have now clearly established the profound neglect of Black bodies in Catholic ethics. Little attention was given to the scandal of white people owning, dominating, harming, sexually violating, lynching, and incarcerating Black people.[39] Historians show that Catholic thinkers, like others, believed myths of racial inferiority that were linked to bodily differences.[40] Black Catholic theologians have called out Catholic complicity with slavery, and the exclusion of

GENDER 127

Blacks from religious orders and parishes. As theologian Shawn Copeland argues, "No Christian teaching has been more desecrated by slavery than the doctrine of the human person or theological anthropology."[41] Black theologians enrich and correct the tradition by offering a more inclusive view of human experience.

Bodily experience involves not only gender, but also race and ethnicity in all of their complexity. Catholic teaching and theological reflection have sometimes missed the mark because they assumed the white male experience. Only with the critical insights of a diversity of scholars, did theology evolve.

Embodied experience is a key source of wisdom in Christian moral thought, but it is not accepted without question. Sometimes development occurs through broadening the sources of experience and through critical examination of initial assumptions. Other times, experience may need a more serious correction. Farley argues that while experience is essential, we need only look to the suffering people inflict on others in their sexual lives to know that it ought not be the lone source of moral norms.[42] In *Sex in Heaven as It Is on Earth*, Patricia Beattie Jung shows how the Christian ideal of sex as a practice that draws a couple together into one flesh raises questions about pornography and hook-up culture, both of which privilege dominance over mutuality.[43] Both Farley and Jung push the boundaries of Christian sexual ethics, but, like many conservative Catholics, they are critical of contemporary sexual practices that fail to enact equality, mutuality, and commitment. Even if people "feel good about" or "are comfortable with" their practice, theologians across the ideological spectrum ask them to question whether their experience measures up to Christian norms of love and justice.

Similarly, the best of secular feminist thought privileges experience without absolutizing it. Women's experience is central to feminism, and, especially for third-wave feminists, listening with generosity to globally diverse bodily experiences without judgment is crucial. Eve Ensler's popular play *The Vagina Monologues*

128 CAN YOU BE A CATHOLIC AND A FEMINIST?

provides a space for women to tell their stories in order to counterbalance the excesses of purity culture and slut shaming.[44] Yet
feminists also raise questions about experience. As I noted in
chapter 2, feminist analysis of sexual violence and what sociologists
call "bad sex" involves critical evaluation of what might seem ordinary or normal. By exposing rape culture, feminists question
desires, practices, and experiences of men and women. By forming
consciousness-raising groups, feminists encouraged women to
unpack internalized sexism and ask the men in their lives to question their satisfaction with patriarchal roles. By holding themselves accountable to their Black sisters, white feminists committed
to understanding their own racism.[45] While few men or women
identified as sexists or victims of sexism, this did not mean that
sexism (imposed and internalized) was not pervasive, or that no
perpetrators or victims existed. While few whites identified as
racists, this did not mean they had not imbibed cultural norms
of white supremacy. As new orthodox feminists note, contemporary sexual norms may seem to free women, when in reality, they
are profoundly oppressive to women. Through critical analysis of
embodied experience, feminists claim that sometimes, what feels
normal needs to be questioned.

Both Catholics and feminists have nuanced ways of valuing experience and critically assessing the implications we draw from it.
Both argue that ethics cannot proceed without it. Neither group
makes it the only source of moral authority. It is not only Catholics
who critically assess experience. Both Catholics and feminists argue
that widely accepted mainstream views of sex and gender have
been wrong—very wrong. Feminists argue for placing more trust
in voices from the margins, including people whose experiences do
not match common ideas about sex and gender ("Trust women").
They call for questioning what has come to seen as natural or right
in order to embrace something more beautiful and more true (e.g.,
"You are enough"). Catholics and feminists stand together against
both the dismissal of experience and uncritical acceptance of it, and

this makes Catholic feminist thinking on sex and gender both possible and irreducibly complicated.

What does this mean for the stories with which I began? Those critical of Catholic teaching on LGBTQ relationships and highly gendered ideas about marriage can, relying on both Catholic and feminist insights, engage experience—especially the experiences of those who do not "fit" within the accepted binaries—with generosity and compassion. The experience of those who are marginalized is especially crucial and has been an important corrective to traditional views. It is the primary source relied upon by theologians who have argued for adaptation in Catholic sex and gender ethics. Yet experience alone cannot suffice. Catholics and feminists know well how experience can be limited. Catholic theologians worked slowly and carefully toward more nuanced accounts of marriage and same-sex relationships, bringing experience (both from individuals and from scientific studies) into dialogue with other sources of moral wisdom, and preserving what was good in the tradition while moving it forward. They trusted the tradition enough to be generous and patient, but were conscious enough of the value of diverse experiences to be critical and prophetic. This complexity allows a Catholic feminist to face today's sex and gender issues with a humble and critical stance.

Gender Is Important but Not of Ultimate Significance

How much does gender matter? So far, I have argued that understandings of gender lie underneath the surface of controversies about LGBTQ inclusion and relational norms. But what about gender itself? Whether one thinks of gender as expression or as identity, how much does it shape who I am? To what extent should I be concerned about it? Critics of feminists sometime argue that feminists want to erase all gender differences. Critics of Catholics sometimes argue that the church makes gender

130   CAN YOU BE A CATHOLIC AND A FEMINIST?

differences too central. But both Catholic and feminist thinkers have a long history of considering the import of gender while insisting on the more important common humanity of women and men. And they have always placed justice at the center of their theory and action. Both understand the importance of gender without making too much of it.

Nuanced views of gender among feminists have a long history. First-wave liberal feminists argued that women deserved to vote both because they were equal to men and because they would bring their greater sensitivity to children and the poor to the voting booth. Second-wave liberal feminists claimed that all people should be able to enter any profession, control personal finances, and trust that society and law would protect them from violence. Yet they also created women's consciousness-raising groups, cooperatives, and art studios so that women could have spaces where issues shaping their lives would be discussed, and they argued that including women in institutions that had previously excluded them would make a difference to the world. Feminists today know that if gender is in part socially constructed or a performance, it is also real enough in its effects to make gendered analysis of oppression and gendered activism necessary. As Farley writes, summarizing recent research, gender matters less than we used to think for many areas of life, and yet we cannot conceive of a world where there is "neither male nor female." In our relationships and ways of being, gender influences the way we see the world and the way others see us.[46]

Balancing the import of gender with its diverse expressions and universal human characteristics has become more complicated with the rise of postmodern feminism. In the third-wave feminist collection *Gender Outlaws: The Next Generation*, a diverse set of authors maps the new landscape.[47] Some trans men and women identify with the phrase "born in the wrong body," but others do not. Some embrace surgical transition; others reject it for themselves without commenting on others' choices. Some view gender as "given," while others see it as a choice. All try to capture what gender means at a time when it has never been more uncertain. One provocative piece rails against the tyranny of the Butler-inspired orthodoxy of gender as performance, arguing that it can be just as oppressive as the claim that gender is natural.[48] Gender as performance, the author writes, does not capture deep feelings about gender identity or concrete changes accompanying hormonal transition. Gender is complicated; it is experienced as personally real, socially shaped, and socially enforced all at once. It is "an amalgamation of bodies, identities, and life experiences, subconscious urges, sensations, and behaviors, some of which develop organically, and others of which are shaped by language and culture."[49]

The activist editors of *Gender Outlaws* stress diversity of perspective, hoping that neither orthodoxies of Left or Right will confine their subjects' diverse gender identities or expressions. They also hope that conflict over gender will not keep those identifying outside the binary from the justice work to which they are committed.

At its core, contemporary feminism affirms human dignity and social justice. In encouraging acceptance of diverse bodies, exposing double standards, and making spaces for people to tell their stories, feminists uphold the dignity of each person in individual uniqueness, challenging the idea that biology is destiny without writing off biology completely. In insisting that social justice is essential to feminism—rather than something separate—the movement signals its broader concerns. Returning again to Audre Lorde's essay on the erotic, we can see how Lorde connects the energy and desires of a person to all of life, inviting readers "not to settle for the convenient, the shoddy, the conventionally expected, nor the merely safe."[50] Of course, as a lesbian whose gender expression was unconventional, she is talking about freedom in one's gender identity, but it is not her major concern. She is much more interested in how owning one's desires can lead to a willingness to "live from within ourselves" and give us "energy for genuine change" instead of conformity and acceptance of "the same weary

132 CAN YOU BE A CATHOLIC AND A FEMINIST?

drama."[51] Lorde lived her life with passion at the center—passion for her partner, her son, and her work. Gender shaped her, but her life was grounded in something larger than herself and oriented outward to the world. In this ordering of gender and justice, she exemplifies the best of feminist consciousness.

Like feminism, the Catholic tradition is attentive to gender but more focused on human dignity and social justice. This may seem counterintuitive, as many people think of the Catholic Church as caring a great deal about gender. But the vast majority of what the Catholic tradition teaches about the nature of human beings and their responsibilities to God and others applies to everyone, regardless of sex or gender. All are baptized; all are invited "to put on Christ," to perform a new role in communion with God and others.[52] In this community of disciples, gender is far less important than fidelity to the work of the kingdom. Even Edith Stein, a favorite of new orthodox feminists, concludes "The Separate Vocations of Man and Woman" with the very traditional claim that the primary vocation of all Christians is "the imitation of Christ . . . [in whom] the masculine and feminine virtues are united and their weaknesses redeemed."[53] Gender is of proximate, not ultimate, importance.

This holds even in the realm of Catholic family ethics—the part of Catholic theology most associated with gender. Yet, apart from a handful of specific passages, contemporary Catholic teaching on marriage is remarkably ungendered.[54] Francis insists that deep, lifelong love is what all human beings are made for. Central to his vision is the goodness of love and intimacy, which need to be cultivated by both partners. Through inevitable disappointments, both spouses are called to embrace "the joy of love," even in the midst of sorrow.[55] In marriage, individuals become partners who promise to be there for each other forever. Together, a married couple is "to bind the wounds of the outcast, to foster a culture of encounter and to fight for justice."[56] In Catholic family teaching, marriage is primarily described as an egalitarian, intimate, outward-facing partnership. To be sure, celebration of feminine virtues continues, as do Francis's worries about gender theory. But this is not what is most significant in Catholic family ethics.

Efforts to improve the way Catholic communities treat LGBTQ people offer another example of the centrality of human dignity and justice rather than sex and gender in Catholic teaching. The work of James Martin, SJ, has been central to these efforts. Martin calls Catholics not to give undue weight to sexual orientation, gender identity, or sexual behavior. Like Pope Francis, he claims not to dispute core Catholic teachings. Instead, he challenges the church to practice the welcoming and inclusion it preaches.[57] He asks that LGBTQ Catholics be called by the names they use to describe themselves and insists that they be recognized for the multiplicity of gifts they bring to the church. Placing gender identity and sexual orientation in a broader context of Catholic teaching makes possible better welcoming of LGBTQ Catholics.

The less than ultimate significance of sex and gender is even more evident in Catholic social thought, where all victims of injustice are deserving of attention and "all people of good will" are called to action. Of course, the latter phrase is also indicative of Catholicism's gender problem. Only recently has the language changed from "men of good will." Moreover, like documents on marriage and family, most social documents include passages calling attention to women's unique roles and, more recently, worries about gender. Yet the overwhelming majority of Catholic social thought is focused on other problems and possibilities for all human persons.

Feminists and Catholics share strong commitments to solidarity, the option for the poor and vulnerable, and activism aimed at making human flourishing more possible for everyone.[58] While some might view both Catholicism and feminism as being centered on sex and gender in opposing ways, arguably both seek clarity on sex and gender in order to move on to more pressing problems.

134 CAN YOU BE A CATHOLIC AND A FEMINIST?

The Potential of Dialogue across Differences

Thus far I have argued that, though Catholics and feminists are tagged with diverging accounts of sex and gender, there is substantial agreement between them that sex and gender are not the same, embodied experience is an important source of wisdom if engaged compassionately and critically, and gender is significant but not of ultimate importance. In highlighting overlap, I do not mean to overlook remaining differences. In the conclusion to this chapter, I suggest a few ways Catholics and feminists could challenge and enrich each other's views. For those seeking authentic Catholic feminist identity, leaning into challenges might be especially important.

For instance, one challenge to postmodern feminists comes from theologians who argue that the Christian tradition on gender is actually more radical than contemporary conversations. The nonbinary nature of gendered imagery in ecclesial language (e.g., all Christians are "brides of Christ") is at least very interesting. Some writers note the presence in the tradition of "gender bending" or "queer" saints and holy people whose lives do not fit a "complementarity" script.[59] It is widely known that some female medieval mystics envisioned Christ as a nursing mother. Religion scholar Amy Hollywood argues the more provocative point that mystics' desire to achieve full union with God led some to a "queering of desire" or a desire for union with God that transgressed heterosexist paradigms while also challenging the need for bodily union.[60] One might say, then, that Catholicism brings something unique to gender dialogue, with its complex set of possibilities for living in tune with one's deepest desires.

British theologian Sarah Coakley highlights the example of Gregory of Nyssa, who embraced both asceticism and gender fluidity. Because he believed gender to be accidental rather than essential to human nature, he envisioned a gender-free heaven. Coakley contends that Gregory's "celebration of the apophatic mystery of divine grace . . . [clears away] . . . the supposed fixities of human 'gender.' "[61] If some postmodern feminists are giving a great deal of attention to gender today, Coakley suggests that reconceptualization of gender is neither threatening nor overly significant, because the main interest of Christianity is union with God. Such a union may require "spiritual purgation and transformation" along the way to "a dizzying adventure into the ecstasy of divine unknowing," which is much more interesting and demanding, according to Coakley, than gender. If some feminists today claim too much for gender as a feature of human identity, the Christian tradition may offer a challenge in its assumption that gender is far less significant than the relation between humans and God.

But Catholics have challenges to face, too. If the Catholic tradition looks to human bodies for wisdom, intersex bodies may disrupt long-held understandings of a sexual binary and allow for deeper discussion on gender identity. Grimes writes, "While God created human beings 'male and female,' the existence of intersex human beings demonstrates that God did not create human beings *only* male and female."[62] If the existence of intersex bodies requires us, as a people committed to using reason to reflect on nature and human experience in order to understand humans and their flourishing, to think again about sex and gender and God, does not the broader variety of gender experiences we encounter require the same? Is human diversity larger than we imagined? If we hold that human beings are made in the image of God, is that not true of human beings in all of their diversity?

Anglican theologian Susannah Cornwall, another theologian committed to encountering postmodern feminists, pushes even further. Some Christians are more comfortable thinking about intersex people as rare exceptions but less open to accepting the claims of trans-identifying people for whom gender identity is not linked to a physical variation. Cornwall asks if we are certain of the distinction between intersex and transgender. She draws attention

136 CAN YOU BE A CATHOLIC AND A FEMINIST?

to ambiguity in how sex has been defined historically (i.e., which characteristics are taken to be more determinative across history and culture) and argues that "the ways bodies are read is affected as much by what one expects to see as by the bodies themselves."[63] She wonders why some are comfortable allowing for surgery to "correct" intersex bodies but not with surgery for trans people who wish to better align their gender identity with their sexed bodies.[64] Are we to accept the bodies we have or not? Are we sure that intersex bodies are not something new altogether? Could it be that those who identify as trans are telling us something new?

Catholic feminists need hear these challenges in the context of the shared Catholic feminist affirmation about the import and limits of experience. In particular, the mixed and evolving data on the effects of gender transitioning or affirming care must be taken into consideration as one aspect of experience.[65] The movement toward gender identity diversity requires critical engagement. But it seems certain that the diversity of human beings is much larger than previously thought. Catholics are challenged to take the body as seriously as they claim to by encountering feminist gender theorists and persons who can talk about how the binary that has been central in the Catholic tradition feels alien to them.

For a Catholic feminist, getting clear about what gender is and what it is not, about what sex is and is not, matters. Our understanding of gender is central to navigating the kinds of moral questions with which I began this chapter. Substantial agreements between Catholics and feminists on the relationship between sex and gender, the significance and limits of experience, and the priority of social justice seem to allow for an integrated identity. But this identity is not obvious or easily forged. It requires sifting through both traditions to find what is common and compelling. Of course, differences remain, and Catholics and feminists can still challenge each other as they seek clarity. In the meantime, perhaps most important is the shared affirmation that living justly does not require a particular kind of body or a specific gender script. Living an authentically human life means moving in response to the Spirit who calls each person into fullness and to freedom and solidarity. It involves striving to become radical disciples who challenge both the Christian community and the world in recognition of our unity in Christ and in each other.

7

Power

In Naomi Alderman's popular 2016 book *The Power*, which became a TV miniseries in 2023, teenage girls suddenly discover they have the power to give people electric shocks, harming or even killing them. While at first this new ability is confusing, girls soon learn how to control and cultivate their power. In time, they are able to help older women discover and access their power. As the story unfolds, more power comes into the hands of women in every sphere, including journalism, politics, the military, and religion. Men without power are stereotyped as weak, frivolous, and submissive. Eventually, women begin to use their power just as men have. There is no "feminine genius" in this brave new world. Women do not create a more humane society with their power. They are every bit as ambitious, ruthless, and corrupt as men have been, and men are every bit as afraid of them as women have been of them. This compelling science fiction novel flips the script, reimagining the future and the past in order to help readers understand the gendered nature of power in our world. It also makes an argument about how power is inevitably abused even, or perhaps especially, when it is attached to religion.

Allie Montgomery Taylor, a central character in the book, emerges from an abusive home to become "Mother Eve," who can heal people by laying her hands on them and feeling their pain. Allie hears a Voice that guides her to gather women and preach a reversal of patriarchal religion that at first seems like a feminist dream in which God is She and girls who have been beaten down are restored to life in a community. There is hope for a new order of compassion and peace. But what begins as an alternative to the

Can You Be a Catholic and a Feminist?. Julie Hanlon Rubio, Oxford University Press.
© Oxford University Press 2024. DOI: 10.1093/oso/9780197553145.003.0008

way the world is eventually turns violent. In Alderman's universe, no one seems capable of imagining a world without domination. Religion is no different from any other cultural force. It is just another tool for consolidating power over others. Optimism about humanity is unwarranted. Darkness is a more rational perspective. "Power has her ways."[1]

How ought a Catholic feminist think about power? The divide between feminists and Catholics on power, as on gender and life issues, is wide. The exclusion of women from the most powerful roles in the Catholic Church is incomprehensible for most who identify as feminists. In each historical wave, feminists have fought for access to power—in marriage, education, and the voting booth; in the professions, healthcare, and politics; in sexuality, especially for those doubly or triply oppressed by race and class, and on a global scale. The women's movement is at its core about female empowerment. Today, though power suits with shoulder pads are long gone, and "girlboss" has become a derogatory term, feminists still mentor other women into power, celebrate women's achievements in male-dominated sectors, and seek to claim more power in every sphere, including most religions. Women's exclusion from leadership roles in the Catholic Church makes little sense for feminists committed to women's liberation,

Yet some Catholics argue that concern about women's power is misplaced. In a piece calling out Pope Francis's failure to act decisively in high-profile cases of priest abusers, new orthodox Catholic writer Simcha Fisher's says she is not optimistic about his recent appointments of women at the Vatican. Because "women are also human, so it might also mean they, too, could be caught up in the politics and power struggles there. They, too, may be tempted by the same vices. This is just human nature. . . . A woman who craves clerical power is not going to automatically make life better for the mom in the pew who's worried about the safety of her altar boy son. It's not men who are the problem; it's power."[2] Giving power to

140   CAN YOU BE A CATHOLIC AND A FEMINIST?

women would not solve anything, Fischer implies. Those truly interested in justice for the vulnerable should shift their focus.

This chapter takes on the difficult and painful question of women's power in the Catholic Church. Like the other chapters in this section of the book, it approaches a hard case by taking a different path. So far, I have used listening to stories and identifying common claims we can agree upon as strategies. In this chapter, instead of drawing a line in the sand, I lean in to the question of ordination and then pull back to ask about the broader landscape of power in the church. What sort of power comes with ordination, why is it still denied to women, and why do feminist theologians think this is a problem? How deep is the problem of power? What overlooked sources of empowerment exist? Can feminist and Catholic thinking about power contribute to a path forward? I will argue that being a Catholic feminist means supporting women's ordination, but, even more significantly, it means opposing structural clericalism, mining sources of female power in the tradition, and cultivating a different kind empowerment. This chapter brings together analysis of a question that is among the most troubling for Catholic feminists, a deeper probing of the Catholic Church's power problem, and an account of its power assets and potential. I claim that authenticity for Catholic feminists means seeing power as problem and possibility, rather than giving into complacency or despair.

Power as Problem: Ordination

What kind of power does ordination confer, and why is it such a big problem for feminists? While church documents on ordination in the early twentieth century tended to speak of a kind of power that sets a priest above and apart from laypeople in the liturgy and everyday life, Vatican II brought an emphasis on power utilized in union with the faithful at Mass and in service of the church. But the early theology had a long history, and its effects continue to shape

POWER   141

Catholic culture. Pope Pius XI taught that, especially in the liturgy, priests "have power over the real Body of Christ," and this power is "received from God."[3] Vatican II documents have a more relational understanding of "sacred power" that is directed to service of the "People of God."[4] Pope John Paul II continued this focus on relationality and service. Pope Francis went further, calling priests to "smell like the sheep," implying that the ordained need to be with ordinary people, not lord power over them. Despite these important developments, an association of priests with the sacred and the laity with the secular remains, and can "imply that priests possess greater holiness, or at least greater access to the holy."[5] Greater access comes with authority. Ordination confers a power that connects a priest to God, and its reach extends beyond the liturgy to leadership in parishes, dioceses, and seminaries, all the way up to the Vatican.

Today women's exclusion from ordination is presented in Catholic teaching not as an indicator of their lesser holiness or worth but as a necessary way of living in fidelity to Jesus's example and identity. In earlier eras, women's lesser capacity for reason, greater capacity for care work, and even their greater susceptibility to sin were offered as rationales for restricting the priesthood to men.[6] However, contemporary official Catholic teaching insists on a differentiation of roles in the church that does not deny the equal dignity of men and women or their share in the *imago Dei*, or the image of God.[7] The documents do not dwell on gender differences, but they do insist on their reality and enduring significance. Embodied sexual difference matters. Because men and women are viewed as equal but different, a differentiation of roles is not understood as elevating men or denigrating women. This theology suggests that both men and women are valued in their uniqueness and make significant contributions to the life of the church and salvation history.

A key claim in current Catholic teaching is that the status quo is unchangeable. Because Jesus chose twelve male apostles and the

142   CAN YOU BE A CATHOLIC AND A FEMINIST?

church has always had an all-male priesthood, there is no possibility of doing otherwise. In an important 1976 document, written
to respond to a growing movement for women's ordination in the
post–Vatican II era, Pope Paul VI highlights the "constant tradition"
of the church and claims that it is tied to Jesus's choice of men to be
apostles.[8] Knowing that some argue that Jesus chose men because
his culture would not have accepted women leaders, he argues that
Jesus's attitude toward women *was* countercultural; he did not seem
worried about challenging the status quo by talking with women,
allowing himself to be touched by women, or including women in
his circle of friends. Still, according to Paul VI, Jesus "did not call
any women to become part of The Twelve." The church "decides
what can change and what must remain immutable," and it chooses
not to change on male priesthood out of fidelity to Christ's example.

In addition to arguing that Catholic tradition cannot change,
Paul VI makes a controversial theological claim central to his case
against women's ordination. He says that because the priest acts
in *persona Christi*, "natural resemblance" between Christ and the
presider in the liturgy is required. Otherwise, the symbol system
that is fundamental to Eucharist (i.e., the priest is like Christ at the
Last Supper) does not work. The document does not suggest that
men are superior to women. Men do not necessarily have more
Christlike virtues or engage in more actions that we associate with
Jesus, but their maleness is still necessary to suggest Christlike-ness
in their priestly role.[9]

Nearly twenty years later, in another document on priesthood,
Pope John Paul II reaffirms Paul VI's claim that Jesus's choice of male
apostles and the constant tradition of the church makes women
priests impossible.[10] Like his predecessor, he does not explicitly
root women's exclusion from priesthood in claims about perceived
differences between men and women. Unlike him, he does not re-
assert the claim that the priest acts in *persona Christi*. Instead, he
asserts his authority to close debate and declares "the question of
the admission of women to the ministerial priesthood" settled.

Further, in a document on women, he claims that women have special gifts and a complementary role, both in families and in the church. The unique work that women do is equally important to the work men do. By respecting differences, the church's teaching and practice uphold women's dignity rather than detracting from it.[11] In this document, John Paul further explains that "it is *the Eucharist* above all that expresses *the redemptive act of Christ the Bridegroom towards the Church the Bride*. This is clear and unambiguous when the sacramental ministry of the Eucharist, in which the priest acts 'in *persona Christi*,' is performed by a man."[12] The church continues to teach that only men can be priests because Christ's maleness is an essential aspect of his humanity and only their bodies can convey this significance sacramentally to an assembly that stands in relation to him as a bride does to a bridegroom.

These arguments have been criticized by feminist scholars for decades. Feminist biblical scholar Elisabeth Schüssler Fiorenza was among the first to question reliance on the twelve apostles as an indicator of Jesus's intentions for the church.[13] She points out that the term "apostle" is used in a variety of ways in the Gospels. It is associated not only with the names of the twelve men traditionally remembered as apostles but also with Paul, Barnabas, and others. It has a much broader usage than the group Jesus is shown calling to ministry and sometimes functions symbolically or rhetorically. Only later were "the twelve" identified as the "apostles." Although only men are included in lists of the twelve, the Gospels include no argument for restricting the designation to men. A narrow focus on the twelve also overlooks the countercultural understanding of the early Christians of their movement as "a discipleship of equals." It cannot make sense of Mark's gospel, in which the twelve are primarily understood as disciples, and women, in contrast to the twelve, appear to be "the exemplary disciples of Jesus."[14]

If biblical arguments for restricting priesthood by gender are flawed, so, too, feminist theologians argue, are claims about sacramental theology and Catholic tradition. Gender is claimed as an

144 CAN YOU BE A CATHOLIC AND A FEMINIST?

essential aspect of Jesus's humanity, necessary for sacramental coherence. But feminist scholars question why gender should carry all of this weight. Why must priests be male but not Middle Eastern, Jewish, or dark skinned? How are we to differentiate some aspects of incarnational embodiment from others? Is a gender binary really so fundamental? The complexity and ambiguity of gendered imagery in Christian theology (e.g., both men and women are somehow understood as brides of Christ) seems to confirm the complex ways women and men embody gender in real life and open the door to a more complex symbolic system. The church's own teaching holds that both men and women are made in God's image, called to model their lives on Jesus, and preach the good news. To argue that Catholics would not perceive a female presider as Christlike seems to dismiss women's relationship to the holy. At its most profound, sacramentality cannot be constrained by gender. Fundamentally, it "expresses the mystery and presence of God-for-us in the Incarnation."[15]

Arguments for maintaining an all-male priesthood rooted in the constancy of tradition are also problematic. Tradition is an important source in Catholic theology, and feminists take seriously magisterial teachings, the witness of saints and holy people, the ritual and ethical practices of Catholic communities in history, and the writings of important theologians such as Saint Augustine and Saint Thomas Aquinas. However, feminist theology also assumes a post–Vatican II understanding of tradition as not static or dead but flexible and living. Like most theologians today, feminists believe that tradition has changed in the past (e.g., on slavery religious liberty, usury, and the death penalty, to name a few), and can and should continue to develop, slowly and carefully, when new insights such as women's equal dignity and capacity to lead and minister emerge. Theirs is a critical fidelity based on an understanding of tradition as "a process—the transmission or handing on of the mystery of God's self-communication in creation and history."[16]

Practically speaking, excluding women from priesthood deprives the church of wise leadership, creative energy, and ministerial capacity. The church suffers from a dearth of good ministers and leaders. There simply are not enough male priests or deacons to do the ritual work of the ordained (e.g., to preach, marry, baptize, hear confessions, preside at Eucharist, bury the dead) or to fill the administrative and leadership roles currently allotted to them. When the gifts of talented women go unused, the whole church suffers.

Counterarguments have been raised by new orthodox Catholic feminists who adhere to a theology of complementarity. Michelle Schumacher argues that male-only ordination does not deny women dignity, but rather recognizes the significance of sexual differentiation and the nuptial meaning of the body.[17] Pia de Solenni similarly offers that women are excluded from this one path not because they cannot do what is required but because their "being" points them away from a role that must be male to complement a female church.[18] Sr. Sara Butler leans heavily on the constant tradition of the church that consistently upholds male-only ordination while speaking to the dignity of women. For these scholars, Jesus's maleness read through the lens of complementarity, gendered theological imagery, and an unchanging tradition is significant enough to raise questions about the arguments of feminist theologians.

While I have argued in this book for a Catholic feminism that is deeply respectful of Catholic tradition and open to seeking common ground, these arguments are not compelling. They seem to be rooted in a failure to believe in the equal capacity of men and women to connect to the holy in service of the church as well as an unwillingness to encounter tradition with that judicious mix of generosity and suspicion that is essential to feminism. Since the beginnings of the women's ordination movement in the 1970s, feminists have raised critical questions about women's exclusion from the full range of ecclesial ministries to which they are called and for which they are needed. They have done so with

146   CAN YOU BE A CATHOLIC AND A FEMINIST?

a deep respect for church teaching, Scripture, embodied human nature, and Catholic tradition. But drawing on developments in the tradition itself and on commitments to interpret tradition with knowledge of its strengths and limitations and to seek the full flourishing of all humans, they have provided powerful arguments for rethinking not just who is ordained but how power is distributed.

The Deeper Problem: Clericalism

Being a Catholic feminist means not only seeing women's exclusion from priesthood, but also analyzing the larger power structure impeding women's full participation in the church. It means acknowledging structural clericalism. In chapter 2, when I discussed sexual violence, I described some of the structural problems that lie underneath both bad sex and sexual violation. Here I turn to sexual violence again because it is in grappling with clergy sexual abuse that many Catholics have grasped clericalism as a structural problem of gender and power. My own research shows just how significant a problem it is.

When the news about the Pennsylvania Grand Jury Report broke in August 2018, I had just arrived at the Jesuit School of Theology in Berkeley, California. In response, our community gathered to lament and pray; we hosted panels and lectures; and we offered workshops about preaching and pastoral care. But the most radical thing we did was to begin examining ourselves—our school of ministry and theology where we train ministers (lay and ordained) for service in the church. We agreed that clericalism was a key root cause of clergy sexual abuse.[19] We designed a simple self-study to help us consider our own complicity with and resistance to it.[20] To our knowledge, we are the only seminary in the United States to undertake this work.

We defined clericalism as "a systemic bias that isolates clergy and sets them apart, granting them excessive authority, trust, rights, and responsibilities at the expense of lay people." We were trying to get at the systemic dimensions of clericalism instead of viewing it simply as a vice of some particularly bad priests.[21] We held focus group sessions and asked two questions: "How does our school challenge clericalism?" and "Where is clericalism still embedded in the culture of our school?" Community members expressed pride in the school's model of educating lay men and women alongside scholastics and priests, the spare use of clerical titles or clothing, and our participatory liturgies. Most agreed that though extreme forms of clericalism were absent from our school, certain kinds of clerical privilege still needed to be addressed. But while some community members named as evidence of remaining clericalism the rarity of female preaching in liturgies, the financial disparities between lay and Jesuit students, and women's exclusion from priesthood, others protested. This was not clericalism; it was just the church.

Though some scholars use the language of "structural clericalism," to indicate the presence of a problem that is bigger than individuals, our study revealed the difficulty of naming these structures. Understanding clericalism as a structure means seeing not just flawed individuals but patterns, assumptions, and practices that are endemic to institutions. In a follow-up study I conducted with colleagues at Santa Clara University, we found evidence of structural clericalism that continues to set priests "above and apart" in spite of individual opposition to it.[22]

Why does clericalism continue when most Catholics (lay and ordained) do not believe priests should be set above lay people? Racism provides a helpful analogy. In June 2020, the deaths of African Americans George Floyd, Ahmaud Arbery, and Breonna Taylor inspired mass protests in the streets in the United States. Though similar to past protests of the Black Lives Matter movement, these gatherings included more white people, signaled broader acceptance of structural racism, and indicated increased general concern about policing.[23] Most Americans do not support activists'

148   CAN YOU BE A CATHOLIC AND A FEMINIST?

call to "defund the police." But a growing understanding that police killings of unarmed Black men and women do not arise from "a few bad apples" is taking hold. A large majority of Americans now support targeted policing reforms. More people are coming to see racism in policing and elsewhere as something "baked into" their society that requires unmasking and dismantling. They are beginning to see racism as a structural problem.

Catholic social teaching has come to a deeper understanding of sinful social structures since Vatican II.[24] Today social sin is an essential part of Catholic social thought. Recent advances in Christian social ethics progress even further toward an understanding of sin as structural. The important work of theological ethicist Bryan Massingale connects Catholics to the broader rising social consciousness of structural racism. In his book *Racial Justice and the Catholic Church*, he employs US history, the history of the Catholic Church, and the experience of Black Americans to help readers understand racism as something that is pervasive and invisible in American culture, including the culture of their local Catholic parish. He defines racism as "a set of meanings and values that forms a people's way of life."[25] His evocative image of racism as a "soul sickness" has penetrated US Catholic consciousness, reshaping previously limiting conceptions, despite the official categorization of racism as an "intrinsic evil."[26] While previously Catholics understood that racism was evil but only rarely saw that they were participating in and benefiting from it, the emerging understanding of racism is now enabling a deeper sense of personal complicity with social sin.

A second significant development in social ethics is the work of ethicist Daniel Finn to better define the "structure" in structural sin. Previously social ethicists often used the word "structure" without reference to relevant social theories. However, Finn has engaged in substantial dialogue with sociologists for years, and he uses critical realist sociology to describe structures as real "systems of human relations" involving "restrictions, enablements, and incentives."[27]

Finn shows how even persons with good intentions often participate in sinful social structures via their free but "influenced" actions. Structures do not force people to do evil, but they subtly exert pressure on people, making alternative choices difficult.

These recent movements in Christian theology do not suggest that structures *determine* actions, but they do offer powerful descriptions of meanings and values that *shape* daily practices, structures that subtly coerce choices, and ways of seeing that enable violence. Theological analysis of racism as structural sin is revelatory.

With this lens in hand, we can see that though ordination may appear to be the dominant restricting ecclesial structure, the exclusion of women and the setting of priests above and apart is much broader. For example, only in the last one hundred years has ordination been a requirement for cardinals, yet no woman has ever held this office, and deacons, who are ordained, cannot be women, even though tradition here is far more ambiguous.[28] The vast majority of Vatican congregations are led by priests, despite the absence of rules requiring ordination. Pope Francis has opened up some offices to women, though these moves have not been uncontroversial and have yet to significantly alter the gender balance at the Vatican.[29]

Structures that restrict women's participation in church governance at the highest levels also incentivize and enable men's control of authoritative theological writing, administration, and public ritual, making women's participation less likely. Women's voices and bodies are literally and meaningfully absent from powerful spaces in the church like seminaries and rectories. Women's bodies are not in the seminars or the meeting rooms, nor are they at the dinner table or in the common room. Women's voices are likewise missing—from most pulpits, most seminary teaching, and much of administrative decision-making. Male dominance is so structurally pervasive to Catholic life that it seems normal. Gendered division is a part of the power structure.

150 CAN YOU BE A CATHOLIC AND A FEMINIST?

Like racism, sexism lives in the church. Racism lives inside of individual Catholics and Catholic institutions in spite of and even through good intentions, for "Anti-Blackness is a spiritual malady, a soul sickness, an interior malformation of a magnitude for which we lack words. An affliction that can only be healed when we learn how to love Blackness. Black bodies. Black people."[30] Clericalism, too, lives inside of individual Catholics and Catholic institutions, in the form of meanings and values that inform explicit restrictions and filter down to ecclesial culture. It lives when women's absence becomes the expectation even where women are technically allowed and women's gifts are in some way affirmed. It shapes Catholic sensibilities about who leads the community in prayer, who represents or speaks for the church, or who heads the parish council, the board of directors, or the search committee. Despite the rhetoric of "equal dignity, different roles," clericalism reflects a profound failure to see or love female bodies, voices, and lives.

Ecclesial enablements that advantage men and disadvantage women are significant. Despite the fact that women are the majority of ecclesial ministers, men constitute the vast majority of students studying theology in seminaries and are much more likely to have their studies funded and their housing provided. The extraordinary dominance of men in leadership roles not requiring ordination occurs via the free choices of other men who occupy high-level administrative roles. Even when offices do not officially require ordination, custom often does not allow for consideration of any other option, especially if women would be placed in roles requiring ordained men to report to them.

Restrictions on preaching and presiding at Eucharist contribute to incentives for men to preach, preside, or bless in other contexts. The many prayer forms that can be led by laypeople are rarely used because Mass is assumed to be the ordinary way Catholics gather to pray. Officially, until 2021, women who served as lectors and eucharistic ministers did so as "extraordinary" ministers.[31] It is worth remembering the controversy that accompanied even this limited opening in the years following Vatican II, due to worries over women being on the altar and doing work traditionally assigned to priests and altar boys.[32]A similar debate ensued and continues in some places over female altar servers.[33] In practice, women and girls have served in these roles for decades, but the absence of theological affirmation until recently has rendered women's touching of sacred objects and reading of sacred texts exceptional and seemingly unfortunate, rather than ordinary and in alignment with their lives as people of faith and leaders of faith communities.

Incentives to grant power to men are also significant, even apart from restrictions due to ordination. Decision-making power is often awarded to pastors even if they are less experienced or less involved on the ground than lay ecclesial ministers. After Vatican II, some women became parish administrators, but since the 1980s, these roles have largely disappeared in the United States, though women continue to do much of the work of keeping parishes running. Similarly, lay preaching was for a time more possible, but has become increasingly rare.[34] Seminaries and schools of theology and ministry that once opened their doors to women have returned to excluding them. Catholic men continue to be more prominent than Catholic women as spiritual leaders, retreat leaders, social media voices, and even pundits. Catholic women with similar or greater qualifications struggle to find a platform.[35] The elevation of men is a structural feature of Catholic life.

The absence of women's bodies and voices matters. Excluding women's voices and bodies from spaces of leadership and power blinds the church to the fullness of humanity. The church whole suffers when it marginalizes the bodies and voices of women and elevates men in unhealthy ways.

By describing the gendered nature of the clericalist structures in the Catholic Church, I hope to illuminate the depth of its power problem. It is not just that women cannot be priests, but that they are restricted structurally from all kinds of other roles in the church, and that the structure itself concentrates power in the

152 CAN YOU BE A CATHOLIC AND A FEMINIST?

ordained men in ways that impede the full flourishing of all the church's members. Being a Catholic feminist means seeing the full scope of women' exclusion from power and criticizing the power structures that reify men's power-over and women's submission to it. It entails both seeking empowerment for women and daring to imagine a different way of embodying power.

Empowered Catholic Women

Though a feminist cannot look away from the power of the ordained or the power dimension of structural clericalism, stopping there would mean failing to see the many ways in which women do hold power in the Catholic Church. Mary, religious sisters, and laywomen hold power and can be empowering in the lives of Catholic women. Each of these sources of female power is real but limited. Yet, through deeper engagement with Catholic tradition in conversation with feminism, they can be reconstructed and redeemed.

In the Catholic tradition, Mary is a woman with an essential role in history of salvation. She is the all-important "Mother of the Redeemer," or "Theotókos" (Mother of God) according to John Paul II.[36] There is no Jesus without Mary, no Christ without Mary, no salvation without Mary. Her "fiat," or faithful "yes" to God's will, is both free and essential. With her, pregnancy and childbearing assume inestimable worth, but so too does a woman's word in response to God's invitation. If Catholic women and men pray to Mary and are invited to imitate Mary, is this not enough power? Could a deeper understanding of Marian power defuse some of the Catholic feminist tension about women and power in the church?

New orthodox feminists think Mary provides more than enough empowerment for Catholic women. Why worry about priestly power when Mary looms so large, providing plenty of space to live as a faithful disciple in one's daily life as a Catholic woman? Why not embrace the particularity of feminine ways of exercising power, especially in motherhood and humble service? Yes, Mary gives her "fiat," her submission, her "yes" to God, but in giving her life she, like other heroic figures, sacrifices herself for the sake of something greater, for the sake of the whole world. Surely, a feminist should acknowledge the centrality of Mary in the Catholic tradition as a win for women.

Yet even acknowledging the powerful place of a woman in the Christian narrative of Incarnation and Salvation, as well as in Catholic theology and piety, a feminist also must grapple with *Marianismo*, or the negative ways Mary functions in the lives of Catholic women. When Mary is upheld as a model for women, very often it is not her strength or prophetic witness that is singled out but her willing obedience in giving up her body and life. Her courage and strength are downplayed. She is domesticated and used to justify male dominance. As Asian feminist theologian Chung Hyun Kyung says, "Mary is tamed as a passive, obedient, yes-woman or humble maid who does everything men want."[37] The qualities held up for women to emulate are humility, sacrifice, and service.[38] And when women are told to be like Mary, often they are not hearing that they should be like Jesus.

The consequences of this domesticated Marian piety are real. Rather than empowering, a focus on Mary can encourage women to hide their gifts, turning over their lives in service to their families without ever considering that they might be able to contribute to the church and the world in other ways. Mary's attainable status as all-giving virgin mother "becomes a source of disempowerment."[39]

Though Catholic feminists can celebrate the ways Mary is depicted in different cultures, knowing that Marian art and piety signal her significance in people's lives, they must also be critical of the paradigm within which these portrayals exist. As Elizabeth Johnson aptly shows, summarizing decades of feminist critique, the basic problem with Marian tradition is that it "is saturated with sexist construals of gender."[40] To be sure, Asian, Latina, African,

Indian, and European renderings of Mary show the ability of different peoples to imagine Mary as someone like their mothers or sisters, someone close to them who can understand their problems and accompany them in their suffering. Mary imagined as compassionate Mother may be easier to approach than God conceived as all-powerful Creator or Father. We see her portrayed in religious art time and again pregnant and with the baby Jesus, which gives women a place in the world of the sacred. But because they drew from their own culturally shaped experiences of women, male theologians and artists shaped an image of Mary as ideal woman. They upheld her as a norm for all women, allowing the symbol of Mary to "legitimate patriarchal social structures."[41] Stories of Mary that are prominent in the tradition (e.g., Annunciation, Visitation, Wedding at Cana) typically sidestep the central gospel theme of the Kingdom of God. Her role in the story of Jesus the Liberator is often missed. Instead of a powerful woman of faith who answers the call of the God of justice and is a part of the early Christian community of disciples, Mary is limited relegated to role of patient mother or healer of our individual sorrows, and Catholic women who seek to imitate her can be similarly limited by this partial vision.

Feminist theologians have recovered the power of Mary's witness by situating her in her historical context and reading her alongside other prophetic biblical figures. As a young, unmarried, pregnant woman Mary would have been very vulnerable and courageous. Her Magnificat gives witness to her fierce faithfulness to a God who sides with the oppressed. Literary analysis of her dialogue with the angel Gabriel (Luke 1:26–38) reveals that it is very much like other conversations in which young men are called into prophetic roles, suggesting that Mary, too, can be seen as a prophet.[42] Mary is important not primarily because of her submission but because of her willingness to participate in God's reign, best captured in her Magnificat (Luke 1:46–55). She can be a model for both men and women seeking to collaborate with the God who is laboring to bring about a kingdom of justice and peace.

POWER 155

A reconstructed Mary offers liberating possibilities for Catholic women. Here is a figure who can be claimed as a legitimate source of empowerment, central to the Christian story because of her willingness to take up the challenging work of discipleship, which includes but is not limited to childbearing, which includes but is not limited to accompaniment during times of suffering. This is a Mary who can also be a source of power for Catholic women who take active roles in the church and the world.

Are Catholic women already powerful in the church through their ability to enter religious life as sisters? Sister power, like Marian power, is sometimes held up in just this way. However, the power of religious sisters is not the same as ordained power. Sisters are technically laypeople, despite their vows, with all of the rights and responsibilities of single and married laypeople and none of the privileges (e.g., preaching, presiding, administering parishes, becoming a bishop, cardinal, or pope) of the ordained. Canonically, they are subject to ordained men. Still, sisters do have a certain kind of power in Catholic life. They are women who defy social conventions, giving up marriage and motherhood in order to focus solely on God and service to the church. They run schools, hospitals, universities, nonprofits, and retreat centers. They are scholars, mystics, and activists. Because of their large numbers and the concentrated work with people, they have been significant influences in the lives of many Catholics. Moreover, many Catholics pray to women who lived as sisters, seeking help when they are in crisis. If one looks closely not just at church structures but at the lived religion of ordinary Catholics, it is difficult not to see the role of powerful sisters.

Still, like Marian power, sister power must be investigated using a feminist lens. Sisters are never completely self-governing but rather stand under ordained men who govern the church. The six-year (2009–2015) investigation of communities of religious women by the Vatican's Congregation for the Doctrine of the Faith is one recent example of how men with power in the church use

156 CAN YOU BE A CATHOLIC AND A FEMINIST?

their authority over religious women. Though communities of women had used their independence to forge new ways of praying and new priorities for ministry and advocacy, men had the authority to ask about what they were doing and attempt to correct them. No woman could be a part of the investigating body. Religious sisters responded gracefully and worked hard to establish their faithfulness while maintaining their independence. The visitation was largely ineffective in meeting its original goals and, in defending themselves, many religious sisters found new life in their vocations and communities.[43] Some women religious now have roles in Vatican agencies, on important committees, and in synodal discussions, though these roles remain largely consultative and exceptional, though some did vote in the 2023 Synod on Synodality. In their own communities, religious women have an independent communal prayer life, yet need to call upon a male priest to preside at liturgy, unlike men who are able to pray in their own communities without the help of a woman.

While these structural issues in the lives of religious sisters are substantial, reconstructing sister power is possible. Second-wave feminism inspired changes in the lives of sisters in the post–Vatican II era, leading many to forgo habits for secular dress in order to stand among rather than apart from the laity, take up justice work rather than remaining enclosed in convents or schools, and change their community structures so that mutuality rather than hierarchy was central.[44] For instance, some congregations of sisters have a "Responsible" rather than a "Superior," and many operate by communal discernment rather than obedience. Not only have they empowered themselves, they have reconceived how power is distributed, understood, and utilized.[45]

Despite the ongoing limits on what religious sisters can do, especially with feminist reconstruction, they stand as prophetic witnesses to a different kind of power for women to embody in the world. Their simple way of living contrasts with the popular feminist icon of the women in the power suit with the baby in one hand

POWER 157

and the briefcase in the other but also with third-wave feminist pop culture icons using sex as power. The lives of religious women have offered a set of options for women that few secular organizations can match. Long before modern feminism, sisters defied stereotypical views of womanhood, had plentiful vocations other than marriage and motherhood, created and led important social institutions, and embraced radical lives of faith. Though lacking the power of ordination and never fully self-governing, they have found alternative ways of claiming and sharing power. Through encounter with feminism, religious life has become a source of empowerment for Catholic women. Sister power does not suggest that ordination is unnecessary, but it does show what women have been able to accomplish, even without it.

Finally, lay power, like Marian power and sister power, is a force that contravenes the limitations on women's power in the Catholic Church, though it, too, stands in need of further development. Laywomen today constitute 80 percent of all lay ecclesial ministers, including directors of religious education, catechists, youth group leaders, campus ministers, and coordinators of parish life.[46] With the increasing shortages of priests, practically speaking, this means that women are the ones introducing children, teens, and adults to the sacraments, teaching theology, planning retreats, leading people in prayer, visiting those who are sick and dying, and comforting those who are seeking or lost.

Catholic laywomen are limited in what they can do both by structures and by culture. Structurally, within parishes, dioceses, and other institutions, they work under men who hold the ultimate authority. Culturally, they can still be relegated to tasks at which women are thought to excel and blocked from roles like preaching and leading regardless of their actual gifts. Working largely within the power structures of the Catholic Church, remarkable laywomen like Dorothy Day and Flannery O'Connor, as well as the countless unknown women who are the backbone of Catholic organizations, have influenced generations of Catholics. In recent decades,

158 CAN YOU BE A CATHOLIC AND A FEMINIST?

single and married laywomen have taken up more powerful roles as Catholic university presidents, theologians, and administrators, and in every kind of secular institution. In addition, women are taking new roles as leaders in Catholic organizations, consultants for Vatican commissions, and theological experts.[47] Influenced by feminism, they have challenged cultural ideas about what Catholic women are capable of, and, daily, they shape the lives of Catholics and contribute to the work of the church in the world.

Though limitations imposed by the restriction of ordination to men and structural clericalism cannot be dismissed, women are not totally bereft of power in the Catholic Church. From Mary to religious sisters to laywomen, women are central actors who wield power in the lives of Catholics. Feminist critique is necessary to see limitations to the ways women are able to hold and utilize power, but feminism has also inspired revisioning that has contributed to women's empowerment and to the reconstruction of power by women. Working within and around existing sexist structures, women have found creative ways to claim and exercise power.

Saving Power

In the movie *The Power*, with which I began, all of the female characters wield considerable power. The two most memorable characters—Allie, the matriarch of a religious movement, and Roxie, a military leader—are initially inspiring, as each transcends abusive childhoods and comes into power that was never meant to be hers. And as the girls and women around Roxie and Allie realize how to use their power to defend themselves from potential and real male attackers, it is hard not to feel encouraged. Finally, there is safety and freedom. Finally, women are in charge of their lives. Yet as the women begin to wield power ruthlessly and violently, it is clear that only the identity of the victims and victors has changed.

Power remains a problem in this narrative universe, no matter who has it.

I have argued that for a Catholic feminist, women's lack of access to the power of ordination is inherently problematic, as is structural clericalism that restricts women and concentrates power in the hands of ordained men. Even still, I have recognized a diversity of imperfect but nonetheless real ways Catholic women have exercised power in and outside of the church. In this last section, I want to point toward a feminist path of empowerment. While acknowledging the worries of Simcha Fischer and Naomi Alderman about power no matter who has it, I contend that Catholic feminists can advocate for women's ordination and legitimately hope that women and men have the potential to wield power differently, whether they are ordained or not.

In *The Power*, power is portrayed an ability people have to make other people do things because of their ability to hurt them. It is power-over that comes to someone because of a threat, implied or actual. The assumption is that people wield power because they can. Men have held power over women because they have greater strength, and if women had a similar kind of power at their fingertips, they would use it in exactly the same punishing way. This may be one kind of feminist utopia. But this is not what most feminists have sought for women when they fought for education, the vote, equal access to professions, financial independence, or freedom from bodily harm. It differs profoundly from the power Catholic feminists have spoken of as being inside of themselves, waiting to be utilized for good.

A Catholic feminist account of power is not about control over others. Ultimately, power comes from our Source, from God. According to Psalm 96, God "comes with power." God does wondrous deeds, governs, and stands forever. Before God, the trees, sea creatures, heavens and earth rejoice. Yet this powerful God also feeds, gathers, carries lambs in his bosom, and leads with care. God "comes with power." But it is a power both gentle and fierce, as

160 CAN YOU BE A CATHOLIC AND A FEMINIST?

present in care as in justice. This same kind of power exists in each person and can be harnessed, claimed, and actualized.

Though we commonly think of God's power as power-over, the gospel upends that conception. This God chooses to save not by imposition but by choosing an imperfect people, sending prophets, giving signs, none of which are received by everyone. Free will remains. Even when drawing near to us in Christ, he chooses to empty himself of power-over, "taking the form of a slave, assuming human likeness" (Philippians 2:7). The power he retains is power-in-relation. The gospel spreads by attraction rather than by fiat, as the stories of growing crowds and the many metaphors Jesus gives for the Kingdom (e.g., mustard seed, yeast) attest. When Jesus's message threatens the authorities, they conspire to kill him, and while Jesus is steadfast in his mission, he does not interfere. The game-changing power of Jesus's witness in history is that he does not do what is expected of the powerful—he does not return to enact revenge on his enemy. Rather, he offers peace.[48] In the gospel, glory is not found in domination but in the cross.

Yet, while sympathetic to worries about hierarchy and domination, feminist theologians have rightly questioned the way power is talked about Christianity without diminishing the undeniable importance of power. We cannot avoid the question of power. Certainly, it must be approached with caution. But if Jesus did not enact power in typical ways, neither did he eschew it altogether. Drawing power from our Source, feminists have argued, we can use it for good, just as Jesus did. Sometimes this will involve confrontation. Just because power is not violent or "over" does not mean it lacks force. In a groundbreaking essay, "The Power of Anger in the Work of Love," ethicist Beverly Harrison argued that God's grace can be seen in the "power to struggle and to experience indignation."[49] Anger can be a powerful tool motivating necessary confrontation. According to Harrison, faithful people are called not only to sacrifice but also "to confront, as Jesus did, that which thwarts the power of human personal and communal becoming."[50]

POWER   161

There are good reasons to claim and use power, to stand against injustice, and insist on change. Power can be drawn from, shared, and used in the service of others and of the good.

The Power is compelling as a novel that reveals the injustice of the present by flipping the script. By viewing a world where women are in charge and men fear them, we can better see unjust structures and accompanying assumptions that we fail to notice simply because they are so pervasive. This upside-down view of the world is helpful because of what it reveals, but the narrative that follows is far too unimaginative and pessimistic.

The Christian narrative, in contrast, names hording and abuse of power as sinful, but is more hopeful about human nature and potential. It offers an alternative vision and holds that Jesus's death and Resurrection open a door through which we are now better able to walk. It can seem that to be Christian is to give up power, to sacrifice, to cast off influence and privilege, that power is something bad people lord over others and good people renounce. While there is no reason to doubt that power can be exploited or that the powerful have unique potential to harm the vulnerable, if "God comes with power," and people are created in God's image, if Jesus changed the rules of the game by the way he claimed power, it seems possible for Christians to figure out a way to use power well.

Feminist Audre Lorde, whose work I have frequently drawn upon in this book, helps us see why it is important to move past a reluctance to use power. In "Poetry Is Not a Luxury" she writes of the dark "places of possibility" hidden deep inside ourselves. "Within these deep places, each one of us holds an incredible reserve of creativity and power, of unexamined and unrecorded emotion and feeling." To give up poetry would— she believes —be to "give up the core—the fountain—of our power."[51] And in another place, she writes of having been afraid to speak, but gradually realizing, with a diagnosis of a serious illness, that there was no time for silence and nothing really to fear. "And then," she said, "I began to recognize a source of power within myself."[52] Lorde identifies power with depth

162 CAN YOU BE A CATHOLIC AND A FEMINIST?

and emotion, with authenticity and courage, with passion flowing through us. Power is something to discover, own, and use for good.

Authentic Catholic feminist engagement with the problem of power in the church is not as simple as saying, "Ordain women!" The argument begins but does not stop here. A Catholic feminist must also see the broader problem of power and call for changes in the priesthood, so that ordination for women would mean that they would join in a ministry of service in which power was shared rather than guarded. It must include continued exploration and reconstruction of female sites of power in the church. It is essential for Catholic feminists to seek a share of the power of ordination for women who feel called to use their gifts to serve the People of God. But being a Catholic feminist also means acknowledging the radical potential opened up by the Christian tradition, in dialogue with feminism, which requires a different vision power and offers hope for future possibilities. With this vision in hand, Catholic feminists should also seek to reform structures of power in the church so that all Christians can be invited to connect with power from their Source and use it for good.

8

Prayer

I Close My Eyes

"I close my eyes," my student tells me. When she looks around in the chapel of our school of theology and ministry, most of the faces are male. The walls are bare; no images of Mary or statues of female saints break the dominant masculinity. To make it through Mass and to connect with a God she is coming to understand as authentically called by female names and depicted in feminine symbols, she closes her eyes and goes within to a space where the images of God are less confining. She did not always have this difficulty, but once she understood the feminist critique of Christian ritual, she could not unsee it.

Another young friend tells me she can no longer even enter a church. The space that has long been a source of joy is now a site of pain and contradiction. The male language, imagery, and leadership are making her "Amen" impossible. Occasionally, she tries to return, but soon finds herself walking out; she is more comfortable in a church that values the feminine. In interviews, some women of color who led Black Lives Matter protests in my former hometown of St. Louis say they are tired of waiting for real commitment to the justice issues that should be the concern of more Christians. Unlike their parents, who found strength in the church, they say, "This is not your mother's civil rights movement" and seek inspiration elsewhere.[1]

It is not only young women. Another friend, mother of a trans son, shares that she is "changing teams." For this longtime Catholic woman who learned to love liturgy and theology as a student at a

---

Can You Be a Catholic and a Feminist?. Julie Hanlon Rubio, Oxford University Press.
© Oxford University Press 2024. DOI: 10.1093/oso/9780197553145.003.0009

164   CAN YOU BE A CATHOLIC AND A FEMINIST?

Jesuit university, a wedding homily that left her child sobbing in the pew was the last straw. A friend my age who works with a primarily Latina nonprofit shares that most Latina mothers she works with rarely participate in parish liturgies; they are Catholic, but they do not feel they belong in church, so they do not often pray there.[2] Catholic women I know who experience a call to ordination themselves or seek women leaders of worship for themselves and their daughters go elsewhere to pray because they are tired of waiting for the church to change.[3] Others give up when they find that the prayers and rituals they know are no longer life-giving. When traditional prayer practices and Mass no longer provide beauty, transcendence, or community, some go elsewhere to worship, while others reclaim Sunday morning for family, nature, or brunch.

Dorothy Day once said, "Without prayer, we could not survive. As breathing is to the body, prayer is to the soul."[4] Still, prayer is more of a problem for many religious feminists now. Most early feminists were religious and, though some raised questions about their faiths, most maintained religious practice as they deepened their feminist commitment.[5] The language, imagery, and leadership they encountered in church did not differ significantly from those found in other institutions, and they were more concerned with social than ecclesial reform. But the twentieth century was a time of progress for women on many fronts. Today the absence of women's voices and leadership inside the church is now more at odds with women's leadership in other parts of public life. Many Protestant churches began allowing women to pastor and preach— and became more attentive to gendered language and symbols—in the 1970s. In the twenty-first century, consciousness about diversity in imagery and representation is rising. In academia, we are critical of "manels" or all-male conference panels, and we know a syllabus is flawed if it fails to include a diversity of authors and their perspectives. But, Catholic feminist theologians note, the sacred texts of liturgy and prayer are all written, proclaimed, and preached by men, and the theology expressed in them has yet to incorporate feminist critique.[6] Today, as women gain power and claim their voice in nearly every sphere, the contrast between ecclesial and secular spaces is starker; male dominance, more noticeable; the absence of women's voices, the lack of opportunities to participate, inexplicable.

For many women of color, however, religion is a place of affirmation and strengthening and, even if they do much of their praying on the other side of church walls, feminist questions about prayer are often less salient. Latina popular religion centers on rituals that take place outside parishes.[7] As in earlier generations of Catholic immigrant communities, women play significant roles in religious processions and festivals. They are in charge of home altars, family visits to the cemetery, and quinceañeras. Priests and Eucharist are less central to their faith and practice. For many Black Catholic women, too, church is a place where the authority and gifts they utilize in family and community are recognized.[8] They are the mothers of the church. They run church raffles, organize the rosaries, offer spiritual direction, and pray when given the opportunity in and outside of liturgy. They pass on the faith to their children and grandchildren. In these Catholic communities, women play central roles in faith transmission, and Catholic feminist tension is not a primary concern.

New orthodox feminists are also less worried about prayer. Though they may share the desire to participate more fully in Catholic prayer life, they are less concerned about traditional prayer forms and more active in claiming space elsewhere. Several years ago, campus ministers at my university asked me to engage with a group of women students who wanted to start a spirituality group. I was excited to meet them and suggested that we could read some feminist theologians to get started. They were not interested. At first, I was confused, but I soon realized that they had been formed by youth ministry, altar service, retreats, and their families to lead prayer. They had no interest in critically engaging Catholic tradition. These women just wanted to pray and they were

166   CAN YOU BE A CATHOLIC AND A FEMINIST?

absolutely equipped to do it on their own. These new orthodox feminists treasured Catholic liturgy and were not interested in engaging critical questions about its substance. Catholic Feminist creator Claire Swinarski's website offers a new orthodox feminist creed that begins with the Apostle's Creed and has a whole separate section on belief in the church: "We believe The Catholic Church is a perfect institution made up of imperfect people, striving to lead the flock closer to Heaven. We believe Pope Francis is the bomb. We believe getting out of bed to go to Sunday Mass is hard, but vital."[9]

Though they can be critical of cultural norms, such as the pressure to be a perfect Catholic mom, these feminists are not troubled by the substance of Catholic faith. Claire Swinarski's "40 Days to a Feminist Faith," a program to encourage daily prayer, is a good example. Like many feminist theologians, she notes Jesus's interactions with women and highlights strong women in Scripture. Unlike them, she offers no critical analysis of the tradition. She writes, "The Church refuses ordination to women because although Jesus loved, cherished, and respected women, he only passed along the sacrament of priesthood to men," and moves on.[10] The spaces and practices of Catholic prayer and liturgical life provide crucial grounding to this group of women. Male leadership and language present no obstacle to participation. Inspired by Mary and female saints, they keep silence when tradition compels it and speak where their voices are welcomed. Some are converts who fell in love with traditional liturgical forms and practices. Others are cradle Catholics who grew up as active participants in faith communities like Life Teen or Focus. In social media communities such as Blessed Is She, Catholic Feminist, and FemCatholic, they embrace their faith and limit feminist critique to secular and Christian subcultures rather than Catholic tradition.[11]

Catholic women in between these different types of feminists who might prefer greater inclusivity accept the church as it is, refusing to let it get in the way of traditions and family relationships they value, but they may not pray in the same way that previous

PRAYER 167

generations of Catholic women did. Sociologist Michele Dillon notes that "women have been the backbone of the Catholic Church in the U.S. . . . since at least the beginning of the 20th century."[12] They were the ones who most appreciated the beauty and aesthetics of liturgy and prayer. They prepared the church, washed the altar linens, and decorated the altar with flowers. But today, only about one-fourth of women go to Mass every week, and fewer see Mass as important to their Catholic identity.[13] Gender imbalance in liturgy is troubling, but it is not the primary concern of these women because liturgy is not the center of their faith.

After a first chapter establishing a vision of authentic human life drawn from a synthesis of Catholic and feminist thinking, this book has offered analyses of six issues. The second set of chapters was more difficult than the first. On these issues, I anticipated that readers would feel deeper divides and need more creative strategies. This chapter is different because for many Catholic women, prayer is not a problem. Yet I will argue that it should be. In this chapter, I claim that for Catholic feminists, it is crucial to face the problems feminist theologians have raised about traditional Catholic prayer forms, to acknowledge the significance of prayer and liturgy nonetheless, and to explore authentically Catholic and feminist ways to pray.

Facing the Problem

Why is so hard for a Catholic feminist to pray? I have defined a feminist as someone who sees sexism in its intersecting reality and works to overcome it so that women and all people are better able to flourish. Sexism is one part of an intersectional analysis that also involves attention to race and class. Concern with structures impeding women's flourishing is central to feminism. In this chapter I consider sexism in the sacramental, liturgical, and prayer life of the church itself. As the anecdotes in the previous section

168   CAN YOU BE A CATHOLIC AND A FEMINIST?

illustrate, some Catholic women find conventional practice difficult even though they continue to pray, and a feminist analysis can help us understand why.

Though many Catholic women, including some who identify as feminists, are not troubled by the issues raised in this chapter, being a feminist requires one to grapple with what feminist scholars have identified as structural sexism—though it does not necessarily obligate a particular response. As we saw in chapter 1, feminism has always included consciousness-raising, whether in the form of speeches and writings or groups of women analyzing their own experiences together, finding they are not alone, and coming to see and even regret their own participation in sexist structures they previously had not noticed. Feminist theologians help religious feminists see structural sexism in their traditions, and their work is especially crucial to this chapter.

I remember the moment in a New Testament class during my master's program when my feminist professor analyzed the term "Lord," which is often used for God in Catholic piety. She made the point that "Lord" has its roots in cultural and political arrangements from another time and implies submission to a master. This obvious connection had never occurred to me. I used the word in prayer and preferred it to "God" because of its sound, which reminded me of "love." Once I knew where the word came from, I could not hear it the same way. It no longer resonated. I had to search the tradition for other words that enabled growth in my relationship with God, though sometimes I found myself using the word anyway, convinced it meant something different to me. Learning about sexism in Catholic prayer practice made me excited about the potential of feminist analysis, but I also felt that something valuable was being taken away from me. I remember thinking, "What else would I learn? What else would I have to let go? And would there be something better to take its place?" Facing sexism in the tradition—including in one's own prayer practice—is not easy, but it is unavoidable.

Liturgy is where sexism in the church is ritualized. In women's exclusion from ritual leadership and interpretation of holy texts, in male language and imagery for God, and patriarchal theology, sexism is present and reinforced through repetition. The rite calls for participation, which signals affirmation; for our "amens" and our "I believes;" our postures of standing, sitting, and kneeling; our singing, and our silence. Of course, women are very present in Catholic liturgical space. Women are part of the Body of Christ that celebrates the Eucharist. Women fill the pews and now serve as acolytes, lectors, and cantors. Women, like men, find beauty, meaning, solace, and challenge in liturgy. Similarly, women in my extended Italian family find meaning when we gather for Sunday dinners even though we still end up doing most of the cooking and dishwashing. Like my ongoing use of "Lord," and my family's gatherings, Catholic liturgies are multivalent rituals with multiple layers of meaning. They "disclose as they reveal."[14] They ritualize sexism while speaking truths about God, the world, and human existence: the goodness of the natural world including the body, the potential of all creation to reveal the divine, the joy and necessity of communal meaning-making; the awesomeness and closeness of God.[15] To say that the Sunday dinners of my extended family reify sexism is not to deny their value as family-strengthening events. To say sexism is ritualized in liturgy is not to say that liturgy is *only* sexist, or to deny ways liturgy can be prophetic, powerful, and nurturing.

Yet feminist theologians have spent decades unmasking the sexism in Catholic liturgy and prayer. There is a high level of consensus on the general problem and its central importance. These arguments are not new or experimental; they are essential elements of scholarly Catholic feminist thought, which authentic Catholic feminism must engage. In chapter 7, I addressed ordination as an issue of power, along with broader structures in the church that disincentivize women's leadership. In analyzing Catholic practices linked to Mary and the saints, I argued that problematic gender

170   CAN YOU BE A CATHOLIC AND A FEMINIST?

dynamics had to be understood before the practices could be reclaimed. Here I reflect more particularly on Catholic practices of prayer, both individual and communal. While I cannot do justice to all of the relevant feminist theology on this topic, I will highlight four key themes: male presiding, androcentric sacred texts, male-dominant imagery for God, and hierarchical theology.

Catholic Eucharist or Sunday Mass is by definition male-led. Because only men can be ordained, only men can preside at or lead Eucharist. Catholics who experience female leadership in most other spheres of their lives can sometimes overlook the sexism inherent in this structure, but it is important to become conscious of its oddity. In this most central Catholic ritual, when half (or more) of those gathered are women, a woman almost never addresses the community on matters of faith.

According to Catholic liturgical theology, presiding and preaching roles within the liturgy are connected, and both belong to those who are ordained. It is important to see the impact of women's exclusion from this role. The Eucharist is, theologically speaking, the most significant Catholic ritual, when the whole community gathers, and at that ritual a woman is almost never heard leading the prayer or blessing members of the community or interpreting sacred texts. Occasionally, exceptions are made for laypeople to preach during the liturgy but, officially, their remarks are not called the "homily" and cannot take place at the time the homily would be given or substitute for the preaching of the presider on the texts of the day.[16] Laypeople can preach outside of Mass. Preaching is a calling of all baptized Catholics. Theologians, Scripture scholars, and other experts frequently speak about theology and lead prayer on Catholic university campuses, at retreats and conferences. Women can write prayer petitions, serve as lectors and Eucharistic ministers, and make announcements at the end of liturgy. But women's exclusion from the preaching and presiding that accompanies male leadership when the community gathers for Mass continues to perpetuate sexism by signaling that only men

PRAYER   171

have the capacity to lead the community in the main space in which Catholics experience public prayer and preaching.

The liturgy that is led by men has at its center sacred texts written by men. The Scriptures read at every liturgy are of central importance. Catholics believe that as these stories are repeated over and over, they become lenses through which their lives are interpreted.[17] This immersion in the core stories of Christianity is part of going to Mass, and often women who struggle to stay in the church say that it is the prophetic wisdom of Jesus and the gospel that keeps them returning.[18] Catholics believe that the Scriptures reveal God's wisdom in a particularly significant way. Yet both the Hebrew Bible and New Testament are written by men, center male characters, and are androcentric (or told through a male lens) and not infrequently sexist.[19] Feminist biblical scholars have done remarkable work to promote nonsexist translations, recover the stories of women, lift up texts that challenge sexism, and offer ways to reinterpret "texts of terror" that are dangerous to women.[20] They have helped us to notice the women who are present in the texts even if the church has forgotten or misremembered them. For instance, because of their work, more Catholics are aware that Mary Magdalene should be remembered not as a former prostitute but as the first witness to the Resurrection and an important early Christian disciple. But the Bible remains limited by the patriarchy of the culture in which it was written. When only this text is read, the voices, stories, and perspectives of women remain marginal. When no feminist biblical interpretation is employed, models of Christian life are limited and imaginations are skewed.

Moreover, in the Scriptures, in the language of the Mass, and in sacred art, God is imaged primarily as male. Catholics pray "in the name of the Father, the Son, and the Holy Spirit." Theologian Elizabeth Johnson has powerfully argued that male God language matters because "the symbol functions" to encourage or justify the subordination of women and is idolatrous as it fails to recognize the mystery and incomprehensibility of God, who cannot be captured

172   CAN YOU BE A CATHOLIC AND A FEMINIST?

by any one name.[21] Feminist theologians have pointed to greater diversity of God language that exists in Scripture and tradition, and advocate using a diversity of names for God, including female names. Such diversity challenges "the idolatry of maleness in classic language about God, thereby making possible the rediscovery of divine mystery; and points to a recovery of the dignity of women created in the image of God."[22] Using many names is both theologically and ethically important. Yet liturgy and prayer remain for the most part stubbornly stuck in male God language and symbol, limiting both our ways of thinking about God and our ways of relating to human beings.

Work that feminist theologians have done to challenge hierarchy in theology and piety raises additional questions about Catholic liturgical and prayer practice. Elizabeth Schüssler Fiorenza's scholarship uncovered the importance of the "discipleship of equals" in the early Jesus movement in which women and men who followed Jesus participated in a uniquely egalitarian community. She argues that working for the *basileia*, or kingdom of God, where "wholeness" and justice would reign, was central to Jesus's mission.[23] The Spirit, according to Schüssler Fiorenza, moved not just *in him* but *among the people*, enabling them to challenge gender-confining stereotypes of their time and adopt a "egalitarian ethos," for in Christ there was "neither male nor female" (Galatians 3:28).[24] Feminist scholars like Schüssler Fiorenza focus attention on following the example of Jesus and forming a community of disciples. Liturgy and prayer, feminists argue, should be more tethered to Jesus's life and to the lives of the ordinary men and women who make up the church. It should encourage prophetic work for justice rather than submission.

Much of the feminist critique too briefly summarized above is tied to the Eucharistic liturgy, but other Catholic prayer forms escape some but not all of these difficulties, according to feminist theologians. The practice of Eucharistic Adoration offers all believers the same access to the presence of Christ in the Eucharist.

PRAYER 173

With this practice, anyone can sit in the presence of the consecrated host, which Catholics believe is the real presence of Jesus, and pray silently. But it can also promote a focus on Christ in the host separated from the life of Jesus and the community gathered to worship, along with a privatized faith unconnected to justice. The rosary can be led by anyone and centers a scriptural text glorifying a woman, Mary, the Mother of God. It can anchor those who pray it via repetition and connection to the tactile in beads, which are sometimes gifts passed down in families or purchased and blessed in holy places. It can be a source of comfort in difficult times. But the words of the rosary and its accompanying "Mysteries" are unconnected to Jesus's essential mission to "bring good news to the poor" (Luke 4:18–19) and distanced from key aspects of his life—his prophetic preaching, meals with outcasts and sinners, and healing of people at the margins of his society. They make no reference to Mary's connection with this mission in the Magnificat, the prayer she speaks in response to the news that she will bear the Christ child (Luke 1:46–55). The prayers of the rosary focus on Mary's humility and ask for her to intercede "now and at the hour of our death," reinforcing a sense of the believer's reliance on someone to intercede on their behalf rather than encouraging an intimate relationship with God and empowering active discipleship.

Similarly, practices centered on saints offer a diverse set of stories of holy men and women, a "cloud of witnesses" from which believers can draw inspiration. A range of Catholic feminists have found them to be empowering, because "Many of these stories did not limit women to the roles of wife and mother within the nuclear family; rather they told of women's outstanding contributions in the history of church and the Western world. These women were creative, independent, and influential." Yet, in practice, the stories of female saints "stressed suffering, sexual purity, submission, outmoded piety, and total obedience," and they can also be a hindrance to women's faith.[25] They have to be critically analyzed and retold before they can serve as authentic sources of liberation. Likewise,

174   CAN YOU BE A CATHOLIC AND A FEMINIST?

Catholic practices around saints need to be approached critically, because they can easily devolve into asking for special assistance from figures who are linked to everything from lost objects to buying a house, suggesting that God will pay more attention to those with special influence in a divine economy. As Johnson shows, this way of praying owes a great deal to hierarchical medieval patronage systems, rather than a feminist sense of saints as "friends and prophets of God" whose lives continue to inspire and whose presence can be a source of strength.[26]

As I wrote in chapter 1, many well-known prayers rely on a model of submission to God that feminists find problematic. Feminist prayers are more likely to be dialogical, encouraging closeness with God and leaving space for expressing a range of emotions—trust and anxiety, rage and joy, gratitude for and frustration with life and religion.[27] In contrast, popular spirituality often leaves little room to imagine that Scripture, liturgy, or liturgical tradition might stand in the way of prayer or that believers could ask for the power of the Spirit to engage in prophetic witness.

This is why, in fall of 1981, Mary Daly (then a theologian at Boston College) led a procession of women out of Harvard Memorial Church, where she had been preaching—the first woman ever to do so.[28] Daly came to believe that the Christian tradition she had been trying to reform was incompatible with her evolving feminist consciousness; many of those who walked out with her shared her frustration with tradition and rejoiced in the freedom they found gathered outside its confining walls. In the years since, some women have continued to gather in spaces where they can create feminist liturgies and bathe in feminine images of God that do not make it into traditional liturgical spaces or spiritual practices, though these groups are not nearly as common as they once were.[29]

But most Catholic feminists do not opt out because, while recognizing the liturgy's profound ambiguity, they are convinced that what is prophetic in it outweighs what is sexist. Being a Catholic feminist means facing structural sexism in the church and its rituals and not walking away. Though not everyone experiences it, tension between Catholicism and feminism comes to a head in prayer and ritual in a unique way; it cannot be explained away or passed over. Being a feminist means seeing, analyzing, and confronting structural sexism even if, as for many Catholic women, one's primary experience is of being nurtured and empowered by faith, despite it all.[30] Feminist theologians who point to structural sexism affirm enduring truth in the tradition, but part ways with their Catholic sisters who argue for acceptance of the status quo.[31] Feminist criticism of the church is rooted in love for the church, knowledge that the church has changed over time, and in hope for continued renewal.[32] Once a feminist sees, she may choose to stay, but she cannot unsee.

And Yet: The Need for Prayer

In this chapter my concern is how one can hold together feminist criticism of sexism in Catholic liturgical and prayer life with a practice of Catholic personal and communal prayer. Given the tensions between feminism and Catholic piety and acknowledging that the words, images, and concepts embedded in religious rituals of the Catholic tradition can be alienating, how can a Catholic feminist go on praying?[33] A young friend tells me she longs for prayers "with words you actually want to say." Why would a feminist continue to participate in liturgy and prayer despite their ambiguity, using words she does not always want to say?

In the broadest sense, feminists who practice any form of spirituality attest to the human need to worship, to honor the divine within, among, and beyond themselves through ritual. Though secular feminism today can be dismissive of ritual practice, it is congruent with feminism both in theory and practice. Most feminists in the early and middle twentieth century were religious.[34] The second wave drove many out of religion, but if one includes in the

176   CAN YOU BE A CATHOLIC AND A FEMINIST?

story of feminism the many Catholic laywomen and religious sisters active in the 1960s, 1970s, and 1980s, the picture of feminism looks different.[35] Even those who did not stay in religious traditions did not always abandon ritual; they created new women-centered rituals instead. Feminists have long recognized the authenticity of a desire for ritual practice.

Catholic feminists can find resonance with the Catholic sacramental imagination or the idea that the world is infused with God's grace.[36] All prayer involves a centering, a reorienting from endless tasks, that focuses attention. In ritual, everyday objects (bread, wine, oil, water) carry deeper meaning, offering participants a way to attend to the holy through the ordinary. Regular participation in liturgy and prayer gives Catholics practice in attending to grace. With liturgy, we mark time, prepare, celebrate, repent, and rejoice, but we spend most of the liturgical year in "ordinary time," practicing awareness of grace.[37]

Liturgy also involves gathering with others in community. For Catholics, it also means joining with the living and dead in a ritual that transcends time and space. Many Catholic feminists value the parish as a place where a very diverse group of people who would not otherwise socialize come together to pray and support each other. A wise friend tells me, "The more that is going on horizontally, the less important the vertical becomes." Male-dominated presiding, preaching, symbol, text, and theology fade into the background when those who gather are neighbors to each other, united in faith, working on common projects, praying for each other's needs. Just as sexism is ritualized in the ritual, so, too, when the people of a church community come together, they practice being the body of Christ they hope to become.[38]

Near the beginning of Catholic liturgy, the community confesses its sins. To be sure, the practice can be misconstrued as admission of human unworthiness to stand before God. But in the post–Vatican II liturgy, the confession of sins in community is a recognition of "the brokenness of the world, and specifically the brokenness of relationships among humans and of humans with God."[39] We are enmeshed in social structures that harm human and nonhuman creatures and the earth. The Mass offers an opportunity to say out loud, in unison, that we have fallen short. Conscious that we are called to holiness, we admit our failings. In the face of sin, we also pass the peace, offering and receiving forgiveness.[40] And through psalms and litanies, we lament injustice, crying out in pain, confusion, and solidarity. The liturgy has room for all of these ways to grapple with the presence of sin. Even as feminists criticize an overemphasis on sin as pride, they can affirm ritualized ways of engaging with the world's brokenness and their own.

In times of struggle, believers seek out communal prayer out of a need for the strength of God and others. Feminists can affirm that moving through life's difficulties alone is untenable. Asking for one's own needs to be met and praying for the needs of others can be a practice of faith and solidarity. By practicing prayer, we reaffirm connection to and concern for God and others. María Pilar Aquino notes that for Latina women, when it is hard to feel the truth of God's presence, having others there to help them remember God's care for them makes it possible not to give into despair.[41] Singing hymns, too, functions as embodied practice of love and accompaniment, human and divine.

In communal prayer, as Scripture is read and hymns are sung, the community recalls and meditates on its central stories, hoping that "by hearing this story in worship, we come . . . to see all the world differently, to see the world truthfully."[42] For feminists who embrace Jesus as the liberating core of the Gospel, these are stories that cannot be told enough. In the telling and retelling, they hope to be formed as disciples by the life of their teacher. While recognizing the patriarchal and androcentric character of this ancient text, they can also appreciate that it can be a "revelatory text" when interpreted by the Christian community today.[43]

Eucharist is the heart of Catholic liturgy. Though feminists express legitimate worries about the overemphasis on the "sacred

178   CAN YOU BE A CATHOLIC AND A FEMINIST?

power" of the priest who blesses the bread and wine, contemporary theology understands Jesus as truly present in the bread and wine as well in the Word (Scriptures), and the community that gathers. The Eucharist is meant to be an invitation to deeper discipleship. The Eucharistic prayer takes believers back through Jesus's life and death on the cross and invites us to become a part of that radical story. As Lisa Sowle Cahill has written,

> In a Catholic sacramental vision, Christ's last supper and sacrificial death are reenacted in memory of his table fellowship with those who were social "outsiders," in honor of the mission of the early church to all peoples and nations, and in continuity with our historic Catholic social justice tradition that is committed to transforming the world.[44]

In sharing the bread and wine of Eucharist that becomes the Body of Christ, we "risk becoming the bread of life we eat."[45]

Personal and group prayer in many forms (e.g., centering prayer, contemplative prayer, the rosary, popular devotions, Adoration) speaks to Catholic women. Above, I noted potential problems from a feminist perspective that must be faced, but these structured practices are adaptable forms within which many women find they can rest in God's presence, and come to feel the power of the Spirit calling them to action.[46] They are worth reclaiming. Most of these prayer forms can be led by laypeople. Susan Ross notes that though the liturgical reforms of Vatican II were intended to emphasize the community gathered at Sunday Eucharist, they had the unintended effect of focusing attention on the presider and discouraging other forms of prayer.[47] Catholic feminists can acknowledge their limitations and reclaim them by reinterpreting them, by centering the core of prayer—the quest to know God and themselves better, to be more attentive to the presence of grace, to gather with others, to be comforted, to be challenged, to be changed.

PRAYER 179

Must prayer be reclaimed in order to be feminist? On the one hand, women's experience confirms that prayer and liturgy can "work" despite sexism. Anne Arabome writes of African women who pray constantly throughout their days, often calling God "Father."[48] Sure that they are empowered by prayer (and thinking more expansively about God despite their words), she argues that despite the androcentric language, the grounded and joyous way African women pray is not bound by sexism. Women's experience in prayer can transcend sexist structures. Still, my argument in this chapter that being a Catholic feminist requires one to do the hard work of confronting sexism in prayer while never losing sight of the need for it.

Being Authentic: Catholic Feminist Prayer Spaces

While the considerable difficulties prayer presents for a Catholic feminist cannot be denied, many paths of authentic prayer practice are possible. Earlier generations of feminists sometimes spoke of two groups—those who leave (and no longer regularly attend Mass) and those who stay, but today these groupings are more fluid, like Catholic identity itself. In chapter 1, I built on Charles Taylor's work to argue that authenticity involves freedom and choice as well as truth and relationality. Though excessive sacrifice and circumscribed freedom are incompatible with authentic selfhood, being authentic is not at odds with duties to others, truth, or tradition. A Catholic feminist discerning an authentic prayer practice is balancing her needs and desires, her commitments to others, and her beliefs about and ties to a tradition, and this can point her in at least three overlapping directions: choosing to be at Mass, choosing to be elsewhere, choosing something in between. The strategy for dealing with the tension identified in this chapter is creative fidelity.

180 CAN YOU BE A CATHOLIC AND A FEMINIST?

The Eucharist is, theologically speaking, the center of Catholic faith life, and a Catholic feminist may approach the practice in a variety of creative ways. Seeing the sexism of the rite in male presiding, preaching, language, and symbols, and acknowledging that the theology embedded in rite does not yet reflect the best insights of feminist theology, a Catholic feminist may nonetheless embrace "fully active and conscious participation" at Mass.[49] As rituals have multiple meanings for participants, for her, participation may signal many things at once: loyalty to family and culture, hunger to be one with Christ, a desire to be in solidarity with the most vulnerable, a belief in God's presence in the people gathered as a body, a desire to seek the sacred in sacrament and beauty, a belief in the real presence of Christ in the Eucharist. For these reasons, she shows up and participates, daily, weekly, or less often.

Both new orthodox and liberal Catholic feminists who have studied theology affirm that they carry with them richer understandings of liturgy and symbol that function to create an overlapping or deeper set of meanings. Their knowledge allows them to see more than the average person, and this allows for more authentic participation in the rite.

But a Catholic feminist may also adopt strategies that straddle the tension of her identities, as many women I spoke to while writing this book told me they did. She may, for instance, choose not to say certain prayers or parts of prayers. She may substitute inclusive language where it is lacking, either out loud or in her head. Some may choose to go to Mass less often, to read something else during (or otherwise avoid listening to) the homily, or to pray as they need to rather than following every word. Theirs is an alternative version of the "fully conscious, and active participation" hoped for by Vatican II. It is perhaps, not so different from what their grandmothers might have done by focusing on their rosaries or prayerbooks. In any congregation, Catholic feminists present at Mass may be drawing from its rich meanings with varying levels of affirmation, participation, and resistance.

At least since Mary Daly's exodus and second-wave feminist critiques, some Catholic feminists have chosen to be elsewhere on Sunday mornings. Other options may take the place of Mass, especially those for whom the desire to seek life-giving spirituality has grown in importance relative to obligations to family, community, and tradition, which have become too much to bear. After the experience of Covid-19, more people had a taste of what Sundays could be if they did not go to church, and not everyone is going back.[50] Some will continue to enjoy Sunday morning at home, perhaps with music, silence, reading, walks, and good company. Others might join the crowds at brunch, with new appreciation for how sacred gathering around a table to share a meal can be. Still others might join a weekend yoga classes, where female teachers might be seen as presiding, preaching, and leading prayer in a different key. Some, who might have explored other options virtually during Covid, may visit or join congregations elsewhere instead of always relying on their local parish. All of these options might coexist with participation in family-based religious practices and occasional Mass-going. Both can be ways of honoring commitments to truth, relationships, and solidarity, while providing avenues for nourishment and challenge. Absence from community worship can be understood as "ambiguous loss" both for the feminist and for the church, but this form of resistance feels necessary to some Catholic feminists for whom parish life is not enough.[51]

Apart from Mass, there is a lot of space in Catholic spirituality for Catholic women to occupy. Today, many women are finding other ways to practice their faith. In contemplative prayer groups and moms' Bible studies, retreats and rosary groups, blogs and online communities, as well as at home altars, home liturgies, and neighborhood festivals, Catholic women are praying. Those sympathetic to feminist critiques are committed to finding prayer spaces where women's voices are welcome and feminist theological commitments are honored. Those who are not may nonetheless be understood as contributing to a more feminist church.

182 CAN YOU BE A CATHOLIC AND A FEMINIST?

Catholic Women Preach is a good example of an alternative space structured to confront the problem of male preaching I addressed in the first section in this chapter. Created as a project of Future Church, a group working for church reform, the site follows the official Catholic lectionary and offers preaching by women every Sunday on the readings of the day. They specifically invite priests and deacons who preach to take advantage of content provided on the site, and they make sure to say that their resource is to supplement rather than replace Mass, though in practice it may serve as an alternative. Some women preach from a pulpit or something like it, while others speak from an office or home setting. The word "homily" is not used, and it does not take place during Mass, so it does not violate any rules. But the visual reality of women doing something they are not allowed to do at Mass is powerful. The creators, including priests and feminist theologians, hope "to inspire Catholics to appreciate the giftedness of Catholic women's preaching."[52] Like liberal and socialist feminists, they are reformist. The preaching is often theologically learned, deeply spiritual, and tied to social justice. With five years of reflections by hundreds of Catholic women from all over the world, Catholic Women Preach is opening a new space for feminist prayer while staying within Catholic tradition.

Blessed Is She is a very different in-between space with no explicit mission to increase women's participation in the prayer and liturgy of the church. According to its website, it is "a sisterhood of women who desire two things: prayer and community."[53] Started in the diocese of Phoenix by a laywoman named Jenna Guizar, it is younger and savvier, with an evangelizing mission to reach women, "no matter where you are on your walk with Christ." In this online community, there is more talk of Catholic mamas, coffee, and fellowship. Blessed Is She sponsors small groups for women in cities all over the country. These new orthodox feminists are not concerned about inclusive language or symbol; they have ties to conservative priests and a strong emphasis on "surrender" that suggests little familiarity with feminist theology. And yet they have sponsored a women's retreat called "Rise" and seem to be successful in uniting and empowering young Catholic women. Here, too, women are claiming space and sustaining each other. On Instagram, they preach with zeal, confidence, and a clear sense of calling to reach their virtual congregation of tens of thousands. They may not call this resistance, but functionally, their project centers women's experience, lifts women's voices, and creates community among women that is not available with Mass-centered piety. With roots in first-wave feminism, as well as contemporary evangelicalism, this group takes full advantage of existing possibilities and shows the church what greater inclusivity looks like. While it does not claim a feminist agenda, it may nonetheless create more space for women to speak, interpret sacred texts, and testify to God's movement in their lives than many more explicitly Catholic feminist organizations.[54]

Both of these movements are ways women are claiming space in a church structured by sexism. I noted above Susan Ross's point about the paradoxical effects of Vatican II. Though the liturgical reforms of the council were meant to emphasize role of the people who gather to pray, they ended up centering the priest-presider. The focus on the Eucharist as the "source and summit of Catholic life" discouraged popular devotions (many women-led), that had been central in the lives of the laity.[55] Women who embrace Mass with strategies of resistance, choose to be elsewhere, or decide to occupy (and thereby stretch) the in-between are finding creative ways to engage in prayer. Though the depth of their encounter with feminism varies, they are changing the tradition through their creative practice.

Praying with Open Eyes

I close this chapter with wisdom from a wise, spiritual woman whose way of belonging to the church over one hundred years ago,

184 CAN YOU BE A CATHOLIC AND A FEMINIST?

like the practices I have already discussed, suggests possibilities for Catholic feminists today. Evelyn Underhill, an early twentieth-century British scholar, brought mysticism to a broad audience at a time when many still viewed it as esoteric, elitist, and potentially dangerous. She did not claim to be a feminist, but arguably advanced women's roles in Christianity and feminist ways of praying.[56] In insisting that spiritual experience was accessible to anyone, she implicitly challenged clericalism, sexism, and hierarchy, opening access to the holy for ordinary women (and men) who had been denied many institutional avenues for spiritual growth. In focusing on communion with God and using a range of symbols, she moved beyond patriarchal images of God as distant and authoritarian, promoting instead a God who always desired to be in relationship. Though she did argue that surrender to God was the goal of the spiritual life, she sought not negation of the self but a letting go of a superficial view of self that prevented authentic relationship with God and others. Her view of Eucharistic worship was an extension of this framework. It is "the communion of the faithful with each other . . . and with the eternal self-offering of Christ."[57]

Like Catholic feminists today, Underhill insisted that spirituality was practical, as "union with Reality" had to spill over into one's life.[58] To those unconvinced of the need for communion with God, she insisted that prayer was decisive:

> The Spiritual Life has everything to do with politics. . . . The occasional dazzling flashes of pure beauty, pure goodness, pure love which shows us what God wants and what He is, only throw into more vivid relief the horror of cruelty, greed, oppression, hatred, ugliness . . . [W]e cannot help feeling the sense of obligation, the shame of acquiescence, the call to do something about it.[59]

By the definitions of this book, Underhill was not a feminist. She chose not to identify with feminists in her own time and she did not explicitly recognize and confront sexism in society or the church. Still, her life can be an inspiration for Catholics feminists. She broke new ground as a woman who studied, practiced, and taught the depth of Christianity through spiritual direction, letters, and talks on mysticism to a wide variety of audiences. Though drawn to Catholicism, she remained outside it as an Anglican due to concerns about its limits. Despite occupying this in-between space, she opened the tradition in ways that Catholic feminists of many types can still appreciate today.

New orthodox Catholic feminists and reformist Catholic women who pray without engaging feminist critique are also, by the definitions of this book, engaging in practices that speak to feminist concerns but are not explicitly feminist. But arguably, all of the women considered in this chapter are occupying a liminal space. Whether at Mass, or not, or in between, they walk an ambiguous path and embrace creative spiritual praxis. All contribute to a more feminist church and, like Underhill, can inspire Catholic feminists today.

However, to be a feminist is to see the sexism in church and society and work to change it. Catholic feminist theologians have spent decades uncovering the sexism in the tradition and its ritual practices. Eventually, a Catholic feminist has to engage that theology and consider the implications for her own practice. Doing so inevitably makes Catholic practice more difficult, but it also opens up creative possibilities for intentional feminist participation.

How does a feminist pray? Elizabeth Johnson closes her book on Mary by reclaiming Mary's Magnificat (Luke 1:46–55) for people of faith today. Taking seriously critiques of language, symbol, hierarchy, Johnson turns to a less-popular Marian prayer that speaks to the mystery and power of God and to human agency. "Rather than praising her, we join with her in praising God and the surprising divine compassion poured out on a world run amok . . . 'My soul proclaims your greatness, O my God, and my spirit rejoices in God,

186   CAN YOU BE A CATHOLIC AND A FEMINIST?

my Saviour.'"[60] Being a Catholic feminist means seeing the limitations of Catholic prayer, connecting with its depth, and forging a path of authentic participation that grounds a life of passionate discipleship. A Catholic feminist can only pray with open eyes and an open heart.

9

Belonging

Standing in Your Truth

When I stand before my students, I inhabit many roles. I am a theologian, a professor who participates in their formation for ministry, and a feminist who stays in the Catholic Church. All of this makes me an anomaly in Berkeley, California, where most people long ago left the church behind in favor of yoga, meditation, or hikes in the local hills. While I teach at a Jesuit school of theology—an institution that is full of religious students and is embedded within the church itself—many of my students share my feminist unease about the church. In teaching them the theology I love, I am also teaching them how to remain within an imperfect system, a system that I, in some way, represent, promote, and collaborate with. I aim to give them hope, to encourage their vocations. Yet I also am teaching them, by example, what it means to live with compromise. They love the church, too, but they are looking at me. They want to know—"How can you work it out in your head and heart?" They interrupt my lectures on this or that theologian—"But what do you think? What do you believe? How can you stand within the Catholic tradition in good conscience?"

I have known many Catholics who struggle with questions of conscience, but today the question of Catholic identity seems the most pressing conscience issue of all. This is why I chose it as the central dilemma of this book. The question is not "Can I *do* this?" but "Can I *be* this?" or "Can I belong?" A large majority of Catholics affirm their right to disagree with church teaching while remaining "good Catholics."[1] Despite church teaching on the obligation

Can You Be a Catholic and a Feminist?. Julie Hanlon Rubio, Oxford University Press.
© Oxford University Press 2024. DOI: 10.1093/oso/9780197553145.003.0010

188 CAN YOU BE A CATHOLIC AND A FEMINIST?

of Sunday Mass, a minority attend church weekly, deciding for themselves the shape of authentic practice.[2] Many also depart from Catholic sexual or social ethics in their personal or political choices. The tougher question for most is whether to continue to claim identification with a tradition when you see it as both graced and sinful, both prophetic and limited, both contributing to the healing of the world and complicit in structural sin.[3] This question becomes particularly salient for those whose very identity places them in tension with Catholic teaching and practice—LGBTQ Catholics, Black Catholics, and, of course, feminist Catholics.[4] So, having spent eight chapters engaging the tensions between Catholic and feminist identities and seeking ways to bring them together, it seems necessary to close by reflecting on Catholic feminist identity and belonging as a question of conscience.

Why Answering the Question Is Harder Now

Though they have wrestled with this book's central question for decades on a personal level, few feminist theologians identify their dilemma as a matter of conscience. In a collection of essays entitled *Women's Consciousness, Women's Conscience: A Reader in Feminist Ethics*, three early Christian feminist ethicists bring feminist consciousness to bear on ethical questions understood as matters of conscience, but they include no essay addressing the central quandary of feminists like themselves who stay in the church.[5] In most feminist writing, *consciousness* is a more important category than *conscience*, and the use of conscience is evocative rather than systematic. Drawing upon women's experience, feminist theory, social analysis, and the best of their religious tradition, Catholic feminists often turn their ethical lens outward. Like others who struggle with the church, they resolve the tension of conflicting identities by combining elements of both, bracketing unresolvable issues, and focusing on other pressing concerns. Why spend time worrying about the conscience of a Catholic feminist when there is so much injustice in the world and so much work for the church to do?

But as Mary Catherine Hilkert argued decades ago in an important essay, it is not clear that the resolution upon which Catholic feminists have relied can be sustained.[6] Thirty years after Hilkert laid out problems that make feminist belonging difficult—daily life in Catholic institutions shows that decades of Catholic feminist thought has had limited influence. In this book, I treat some of those issues in chapters 7 and 8, and frame them as presenting some of the greatest challenges for Catholic feminist identity.

However, for many Catholic women, other issues are more concerning. When women who identify as feminists perceive a disconnect between their understanding of what it means to a good person and what the church asks of them, or between how they believe they should approach work, sex, marriage, or family versus what Catholic tradition requires, the tradition becomes difficult to identify with. I have tried to show that tensions can sometimes be resolved because complex views of Catholicism and feminism challenge the idea of these traditions as hopelessly at odds. On being a good human, the ethical foundation for this book, Catholicism and feminism in their complexity have much in common, and Catholic thought has evolved in areas that used to be contested. As a result, there is little tension left to resolve. With regard to work, sex, and marriage, while I identify some continuing tension, there is substantial common ground and plenty of potential for synergy and collaboration. In other areas (gender, life, power) deep gaps remain, but I have attempted to lay out strategies to enable authenticity. And while prayer may not be as problematic for many, I argue that it should be, and by the time readers get to this point in the book, I imagine they might agree. Some Catholic feminist readers will no doubt disagree with my assessment of what is easy and what is hard. But for all Catholic feminist readers who are willing to look deeply at Catholic tradition, ethics, and practice, the dilemma of belonging remains.

190 CAN YOU BE A CATHOLIC AND A FEMINIST?

In recent decades, the dilemma has deepened, and so has our sense of what it means to be a responsible, authentic self. In chapter 1, I discussed how philosopher Charles Taylor captures something essential in naming the modern "ethics of authenticity," which shapes the individual's search for a meaningful life. Andrew Prevot suggests that Blacks, as well as women and other marginalized groups, are similarly—if not equally—blocked from becoming their true, free selves even now, when authentic selfhood has never been more valued.[7] Today we feel more responsible for what we identify as and with, for the persons we become and the relationships we maintain. We feel a greater obligation to take belonging seriously and to disentangle ourselves from complicity with unjust institutions.

The Catholic moral tradition offers a helpful framework for discerning when complicity—or what is called "cooperation with evil"—is and is not permissible.[8] Despite its off-putting name, there is wisdom in the tradition's recognition of the problem of guilt by association, which many feel in their bones, and in the traditional affirmation of the impossibility of purity. To avoid all cooperation with evil (or all instances when, despite my good intentions, I support actions I understand to be evil), would mean missing out on too many opportunities for good. I vote for candidates who hold a mix of views, buy from companies with mixed records on labor and the environment, give money to charities with a diverse set of priorities and partners, buy real estate in a neighborhood hoping to do good while also knowing I may be contributing to gentrification. When my intentions are good, and my actions are good or neutral, the tradition allows for some cooperation. Yet it also asks me to consider some questions: Is my action substantial or minor, proximate or remote (close to or far removed from the evil), necessary or not (to the furthering of the evil), justified by a serious enough reason or not? The tradition at its best acknowledges the limitations of any one person, especially given their primary responsibilities to loved ones and work. But it also asks us to cultivate a consciousness of moral complexity. Sometimes this consciousness will require disengaging ourselves from sinful structures as a kind of "prophetic witness," while at other times it might encourage remaining as a "pilgrim" so as not to lose out on the possibility of doing good amid imperfection.[9] Cooperation accurately captures the conscience dilemma of the Catholic feminist: one who loves the church while recognizing ongoing problems in its teachings and practices.

Catholic literature on conscience, despite its inattention to this particular dilemma, can illuminate the increasingly difficult Catholic feminist quest for authentic selfhood and can help with discernment about when cooperation is acceptable and what kind of belonging is authentic.

Conscience Wrestling

Conscience was central to Vatican II. European theologians concerned about the cooperation of Catholics with Nazi Germany and fascist Italy reached deep into Catholic tradition to revive the idea of conscience. They insisted that individuals could know the truth without relying on external authority, and that moral agency flows from internal conviction.[10] In a famous paragraph from *Gaudium et spes*, conscience is described as a secret core or sanctuary where we are alone with God, whose voice echoes in our depths.[11] Here, in our hearts, we perceive "a law written by God." We are called to good, away from evil. We experience a pull to do this, not that; to stand here, not there; to speak truth rather than to lie. Recently, Pope Francis acknowledged that this long-standing Catholic teaching has not always been clearly affirmed or communicated. "We have been called to form consciences, not replace them," he said, the propensity to identify the dignity of conscience with its conformity to church teaching is misguided.[12] In expanding the space for conscience, Francis has also underlined the need to approach the holy ground of the other with reverence.

192 CAN YOU BE A CATHOLIC AND A FEMINIST?

As I noted in chapter 1, secular feminist thinkers have likewise claimed space to nurture a sense of self and listen to the voice within. In 1929, Virginia Woolf tried to answer the question of why so few women have been writers, by describing how difficult it was for a woman "to have a room of her own."[13] Occupied by serving the needs of others, and told repeatedly of their lack of suitability for the creative arts, few women have had the freedom to be artists, despite the art they had inside them.[14] Nearly forty years later Tillie Olsen would write of the silences that remain in history because women were so busy being "the angel in the house" that they had no time for creative work of their own.[15] Around the same time, Betty Friedan looked closely at "the feminine mystique," the pervasive belief that women should be fulfilled by their role in the home, and the devastating effects on the many women who wanted more from life than housework and parenting.[16] In these representative voices of liberal feminism lies an implicit recognition of a stirring deep within that needs to be recognized, respected, and given space to grow.

Catholic feminist theologians, too, have identified a space within from which strong convictions arise, though they differ from many of their secular sisters in connecting interiority with the Divine. Anne Patrick identifies the law written on the human heart as "the presence in us of the Holy Spirit."[17] Linda Hogan calls for a "personalist theology of conscience," rooted in recognition of a person's discernment of the Spirit in ethical decision-making, in light of the imperfections of the church and the fact that it is a living tradition.[18] Both hoped that a better theology of conscience would ground mature faith and make space for authentic belonging.

Catholic feminists today who claim an interior space of their own stand within this tradition of Catholic thought on conscience. And while they appreciate those who came before them, they insist on recalling that the authors of *Gaudium et spes*, writing right in the middle of the second wave of the women's movement, did not see anything problematic about framing their discussion with androcentric language ("In the depths of his conscience, man detects a law which he does not impose upon himself, but which holds him to obedience"). This framing both opened possibilities for moral wrestling and limited those possibilities by assuming a male subject. Claiming conscience as a space within the self where critical engagement with tradition is welcome gives Catholic feminists freedom to be their authentic selves.

Neither the Catholic tradition nor Catholic feminists see conscience as a voice within that reveals complete truth. This can complicate authentic Catholic feminist identity. In the Catholic tradition a good conscience is not formed in isolation. Rather, it is relational, nurtured through encounters with other human beings (as "Christians are joined with the rest of men in the search for truth") and with Christ.[19] Though Pope Francis urges respect for the conscience-based decisions of adult Catholics, he also affirms the church's part in forming the consciences of believers.[20] Ignorance (vincible or invincible, that is the kind we can reasonably overcome or the kind we cannot) can lead to an erroneous or morally wrong conscience.[21] A believer is both obligated to form her conscience and duty bound to follow conscience once it is formed.

Recent writing on conscience suggests that the work of formation is harder than we once thought. Knowing this can help us reframe the problem of conscience. Catholic theologian Bryan Massingale argues that white Catholics especially have been slow to realize the pernicious influence of cultural forces shaping perceptions and emotions.[22] For white Catholics, responsible conscience formation must include working to overcome the unconscious bias that allows so many to remain unmoved by the social evil of racism. Today, ethicists encourage formation of an "engaged conscience" that "draws us out of ourselves and away from our own concerns" and toward responsibility for social sin.[23] For Catholic theologians, taking conscience formation seriously means being open to coming to see more clearly the many ways we are complicit with evil.

194   CAN YOU BE A CATHOLIC AND A FEMINIST?

Feminists, too, value interior conviction while insisting that openness to critique and conversion is central to living a good life. Friedan's call for consciousness-raising in the 1960s assumed that women were so impacted by the feminine mystique that they could not hear "the voice within."[24] Internalized sexism led to the psychological problems reported by women in Friedan's study. Women's distress, Friedan found, was due to their belief that they should be fulfilled in their purely domestic lives but were not. Women needed to come to terms with the damage done by internalized sexism.[25]

In the language of the Catholic tradition, one might say that women were following their erroneous conscience in believing that domesticity would ensure bliss, but were also heeding a more authentic call of conscience in recognizing and articulating their unhappiness. By internalizing the messages that were everywhere around them, they came to a false consciousness. The remedy was better conscience formation, which would enable them to see things more clearly, claim their own identity, and better love themselves and others.

But feminist conscience formation did not stop there. Women of color challenged white second-wave feminists, including Catholic feminist theologians, to come to a deeper awareness of the narrowness of their concerns.[26] As we saw in chapter 3, many women of color who were already working outside the home were more concerned with racial discrimination than the feminine mystique. White women needed to confront their own dependency on the domestic labor of other women. In the language of the Catholic tradition, conscience formation needed to go deeper. Women needed to ask how their actions and nonactions were impacting the lives of vulnerable people and how they could better contribute to a more just society.

Catholics and feminists both have nuanced ways of valuing the ongoing formation of conscience. Both honor deeply held convictions, challenge themselves to critically assess personal judgments in light of possible "false consciousness," and insist on the need for ongoing formation. For a Catholic feminist today, awareness of the critical edges of both traditions can allow for authentic belonging. Catholic feminists are formed both by feminism and by Catholicism to listen to interiority, to be critical of tradition, *and* to be wary of their own biases. Catholic women first came to feminist consciousness during the second wave not only through secular liberation movements but also through their own tradition.[27] For Catholic feminists striving to listen to both traditions, conscience formation is an ongoing process that requires always being open to being challenged.

Conscience in Catholic tradition is not only a sanctuary or a faculty that can be formed well or badly; it is also a process of decision-making. We draw upon this kind of conscience when we have to decide whether and how to belong to an imperfect tradition. Anne Patrick, the Catholic feminist theologian who has done the most substantial work on conscience, offers a four-pronged model for discernment: (1) focusing on the question to be decided, (2) understanding what is going on inside yourself, (3) critically examining the situation in consultation with others, and (4) acting once a decision is made.[28]

Applying Patrick's process to the dilemma of Catholic feminist identity, we could say that the question is "Is it possible to remain Catholic and feminist?" For a Catholic who holds a position within a Catholic institution, the question is further sharpened— "Knowing the church's deep limitations, is it ethical to remain an official representative of the church, contributing to its witness and to the formation of the Catholic faithful?" Once the question is clear, it is important to assess what is going on inside oneself, asking, "What is God calling me to in this moment?" and "Am I being shaped by a desire for the good or something else?" Social analysis would take a Catholic feminist deeper, allowing her to weigh the good she could accomplish by remaining, as well as the potential damage to self and others, both real and potential.

196 CAN YOU BE A CATHOLIC AND A FEMINIST?

Sandra Schneiders, the first woman to teach at my institution and author of one of the most important books on being a Catholic feminist, argues that the problem only deepens the longer a Catholic feminist stays:

> Once she has begun to see, begun the critical process of analysis, she will necessarily gradually be overwhelmed by the extent, depth, and the violence of the institutional church's rejection and oppression of women. This precipitates the inward crisis which the feminist Catholic inevitably faces: a deep, abiding, emotionally draining anger.[29]

And yet the ability to stand as a Catholic within Catholic institutions and speak feminist truths within the community of faith, to claim ground that has not yet been claimed, to challenge authority on behalf of women of the future, is a powerful thing. It is part of what sustained Schneiders through forty years of teaching in a school of theology and ministry. "My presence was significant," she told me in an interview in 2023. "I've never had the sense that by belonging, I'm legislating something I don't believe in. You'd have to leave the human race! If I only want to participate in something that meets all my standards, I'm going to become a lone ranger, and not be in collaboration with anyone and make change." Instead, she urges Catholic feminists to "find a way to be consistently undermining evil without undermining the project you believe in. Be a part of it and at the same time subvert it."[30]

The significance of the work of feminist scholars is a strong example of what can be accomplished. Theologians like Schneiders, Ada María Isasi Díaz, and Elizabeth Johnson have been broadly influential. The work of new orthodox feminists on social media, like FemCatholic, fills a need for women-centered faith sharing unavailable elsewhere. A recent online post highlights Catherine of Siena, who challenged the church, as a saint for women who are told they are "too much."[31] I imagine that this reading of Catherine was a relief to strong women engaged in this online community. Similarly, one woman who encountered Elizabeth Johnson's interpretation of Mary as "a spirited, scandalous, prophetic, poor, liberated, joyful refugee," instead of an obedient handmaid, wrote, "This is a Mary I can live with."[32] When Catholic tradition is put in dialogue with feminism, women who linger on the edges of the church find space to let go of anger and breathe. They find a faith they can live with. This feminist mission within the church, often understood as a calling, can counterbalance feelings of complicity and allow women to conclude that their belonging is authentic.

But most Catholic women are not theologians, and they, too, need an account of belonging that makes sense of their dilemma. In her most recent book, Catholic feminist Joan Chittister speaks movingly from a foundation in the gospel about the call for Catholics to embrace prophetic speech and action in response to social suffering.[33] One might see her as a modern-day Saint Thomas More, engaging in prophetic witness. But she does not articulate a compelling account of *why* feminists should continue prophetic work from inside the Catholic Church. Perhaps for Catholics of her generation, reasons to stay were obvious and belonging was less complicated. But today, when staying is anything but obvious, it is less clear why prophetic witness would be a choice of integrity. Most people would agree that exercising moral responsibility sometimes means calling the institutions to which one belongs to be better. Yet this still raises the question of why one remains in such a difficult position. We might ask, "What are the morally weighty reasons that justify complicity with the church?" Integrity demands an answer.

Why Stay? Why Belong?

So far in this chapter I have discussed the challenges arising when feminist consciousness conflicts with Catholic teaching, creating conscience dilemmas. But along with challenges, the Catholic

198 CAN YOU BE A CATHOLIC AND A FEMINIST?

tradition offers prophetic wisdom. The same tradition that leads to worries about cooperation compels and inspires. Seven key themes run through this book. They are central to my account of why it makes sense for a Catholic feminist to stay in the church and wrestle with belonging.

From the very beginning, I have argued that the Catholic understanding of human persons as created in the image of God, possessing an unalienable dignity, and deserving of flourishing is essential. Against challenges from many sides, Catholics hold onto the belief that human beings have inherent value and claim that we can know something of God's desires for our lives. We are not completely adrift, unable to discern what life is for. Our attempts to work out what flourishing looks like are always partial and open to revision. But Catholic understandings of the dignity of human person can enlighten us, as long as they are seen through a critical lens. Human dignity is the foundation for seeking sexual relationships of equality and mutuality, for making sacrifices in my own life for the sake of vulnerable others, and working for a more just social order.

A belief in the significance of the Incarnation (or God becoming one of us) is another central theological claim running through the book. In taking human flesh, Catholics believe, God blesses human body and spirit. There is no room for a dualistic split, for valuing bodies but not souls or for thinking that the mind is more important than the body. Human beings are one. To know this intellectually is one thing. To feel it in your bones is another. I remember a professor colleague telling me that one day after teaching about Incarnation in class, a student stayed in her seat long afterward, overwhelmed. "You know it's true, don't you," he said to her. This rich understanding of the nature of persons provides a foundation for fight against sexual violence, approaching work as a vocation, and treating unborn children and the women who carry them with reverence. It changes everything.

Freedom is also powerfully affirmed in the Catholic tradition. M. Shawn Copeland's work is central this book's account of human becoming, as she shows how hypocritical it was for white Christians to deny this freedom to Blacks. The importance of the freedom of individuals to respond to God's call is also important to limiting the influence of gender scripts and opening a variety of life pathways for women and men. Contemporary theologies of conscience have contributed to the recovery of freedom for Catholics to make moral decisions on their won. Freedom in the Catholic tradition is not a thin freedom to do whatever I want but a richer freedom to live the life I am called to live, which may sometimes mean criticizing or defying cultural or ecclesial norms.

Commitment is another fundamental Catholic value. In a world where nearly all commitments seem negotiable, the Catholic tradition insists on the value of binding promises—in marriage and parenting to be sure, but also in religious life, the workplace, and in relation to the common good. Fidelity narratives are more prominent and inspiring than departure stories. Though recognizing the need for times when commitments must be broken, I deeply value the many countercultural models of fidelity enriching Catholic communities.

Solidarity understood as the reality of human connection and the virtue of working for the good of all, is also central to Catholic thought and life. If some religious and cultural wisdom counsels putting "family first," Catholicism offers an alternative vision of family that is much broader. Solidarity is drawn from the life and teaching of Jesus and confirmed in experience. Thomas Merton's memorable vision on the streets of Louisville captures it well. "I was suddenly overwhelmed with the realization that I loved all those people, that they were mine and I theirs, that we could not be alien to one another even though we were total strangers," he wrote.[34] Merton lived a life of radical solidarity because he found the reality of connection so overwhelmingly true. This is the kind of solidarity that is fundamental to being a good human. It is essential to Catholic understandings of social justice across issues discussed in this book, from sexual violence to gender, life, work, marriage, and

200 CAN YOU BE A CATHOLIC AND A FEMINIST?

power. A privatized Eat Pray Love feminism is highly impoverished in comparison.

Community naturally flows from solidarity. Dorothy Day closes her autobiography with an affirmation she lived out in the Catholic Worker movement: "We have all known the long loneliness and we have learned that the only solution is love and that love comes with community."[35] This very Catholic sense that we are called into relationship with others, differs from an individualistic account of a good human life. Because life is not all about me, figuring about who I am and how to live entails not going off on my own but leaning in to community—in prayer, in the workplace, and in life's most difficult moments. The church as a body is the context for all of the moral wrestling I do in this book.

While widely criticized for focusing on sin, Catholic claims about sin—individual and social—are essential to making of sense of the limitations most persons perceive in themselves and broader systems of evil like racism, poverty, and environmental degradation. Understanding of social sin is essential to my analyses of sexual violence and power, but it was also implicit in other chapters. Knowing the depth of what is wrong in the world, I have deeper sense of what my obligations are and how my own complicity goes far beyond personal, intentional failures. My worldview expands.

Understanding myself as sinful is a foundation for humility and inspires a continual openness to being challenged. There is no space for "canceling" others when I know the depth of my own complicity. I need to consider that I might be wrong. This is why, I argued with regard to gender, experience is engaged with generosity and critical distance in the Catholic tradition. This complex approach to experience avoids the traps of giving experience undue weight, just as the freedom helps cultivate a healthy ability to be critical of received wisdom. This seems especially necessary for Catholic feminists to embrace the tradition with integrity. Making space for what Margaret Farley calls "the grace of self-doubt" is as crucial in the church as it is in any other sphere of life.[36] Accountability to a tradition that knows its own failures and can illuminate mine makes more sense than thinking I have everything figured out and can go it alone. I can bear with an imperfect church, knowing that I, too, stand in need of conversion and benefit from being part of a community that continually calls me to deeper discipleship.

Feminism at its best holds many of the same values I uphold here as essential to staying, though not, in my judgment, always with the same depth. Still, I have tried to highlight compatibility that is not always acknowledged, such as the common commitment to the inherent value of work and work-life balance for all, which sets both Catholics and feminists at odds with the antiwork movement, and the common valuing of intimacy, mutuality, and solidarity in marriage. Together, feminism and Catholicism offer essential wisdom about what it means to be a good human and live an authentic life. Feminism pushes Catholicism to look within and apply principles of solidarity, dignity, and sinfulness to its own teachings, rituals, and structures. Feminism pushes the church toward greater consistency on gender, life, power, and prayer. With feminist critique, retrieval, and reconstruction, Catholic faith is made more whole. This is a faith worth staying for.

From Purity to Conscious Belonging

Because of the wisdom Catholic feminists find in the Catholic tradition, they are committed to staying in the church, but they cannot forget about the very real tensions that remain. Their struggles can be described as conscience wrestling, honoring the authentic voice within, conscience formation, discernment, and a search for integrity. All of these ways of talking about conscience provide some assistance in unpacking the undeniable stresses and strains as well as the ongoing work of living with authenticity that are inescapable for a Catholic feminist. Seeing what she sees, conscious of the limits of the church, feminism, and herself, she cannot have the "purity"

202 CAN YOU BE A CATHOLIC AND A FEMINIST?

of uncomplicated belonging, but she can forge her own, more complex path with consciousness and joy.

To be sure, pure belonging is deeply attractive. The formerly Catholic singer-songwriter Audrey Assad seems to have had this kind of faith. Her hit songs (e.g., "I Shall Not Want," "Be Thou My Vision," and "Restless") have been very popular with Christian audiences since the mid-2000s. A convert to Catholicism in 2007, she became a favorite in conversative Catholic circles. She performed at Catholic universities, retreats, and youth conferences, and her songs were part of the spiritual landscape of a good many Catholics. In 2021, however, she announced on Twitter that she was no longer a Christian, and had not been a practicing Catholic for three years. Her many fans were understandably distraught.

Though Assad did not detail the reasons for her deconversion, it seems that the pure belonging that marks her songs was a part of the problem. In an interview published in *National Catholic Reporter*, Assad described awakening to the limitations she had previously accepted. "I really grew frustrated that the Catholic Church, or any church, demanded ideological purity at all times in all situations, and that really bothered me," she told *National Catholic Reporter*. When asked about what she did not miss about being Catholic, she said, "'I can't be myself here' is how it felt. I don't miss that feeling of not being able to show up as my full, authentic self in a space because I'm afraid it would scandalize or offend."[37]

With consciousness of feminist critiques of Catholicism, only a complicated belonging that allows adherents to "show up as [their] full, authentic sel[ves]" makes sense. I noted earlier that belonging has become more fraught as people today feel more responsible to extricate themselves from persons or groups that involve them in cooperation with evil. "Cancel culture" is one problematic manifestation of the reasonable impulse to be conscious of the import of one's associations. Yet if belonging is more complex it is also more important.

Belonging has the power to open the door to relationships among people who are alienated from each other. Padraig O'Tuama, poet and expert in conflict resolution in Northern Ireland, likes to say that belonging "creates and undoes us."[38] In spite of a long history of violent conflict, Protestants and Catholics in a peacemaking community he led are able to talk and pray together because they have decided that they belong to each other.

As a gay Catholic, O'Tuama faces his own dilemma of complicated belonging in the church he calls home. Here, too, he finds a place to stand with integrity, honoring the wisdom of the Catholic tradition from a space of "fluid belonging" that allows for affirmation of the loving relationships in his life.[39] Theologian James Alison makes a take a similarly complicated stance of staying in the church for gay Catholics like himself. He does not shy away from calling out the difficulties. He calls gay Catholics to "love the project," ignore those who don't get it, and build the church as it ought to be.[40]

M. Shawn Copeland's vision of Eucharistic solidarity is another model of complicated belonging. Copeland looks unflinchingly at how the church either stood by or participated in slavery, lynching, and exclusion of Black people, making a mockery of its claims to honor human dignity. Eucharistic solidarity is her response to the depths of Black suffering she narrates. She calls readers to acknowledge their own blindness and trust in a tradition much larger than themselves, embracing the Eucharist as "countersign to the devaluation and violence directed toward the exploited, despised black body . . . [It] forms our social imagination, transvalues our values, and transforms the meaning of our being human, of embodying Christ."[41] Keeping her focus on those who have been harmed while embracing a prophetic faith makes it possible for her to hold Catholic, Black, and feminist identities in balance, to claim integrity.

Finally, Sr. Thea Bowman is a wise guide for the sort of complicated belonging Catholic feminism seems to demand. Sr. Thea was a convert to Catholicism, a teacher and professor, a gifted

204 CAN YOU BE A CATHOLIC AND A FEMINIST?

singer, and a consultant to the bishop of Jackson, Mississippi, on intercultural awareness. She traveled across the country, even after being diagnosed with cancer, leading groups of Catholics in singing, praying, and finding their way across cultural barriers. Though deeply conscious of the racism of the tradition to which she belonged, she embodied joyful participation in the life of the church.

In a fiery speech to the US Catholic bishops in 1989, she called her "brothers" to better accompaniment of Black Catholics.[42] She began with song, telling them that being a Black Catholic sometimes make her feel "like a motherless child." She spoke with urgency, humor, and love, naming the failures, injustices, and neglect that harmed her and other Black Catholics. At the close, she invited the bishops to join her in singing "We Shall Overcome," instructing them on how to link arms, reminding them that Black protestors had linked arms to protect themselves from bullets. And they did as she said—though, of course, the work for a fully inclusive church ready to take on structural racism continues.

To be a Catholic feminist is to feel alienation and cooperation, along with joy in belonging to a church that has offers an authentic way to be human, a wise and challenging balance of freedom and solidarity. Purity is assumed to be the gold standard by those who seek perfection and those who confidently leave tradition behind. In contrast, like Sr. Thea Bowman, a Catholic feminist chooses to belong to the Catholic community and yet continues to feel pained by the church's neglect of suffering and by its refusal to take advantage of the rich resources that those excluded from power have to offer. She continues to be critical of the church when it falls short. Yet belonging also requires her to embrace humility, to acknowledge her own need for conversion and the ways the church's wisdom challenges some feminist ideas. There is no purity in this ambiguous space.

I began this book by telling a little of my own story, from the base community in which I was raised to the school of theology and ministry where I now teach. Teaching in a seminary involves regular confrontation of Catholic feminist tensions on issues of prayer and power, among others. Yet every day I see the incredible work of my lay and ordained colleagues and students. They give me hope for the future of the church. My hope is grounded in powerful witnesses past and present but also in ideas—in the theology of the Catholic tradition, including Catholic feminist theology, where there is space for a critical questioning and fidelity.

I promised to ground this book in experience rather than the-oretical debates, and I have tried to keep that promise through consistently engaging stories, both real and fictional. However, a constant theme running through this book has been the push to fully engage both Catholicism and feminism. That engage-ment deepens the problem many feel at a surface level. As Sandra Schneiders told us, the more you know about Catholic theology and feminism, the worse the problem becomes. But the flip side is also true. Knowing more reveals more of the wisdom of both traditions and more of what they share. With the best of feminism, a credible church emerges with compelling wisdom about living a meaningful life in a broken world. With the depth of Catholic tra-dition, feminist ideals find their place in a richer vision of human flourishing. Because both traditions value experience but demand critical self-reflection, ambiguous and joyful belonging is possible.

The strife of belonging does not disappear. The pain of feeling torn between two traditions does not go away, but it does not in-terfere with seeing all that is held in common, everything that nourishes, all that I cannot live without. With Sr. Thea, with saints and holy people who have always conscientiously challenged the church they loved, Catholic feminists can claim ambiguous belonging and show up as their authentic selves.

Notes

Introduction

1. See Elisabeth Schüssler Fiorenza, "Saints Alive: Yesterday and Today," in *Discipleship of Equals: A Critical Feminist Ekklesia-logy of Liberation*, ed. Elisabeth Schüssler Fiorenza (New York: Crossroad, 1993), 39–48.

2. See "100 Women: The Truth behind 'Bra-Burning Feminists," *BBC News*, September 7, 2018, https://www.bbc.com/news/world-45303069.

3. Rosemary Radford Reuther notes that few Catholics were involved in early feminist movement, in "Catholic Women," in *In Our Own Voices: Four Centuries of American Women's Religious Writing*, ed. Rosemary Radford Reuther and Rosemary Skinner (San Francisco: Harper, 1995), 24–29. Early voices include Mary Daly's *The Church and the Second Sex* (New York: Harper & Row, 1968); Rosemary Radford Reuther, *Sexism and Godtalk: Toward a Feminist Theology* (Boston: Beacon, 1983); Maria P. Riley, *Transforming Feminism* (Kansas City, MO: Sheed & Ward, 1989); Carolyn Osiek, *Beyond Anger: On Being a Feminist in the Church* (Mahwah, NJ: Paulist, 1986); Anne E. Carr, *Transforming Grace: Christian Tradition and Women's Experience* (San Franciso: Harper, 1988); and Sandra M. Schneiders, *Beyond Patching: Faith and Feminism in the Catholic Church* (Mahwah, NJ: Paulist, 1991, rev. ed. 2004).

4. Major feminist theologians include Elisabeth Schüssler Fiorenza, Elizabeth A. Johnson, Margaret A. Farley, M. Shawn Copeland, Maria Pilar Aquino, Lisa Sowle Cahill, Ada-María Isasí-Diaz, and Susan Ross. The most recent significant theological text in the field—Linda Hogan and A.E. Orobator, eds., *Feminist Catholic Theological Ethics: Conversations in the World Church* (Maryknoll, NY: Orbis, 2014)—largely neglects identity. Interview-based books wrestling with identity questions include Sally Cunneen, *Sex: Female, Religion: Catholic* (New York: Holt, Rinehart and Winston, 1968); Jane Redmont, *Generous Lives: Catholic Women Today* (Liguoiri, MO: Triumph, 1992); Jeanne Pieper, *The Catholic Woman: Difficult Choices in a Modern World* (Los Angeles: Lowell House, 1993); Debra Campbell, *Graceful Exits: Catholic Women and the Art of Departure*

208 NOTES

(Bloomington: Indiana University Press, 2002); Angela Bonavoglia, *Good Catholic Girls: How Women Are Leading the Fight to Change the Church* (New York: HarperCollins, 2005); Gina Messina-Dysert, Jennifer Zobair, and Amy Levin, *Faithfully Feminist: Jewish, Christian, & Muslim Feminists on Why We Stay* (Ashland, OR: White Cloud Press, 2015); Catholic Women Speak Network, *Catholic Women Speak: Bringing Our Gifts to the Table* (Mahwah, NJ: Paulist, 2015); and Celia Viggo Wexler: *Catholic Women Confront Their Church: Stories of Hurt and Hope* (Lanham, MD: Rowman & Littlefield, 2016).

5. Helen Alvaré, ed., *Breaking Through: Catholic Women Speak for Themselves* (Huntington, IN: Our Sunday Visitor, 2012).

6. Michelle Boorstein and Sarah Pulliam Bailey, "More U.S. Catholics Are Considering Leaving the Church over the Sex Abuse Crisis, Poll Says," *Washington Post*, March 13, 2019, https://www.washingtonpost.com/relig ion/2019/03/13/more-us-catholics-are-considering-leaving-church-over-sex-abuse-crisis-poll-says/.

7. Here I draw on Matthew J. Cressler, *Authentically Black and Truly Catholic: The Rise of Black Catholicism in the Great Migration* (New York: New York University Press, 2017). There are, of course, profound differences between the dilemmas of Black Catholics and those of feminist Catholics, but there are also key similarities that I explore in this book.

8. There is no one accepted way of describing feminist waves, but they can be a useful shorthand. See Dorothy Sue Cobble, Linda Gordon, and Astrid Henry, *Feminism Unfinished: A Short, Surprising History of the American Women's Movement* (New York: Liveright, 2014). Some identify a fourth feminist wave linked to queer theory, but I see the third wave beginning in 1990s continuing today, and find the broader "postmodern" category (which includes queer feminism) more helpful in capturing the diversity of contemporary feminist thought and activism.

9. Olive Banks, *Faces of Feminism: A Study of Feminism as a Social Movement*, 2nd ed. (New York: Basil Blackwell, 1986), 7–9, gives an overview of radical, liberal, and socialist feminisms. There is no universally accepted typology of feminisms, but I find Bank's categories persuasive and use them throughout the book, though I add postmodern and new orthodox. The latter includes feminists who combine conservative Catholic faith and elements of first-wave liberal feminism. See, especially, Erika Bachiochi, *The Rights of Women: Reclaiming a Lost Vision* (Notre Dame, IN: University of Notre Dame Press, 2021).

NOTES   209

10. Julie Hanlon Rubio, *Hope for Common Ground: Mediating the Personal and the Political in a Divided Church* (Washington, DC: Georgetown University Press, 2016).

Chapter 1

1. Valerie Saiving, "The Human Situation: A Feminine View," *Journal of Religion* 40.2 (1960): 100–112. See also Serene Jones, *Feminist Theory and Christian Theology: Cartographies of Grace* (Minneapolis: Fortress, 2000), 22–48, 94–125. For ongoing debate, see Mark Douglas and Elizabeth Hinson-Hasty, "Revisiting Valerie Saiving's Challenge to Reinhold Niebuhr," *Journal of Feminist Studies in Religion* 28.1 (2012): 75–114.
2. John Paul II, *Letter to Women* (1995), no. 10.
3. Mandy Hale, *You Are Enough: Heartbreak, Healing, and Becoming Whole* (New York: FaithWords, 2018).
4. Elizabeth Gilbert's *Eat Pray Love: One Woman's Search for Everything across Italy, India, and Indonesia* (New York: Riverhead Books, 2007) sold over twelve million copies. It might be seen as the single most influential contemporary book of feminist spirituality.
5. Betty Friedan, *The Feminine Mystique* (New York: Norton, 1963). Friedan's book sold three million copies and is one of many key moments of second-wave feminism. Others include the protest at the 1968 Miss America pageant, the 1966 founding of the National Welfare Rights Organization, and the publishing of *Our Bodies, Ourselves* in 1969. Dorothy Sue Cobble, Linda Gordon, and Astrid Henry, *Feminism Unfinished: A Short History of the American Women's Movements* (New York: Norton, 2014).
6. Virginia Woolf, *A Room of One's Own* (New York: Harcourt Brace, Jovanovich, 1929), 54.
7. Woolf, *Room of One's Own*, 58.
8. Tillie Olsen, *Silences* (New York: Dell, 1965).
9. See Mary Daly, *The Church and the Second Sex* (Boston: Beacon, 1968) and *Outercourse: The Be-dazzling Voyage* (San Francisco: Harper, 1992).
10. Simone de Beauvoir, *The Second Sex*, trans. and ed. H. M. Parshley (New York: Vintage, 1989).
11. J. Jack Halberstam, *Gaga Feminism: Sex, Gender, and the End of Normal* (Boston: Beacon, 2012), 27.
12. Susannah Cornwall, *Un/familiar Theology: Reconceiving Sex, Reproduction, and Generativity* (London: Bloomsbury, 2017), 69.

210 NOTES

13. Colleen Carroll Campbell, *My Sisters, the Saints: A Spiritual Memoir* (New York: Image, 2012).
14. Campbell, *My Sisters, the Saints*, 208.
15. In her book *The New Faithful: Why Young Adults Are Embracing Christian Orthodoxy* (Chicago: Loyola, 2002), Campbell identifies a new religious movement among young adults in which commitment to tradition and sacrifice are sought rather than avoided.
16. Expressions of popular piety are taken from the Prayer of St. Francis, Ignatian spirituality, and the Prayer of Generosity, often (falsely) attributed to St. Ignatius.
17. Mary J. Henold, *Catholic and Feminist: The Surprising History of the American Catholic Feminist Movement* (Chapel Hill: University of North Carolina Press, 2008), 27–28.
18. Gertrud von le Fort, *The Eternal Woman: The Timeless Meaning of the Feminine*, trans. Marie Cecilia Buehrle, new ed. (San Francisco: Ignatius Press, 2010), 11.
19. Henold, *Catholic and Feminist*, 29. Surrender language is still popular in Christian song lyrics (e.g., Israel Houghton, "I Surrender All") and in the Christian blogosphere.
20. John Paul II, *Familaris consortio* (1981), no. 11.
21. John Paul II, *Letter to Women*, no. 12.
22. Joan Walsh, "Amy Coney Barret's Extremist Religious Beliefs Merit Examination," *The Nation*, September 26, 2020, https://www.thenation.com/article/politics/amy-coney-barrett-religious/.
23. Barrett has seven children, including two who are adopted and one with special needs. She told graduates of Notre Dame Law School that their legal careers should be "but a means to an end . . . and that end is building the Kingdom of God," quoted in Tom Gjelten, "Amy Comey Barrett's Catholicism Is Controversial but May Not Be a Confirmation Issue," *NPR*, September 29, 2020, https://www.npr.org/2020/09/29/917943045/amy-coney-barretts-catholicism-is-controversial-but-may-not-be-confirmat ion-issue.
24. See Benjamin Franklin, "The Way to Wealth" (1758), which draws together sayings from *Poor Richard's Almanac* (1732). Franklin juxtaposes sloth and industry. Available at Project Gutenberg, http://www.gutenberg.org/files/43855/43855-h/43855-h.htm.
25. Wendy Wasserstein, *Sloth: The Seven Deadly Sins* (New York: Oxford University Press, 2005) and Jenny O'Dell, *How to Do Nothing: Resisting the Attention Economy* (New York: Melville House, 2019).

NOTES 211

26. Rebecca Konyndyk DeYoung, "The Vice of Sloth," *Other Journal*, http://theotherjournal.com/2007/11/15/the-vice-of-sloth-some-historical-reflections-on-laziness-effort-and-resistance-to-the-demands-of-love/.

27. Aquinas, *Summa Theologica* II-II, Q. 35.

28. Aquinas, ST II-II, Q. 35.

29. DeYoung, "The Vice of Sloth."

30. DeYoung, "The Vice of Sloth."

31. Richard Gaillardetz, A *Daring Promise: A Spirituality for Christian Marriage*, rev. ed. (Liguori, MO: Liguori Press, 2007).

32. DeYoung, "The Vice of Sloth."

33. Cobble, Gordon, and Henry, *Feminism Unfinished*, 79–84. Still, they were limited by their mostly white, middle-class membership who, despite good intentions, often found it difficult to see problems other than their own (92–102).

34. Intersectionalism means analyzing different aspects of a person (e.g., gender, race, class, ethnicity, age, religion, ability) that may contribute to oppression in relation to each other. First- and second-wave feminism focused primarily on sexual oppression, but contemporary feminism is intersectional. See Kimberle Crenshaw, "Demarginalizing the Intersection of Race and Sex: Black Feminist Critique of Antidiscrimination Doctrine, Feminist Theory and Antiracist Politics," *University of Chicago Legal Forum* 1989.1: issue 8, http://chicagounbound.uchicago.edu/uclf/vol1989/iss1/8; and Patricia Hill Collins, *Black Feminist Thought: Knowledge, Consciousness, and the Politics of Empowerment* (New York: Hyman, 1990).

35. Audre Lorde, "The Uses of the Erotic: The Erotic as Power," in *Sister Outsider: Essays and Speeches* (Berkeley: Crossing Press, 2007), 58.

36. Saiving, "The Human Situation," 43.

37. See Kirsten Swinth, *Feminism's Forgotten Fight: The Unfinished Struggle for Work and Family* (Cambridge, MA: Harvard University Press, 2018).

38. Charles Taylor's *Sources of the Self* (Cambridge, MA: Harvard University Press, 1989) is his major historical work on the topic. Here I rely primarily on *The Ethics of Authenticity* (Cambridge, MA: Harvard University Press, 1991) which captures Taylor's core constructive argument.

39. Taylor, *The Ethics of Authenticity*, 28–29.

40. Taylor, *The Ethics of Authenticity*, 39.

41. Taylor, *The Ethics of Authenticity*, 52.

42. Taylor, *The Ethics of Authenticity*, 91.

212   NOTES

43. Andrew Prevot, "Sources of a Black Self? Ethics of Authenticity in an Era of Anti-Blackness," in *Anti-Blackness and Christian Ethics*, ed. Vincent W. Lloyd and Andrew Prevot (Maryknoll, NY: Orbis, 2017), 90.

44. Prevot, "Sources of a Black Self," 91–95.

45. Theresa Delgado, "This Is My Body," in *Frontiers in Catholic Feminist Theology: Shoulder to Shoulder*, ed. Susan Abraham and Elena Precario Foley (Minneapolis: Fortress, 2009), 30.

46. Margaret A. Farley, *Just Love: A Framework for Christian Sexual Ethics* (New York: Continuum, 2006), 215–232.

47. M. Shawn Copeland, *Enfleshing Freedom: Body, Race, and Being* (Minneapolis: Fortress, 2010).

48. Copeland, *Enfleshing Freedom*, 109.

Chapter 2

1. I use the term "sexual violence" to cover rape, sexual assault, and abuse, as well as unwanted sexual attention, stalking, touching, etc., of adults and children. See https://www.rainn.org/types-sexual-violence.

2. See "Catholic Women Strike," https://www.cwstrike.org/about.

3. Early influential texts include Noreen Connell and Cassandra Wilson, *Rape: A Sourcebook for Women* (New York: New American Library, 1974); Susan Brownmiller, *Against Our Will: Men, Women, and Rape* (New York: Bantam, 1975); Andrea Dworkin, *Pornography: Men Possessing Women* (New York: Penguin, 1979); and Catherine A. MacKinnon, *Sexual Harassment of Working Women: A Case of Sex Discrimination* (New Haven: Yale University Press, 1979). Early feminist discourse on rape gave limited attention to women of color and failed to acknowledge white women's role in demonizing Black men. See Angela Y. Davis, *Women, Race, & Class* (New York: Vintage, 1983), 172–201.

4. Available at https://www.cambridgedocumentaryfilms.org/filmsPages/rapeculture.html. The 1975 film was revised in 1983, not long before I encountered it. Prisoners Against Rape collaborated with Black women from the DC Rape Crisis Center on the film, which featured Mary Daly.

5. The church's failures on clergy sexual abuse are well established. Reports such as *Pennsylvania Grand Jury Report* (July 27, 2018), https://www.attorneygeneral.gov/report/, and *The Light from the Southern Cross: Promoting Co-responsible Governance in the Catholic Church in Australia* (August 15, 2020), https://static1.squarespace.com/static/5acea6725417fc059ddcc

NOTES 213

33f/t/5f3f79e41aac2871be0fba5c/1597995610389/The+Light+from+the+ Southern+Cross+FINAL+%2815+August+2020%29.pdf, show the pervasiveness of abuse and a lack of transparency. For a structural analysis, see Julie H. Rubio and Paul J. Schutz, "'Beyond Bad Apples': Understanding Clergy Sexual Abuse as a Structural Problem and Cultivating Strategies for Change" (2022), https://www.scu.edu/ic/programs/bannan-forum/ media—publications/beyond-bad-apples-/.

6. My focus in this chapter will be on women, who account for 90 percent of victims of sexual violence, but they are not the only victims. A minority of men are sexually victimized (mostly by other men) and nearly half of transgender persons are sexually assaulted, James et al., *The Report of the 2015 U.S. Transgender Survey* (Washington, DC: National Center for Transgender Equality, 2016), https://transequality.org/sites/default/files/ docs/usts/USTS-Full-Report-Dec17.pdf.

7. Amy J. Traub and Amanda Van Hoose Garofalo, "#MeToo—a Brief Review," *Employee Relations Law Journal* 44.4 (2019): 4–7.

8. See https://nwlc.org/times-up-legal-defense-fund/; Charisse Jones, "#MeToo One Year Later: Cosby, Moonves Fall, Sex Harassment Fight at Work Far from Over," *USA Today*, October 9, 2018, https://www.usatoday. com/story/money/2018/10/04/metoo-workplace-sexual-harassment-laws-policies-progress/1378191002/.

9. Collier Myerson, "#MeToo Is Changing the Definition of 'Bad Sex,'" *The Nation*, January 28, 2018, https://www.thenation.com/article/metoo-is-changing-the-definition-of-bad-sex/. Ann J. Cahill, "Unjust Sex vs. Rape," *Hypatia* 31.4 (2016): 746–761, argues for commonality as well as distinction.

10. Katie Way, "I Went on a Date with Aziz Ansari," *babe.net*, January 14, 2018, https://babe.net/2018/01/13/aziz-ansari-28355.

11. Kristen Roupenian, "Cat Person," *New Yorker*, December 11, 2017, https:// www.newyorker.com/magazine/2017/12/11/cat-person. See also Alexis Nowicki, "'Cat Person' and Me," in which the author suggests that her personal details may have been utilized for the story, though the relationship she had with an older man was not, in her view, exploitative, https://slate. com/human-interest/2021/07/cat-person-kristen-roupenian-viral-story-about-me.html. Still, the resonance of the story remains.

12. "45 Stories of Sex and Consent on Campus," *New York Times*, May 10, 2018, available at https://www.nytimes.com/interactive/2018/05/10/.../ sexual-consent-college-campus.html; see also Megan K. McCabe, "A Feminist Catholic Response to the Social Sin of Rape Culture," *Journal of*

214   NOTES

Religious Ethics 43.4 (2018): 637–644, for a summary of studies on sexual violence that find the same pattern.

13. Joanne Sweeny, "The #MeToo Movement in Comparative Perspective," *Journal of Gender, Social Policy, & the Law* 29.1 (2020): 33–88, detailing a global pattern of backlash.

14. Jessica Valenti, "#MeToo Is about More Than Stopping Rape. We Demand More," *The Guardian*, January 31, 2018, https://www.theguardian.com/commentisfree/2018/jan/31/me-too-we-demand-more-jessica-valenti.

15. McCabe, "Feminist Catholic Response," 639. I agree with Sweeny, "#MeToo Movement," 87–88, that taking on internalized patriarchy is necessary. Focus on consent alone is insufficient.

16. See http://www.usccb.org/about/migration-and-refugee-services/.

17. McCabe, "Catholic Feminist Response," 636, notes the silence of the US Conference of Catholic Bishops and the inadequate treatment of rape in the Catechism.

18. See US Conference of Catholic Bishops, "Sexual Abuse of Women," for a short list of references in papal documents and the USCCB's own *When I Call for Help* (2002), http://www.usccb.org/issues-and-action/human-life-and-dignity/sexual-abuse-of-women/index.cfm.

19. E.g., "The second blessing of matrimony which We said was mentioned by St. Augustine, is the blessing of conjugal honor which consists in the mutual fidelity of the spouses in fulfilling the marriage contract, so that what belongs to one of the parties by reason of this contract sanctioned by divine law, may not be denied to him or permitted to any third person." Pius XI, *Casti connubii* (1931), no. 19.

20. John Paul II, *Familiaris consortio* (1981), no. 13. For critiques of John Paul II, see William C. Mattison and David Cloutier, "Bodies Poured Out in Christ: Marriage beyond the Theology of the Body," in *Leaving and Coming Home: New Wineskins for Catholic Sexual Ethics*, ed. David Cloutier (Eugene, OR: Cascade, 2010), 206–225; and Cristina L. H. Traina, "Papal Ideals, Martial Realities: One View from the Ground," in *Sexual Diversity and Catholicism: Toward the Development of Moral Theology*, ed. Patricia Beattie Jung with Joseph Andrew Coray (Collegeville, MN: Liturgical, 2001), 269–288.

21. Synod of Bishops, *The Vocation and Mission of the Family in the Church and in the Contemporary World* (2015), no. 27.

22. Francis, *Amoris laetitia* (2016), nos. 62, 124, 13.

23. Francis, *Amoris laetitia*, nos. 53 and 155.

NOTES 215

24. Francis, *Amoris laetitia*, nos. 54, 56, 171, 173–175. Yet note the warning against "controlling" fathers, nos. 176–177.
25. Francis, *Amoris laetitia*, no. 49
26. Joshua J. McElwee, "Backgrounder: What Happened before Chile's Bishops Resigned," *National Catholic Reporter*, May 18, 2018, https://www.ncronline.org/news/accountability/backgrounder-what-happened-chiles-bishops-resigned.
27. Efforts include the Vatican's former Centre for Child Protection, now the Institute of Anthropology, Interdisciplinary Studies on Human Dignity and Care, and the US Catholic Conference of Bishops' Committee on the Protection of Children and Young People, https://www.usccb.org/committees/protection-children-young-people, and the all-lay National Review Board, https://www.usccb.org/offices/child-and-youth-protection/national-review-board.
28. John Paul II, *Centesimus annus* (1991), no. 54.
29. Leo XIII, *Rerum novarum* (1891), no. 107, qtd in John Paul II, *Centesimus annus* (1991), no. 53.
30. Leo XII, *Rerum novarum*, no. 44.
31. Leo XII, *Rerum novarum*, no. 45.
32. Leo XII, *Rerum novarum*, no. 20.
33. John Paul II, *Centesimus annus*, no. 55.
34. L. V. Anderson, "What to Read about 'Cat Person,' the Short Story Tearing Apart the Internet," *dig*, December 12, 2017, http://digg.com/2017/cat-person-think-piece-roundup.
35. Lisa Wade, *American Hookup: The New Culture of Sex on Campus* (New York: Norton, 2017).
36. Donna Freitas, *Sex and the Soul: Juggling Sexuality, Spirituality, Romance, and Religion on America's College Campuses* (New York: Oxford University Press, 2008). In *Consent on Campus: A Manifesto* (New York: Oxford University Press, 2018), Freitas makes rape culture an explicit part of her analysis. In *Consent: A Memoir of Unwanted Attention* (Boston: Little, Brown, 2019), Freitas tells her own story of being stalked by a Catholic priest professor.
37. See Conor Kelly, "Sexism in Practice: Feminist Ethics Evaluating the Hook-Up Culture," *Journal of Feminist Studies in Religion* 28.2 (2012): 27–48; and Jennifer Beste, *College Hookup Culture and Christian Ethics: The Lives and Longings of Emerging Adults* (New York: Oxford University Press, 2017).

216   NOTES

38. On the limits of John Paul II's approach, see Daniel J. Daly, *The Structures of Sin and Vice* (Washington, DC: Georgetown University Press, 2021), 39–43.

39. John Paul II, *Solicitudo rei socialis* (1987), nos. 37–38. Catholic ethicists are working on more complex ways of understanding social structures. Daniel K. Finn, "What Is a Sinful Social Structure?," *Theological Studies* 77.1 (2016): 136–164, as I discuss in chapter 9.

40. Karen Lebacqz, "Love Your Enemy: Sex, Power, and Christian Ethics," *Annual of Society of Christian Ethics* (1990), reprinted in *Feminist Theological Ethics: A Reader*, ed. Lois K. Daly (Louisville: Westminster, 1994), 244.

41. Lebacqz, "Love Your Enemy," 244–45.

42. Christine E. Gudorf, *Body, Sex, and Pleasure: Reconstructing Christian Sexual Ethics* (Cleveland: Pilgrim, 1994), 164.

43. Gudorf, *Body, Sex, and Pleasure*, 171.

44. Helen Alvaré, "#MeToo Women, You Have More in Common with Pro-life Women Than You Think," *Washington Examiner*, January 17, 2018, https://www.washingtonexaminer.com/metoo-women-you-have-more-in-common-with-pro-life-women-than-you-think.

45. Christine Emba, *Rethinking Sex: A Provocation* (New York: Sentinel, 2022).

46. The terms are from Finn, "Sinful Social Structure." Paul J. Schutz and I pursue this line of thought in "Beyond 'Bad Apples.'"

47. Gemma Cruz, "Em-bodying Theology: Theological Reflections on the Experience of Filipina Domestic Workers in Hong Kong," in *Body and Sexuality: Theological-Pastoral Perspectives of Women in Asia*, ed. Agnes M. Brazal and Andrea Lizares Si (Manila: Ateneo de Manila University Press, 2007), 66.

48. Cruz, "Em-bodying Theology," 68.

49. Theresa Yih-Lan Tsou, "Theological Reflection on Sex Work," in *Body and Sexuality: Theological-Pastoral Perspectives of Women in Asia*, ed. Agnes M. Brazal and Andrea Lizares Si (Manila: Ateneo de Manila University Press, 2007), 85.

50. Tsou, "Theological Reflection," 78. See also Nichole M. Flores, "Trinity and Justice: A Theological Response to the Sexual Assault of Migrant Women," *Journal of Religion & Society* 16 (2018): 39–51.

51. Julie Hanlon Rubio, *Hope for Common Ground: Mediating the Personal and the Political in a Divided Church* (Washington, DC: Georgetown University Press, 2016).

52. John Paul II, *Sollicitudo rei socialis*, no. 38.

NOTES 217

53. Meghan Clark, *The Virtue of Solidarity and the Praxis of Human Rights* (Minneapolis: Fortress, 2014).
54. Melissa Browning, *Risky Marriage: HIV and Intimate Relationships in Tanzania* (Lanham, MD: Lexington, 2013).
55. John Paul II, *Centesimus annus*, no. 60.
56. Clark, *Virtue of Solidarity*, 111–124.
57. James McWilliams, "Bryan Stevenson on What Well-Meaning White People Need to Know about Race," *Pacific Standard*, February 6, 2018, https://psmag.com/magazine/bryan-stevenson-ps-interview.
58. Audre Lorde, "The Uses of the Erotic: The Erotic as Power," in *Sister Outsider: Essays & Speeches* (Freedom, CA: Crossing, 1984).
59. Margaret A. Farley, *Just Love: A Framework for Christian Sexual Ethics* (New York: Continuum, 2006), 129.
60. Farley, *Just Love*, 173.

Chapter 3

1. John Paul II, *Letter to Women* (1995), 10–11.
2. See Alicia VanOrman and Linda Jacobsen, "U.S. Household Composition Shifts as the Population Grows Older: More Young Adults Live with Parents," *PRB*, February 12, 2020, https://www.prb.org/resources/u-s-household-composition-shifts-as-the-population-grows-older-more-young-adults-live-with-parents/. For broader context, see Sarah Jaffe, *Work Won't Love You Back* (New York: Bold Type Books, 2021).
3. Gretchen Livingston, "Stay-at-Home Moms and Dads Account for about One-in-Five U.S. Parents," *Pew Research Center*, September 24, 2018, https://www.pewresearch.org/fact-tank/2018/09/24/stay-at-home-moms-and-dads-account-for-about-one-in-five-u-s-parents/.
4. The Institute of Family Studies found both mothers and fathers preferring remote work from home at least some of the time. Wendy Wang, "Homeward Bound: The Work-Family Resent in Post-COVID America," *Institute for Family Studies*, August 17, 2021, https://ifstudies.org/blog/homeward-bound-the-work-family-reset-in-post-covid-america.
5. "Americans Keep Quitting Their Jobs in Record Numbers," *Aljazeera*, November 12, 2021, https://www.aljazeera.com/economy/2021/11/12/americans-keep-quitting-thier-jobs-in-record-numbers.
6. Misty Heggeness et al., "Moms, Work, and the Pandemic," *U.S. Census Bureau*, March 3, 2021, https://www.census.gov/library/stories/2021/03/moms-work-and-the-pandemic.html; Kate Ward, "Theologizing the

218 NOTES

Great Resignation: Dignity, Downward Mobility and Death," *CTWEC Forum*, November 28, 2021, https://catholicethics.com/forum/theologiz ing-the-great-resignation/#disqus_thread.

7. Pius XI, *Casti connubii* (1931), no. 75.

8. Rosemary Radford Reuther and Rosemary Skinner, eds., *In Our Own Voices: Four Centuries of American Women's Religious Writing* (San Francisco: Harper, 1995), 26.

9. Dorothy Sue Cobble, Linda Gordon, and Astrid Henry, *Feminism Unfinished: A Short, Surprising History of American Women's Movements* (New York: Norton, 2014), 10.

10. Cobble, Gordon, and Henry, *Feminism Unfinished*, 18–19. Most "social justice feminists" in the mid-twentieth century had religious, working-class roots.

11. Kathleen Gerson, *Unfinished Revolution: How a New Generation in Reshaping Family, Work, and Gender in America* (New York: Oxford University Press, 2010), 5.

12. Gerson, *Unfinished Revolution*, 12. Arlie Hochschild found in *The Second Shift: Working Families and the Revolution at Home* (New York: Penguin, 1989) that women worked an extra two hours per day.

13. Kirsten Swinth, *Feminism's Forgotten Fight: The Unfinished Struggle for Work and Family* (Cambridge, MA: Harvard University Press, 2018), 240–244.

14. Betty Friedan, *The Second Stage* (New York: Summit, 1981); Swinth, *Feminism's Forgotten Fight*, 236–240.

15. Colleen Carroll Campbell, *My Sisters the Saints: A Spiritual Memoir* (New York: Image, 2014).

16. Joan Williams, *Unbending Gender: Why Family and Work Conflict and What to Do about It* (New York: Oxford University Press, 2000), 38.

17. Swinth, *Feminism's Forgotten Fight*, 251.

18. John Paul II, *Letter to Women*, no. 2.

19. John Paul II, *Letter to Women*, no. 4.

20. For estimates on workers, see Cal Newport, *A World without Email: Reimagining Work in an Age of Information Overload* (New York: Penguin, 2021), 39; and Shane McFeely and Ryan Pendell, "What Workplace Leaders Can Learn from the Gig Economy," *Gallup*, August 16, 2018, https://www.gallup.com/workplace/240929/workplace-leaders-learn-real-gig-economy.aspx.

21. "Always On," available at https://www.techopedia.com/definition/31550/always-on-technology. Italics mine.

NOTES 219

22. See Juliana Menasce Horowitz and Kim Parker, "How Americans View Their Jobs," *Pew Research Center*, March 30, 2023, who show that about only about half of workers express satisfaction with their work, https://www.pewresearch.org/social-trends/2023/03/30/how-americans-view-their-jobs/.

23. Newport, *World without Email*, 35–38.

24. Newport, *World without Email*, 39–47.

25. Newport, *World without Email*, 35–39.

26. Newport, *World without Email*, 60–61.

27. Newport, *World without Email*, 30, 57.

28. Newport, *World without Email*, 39.

29. Juliet Schor, *After the Gig: How the Sharing economy Got Hijacked and How to Win It Back* (Oakland: University of California Press, 2020), 20.

30. Schor, *After the Gig*, 29.

31. Alexandrea J. Ravenelle, *Hustle and Gig: Struggling and Surviving in the Sharing Economy* (Oakland: University of California Press, 2019), 7, 89. Workers lack rights to breaks, just wages limited hours, and unionizing.

32. Schor, *After the Gig*, 49. Schor's sample is somewhat unusual. It was limited to the Boston area, is highly educated, and includes fewer drivers, most of whom are dependent (44–45).

33. Ravenelle, *Hustle and Gig*, 160.

34. Schor, *After the Gig*, 76, 79.

35. John Paul II, *Laborem exercens* (1981), nos. 3, 6.

36. John Paul II, *Laborem exercens*, no. 27.

37. As Patricia A. Lamoureux describes in *"Laborem Exercens,"* in *Modern Catholic Social Teaching: Commentaries & Interpretations*, ed. Kenneth R. Himes (Washington, DC: Georgetown University Press, 2005), 407–408. Yet see David Cloutier, "The Workers' Paradise: Eternal Life, Economic Eschatology, and Good Work as the Keys to Social Ethics," *CTSA Proceedings* 75 (2021): 39–41, https://ejournals.bc.edu/index.php/ctsa/article/view/13831/10477.

38. Jessica C. Russell, "The Use of Narratives to Contextualize the Experiences and Needs of Unemployed, Underemployed, and Displaced Workers," *Journal of Employment Counseling* 48 (2011): 50–62; Frances M. McKee-Ryan and Jaron Harvey, "'I Have a Job, but . . . ': A Review of Underemployment," *Journal of Management* 37 (2011): 962–996, http://jom.sagepub.com/content/37/4/962.

39. McKee-Ryan and Harvey, "I Have a Job," 987–988.

220 NOTES

40. Mark J. Allman, "Participation as Moral Measure of the Economy," in *The Almighty and the Dollar: Reflections on Economic Justice for All*, ed. Mark J. Allman (Winona, MN: Anselm, 2012), 168. See also Kenneth E. Himes, "Work in Roman Catholic Thought," *American Journal of Economics and Sociology* 79.4 (2020): 1085–1109.

41. John XXIII, *Gaudium et spes* (1965), no. 39, and Cloutier, "The Workers' Paradise."

42. Leo XIII wrote, "To misuse men as though they were things in the pursuit of gain, or to value them solely for their physical powers—that is truly shameful and inhuman," and called unjust wages "a crime which cries to the avenging anger of Heaven" (*Rerum novarum* [1891], no. 20.

43. Christine Firer Hinze, *Radical Sufficiency: Work, Livelihood, and a US Catholic Economic Ethic* (Washington, DC: Georgetown University Press, 2021), 7.

44. Leo XIII, *Rerum novarum* (1891), no. 20.

45. Christine Firer Hinze, "Bridge Discourse on Wage Justice: Roman Catholic and Feminist Perspectives on the Family," *Annual of Society of Christian Ethics* 11 (1991): 109–132.

46. Carol P. Coston, "Women's Ways of Working," in *One Hundred Years of Catholic Social Thought: Celebration and Challenge*, ed. John A. Coleman (Maryknoll, NY: Orbis, 1991), 256–269.

47. Mary Devlin Capizzi, "Something Old and Something New," in *Breaking Through: Catholic Women Speak for Themselves*, ed. Helen M. Alvaré (Huntington, IN: Our Sunday Visitor, 2012), 77–92.

48. Toinette M. Eugene, "Moral Values and Black Womanist," in *Feminist Theological Ethics*, ed. Lois K. Daly (Louisville, KY: Westminster, 1994), 160–171.

49. Patricia Hill Collins, "Black Women and Motherhood," in *Rethinking the Family: Some Feminist Questions*, ed. Barrie Thorne (Boston: Northeastern University Press, 1992), 237.

50. Catherine R. Osborne, "Migrant Domestic Careworkers: Between the Public and the Private in Catholic Social Teaching," *Journal of Religious Ethics* 40.1 (2012): 1–25.

51. Janice G. Raymond, "Reproductive Gifts and Gift Giving: The Altruistic Woman," in *Feminist Theological Ethics: A Reader*, ed. Lois K. Daly (Louisville, KY: Westminster, 1994), 233–242.

52. This is the premise of Leah Libresco Sargeant's substack, "Other Feminisms."

53. Jaffe, *Work Won't Love You Back*, 330.

NOTES 221

54. Maggie Levantovskaya, "Keeping It in the Family: On Sarah Jaffe's 'Work Won't Love You Back,'" *Los Angeles Review of Books*, February 12, 2021, https://lareviewofbooks.org/article/keeping-it-in-the-family-on-sarah-jaffes-work-wont-love-you-back/.

55. Arlie Russell Hochschild, *The Managed Heart: Commercialization of Human Feeling* (Oakland: University of California Press, 2012); Kathi Weeks, "Down with Love: Feminist Critique and the New Ideologies of Work," *Women's Studies Quarterly* 35.3–4 (2017): 37–58.
Jaffe, *Work Won't Love You Back*, 329, 331.

56. Jaffe, *Work Won't Love You Back*, 332.

57. Benedict XVI, *Caritas en Veritate* (2014), no. 36.

58. Julie Hanlon Rubio, "Dual Vocation of Christian Parents," *Theological Studies* 63.4 (2002): 786–812.

Chapter 4

1. Hank Stuever, "'Unorthodox' Carefully and Beautifully Depicts a Young Woman's Flight from Tradition," *Washington Post*, March 25, 2020, https://www.washingtonpost.com/entertainment/tv/unorthodox-carefully-and-beautifully-depicts-a-young-womans-flight-from-tradition/2020/03/25/f36ab420-6d2d-11ea-a3ec-70d7479d83f0_story.html.

2. Debra Campbell, *Graceful Exits: Catholic Women and the Art of Departure* (Bloomington: Indiana University Press, 2003).

3. E.g., Author Alex Elle (@alex_elle) has a one-million-follower-strong Instagram presence focused on helping women feel worthy. A popular post reads, "Note to Self: You deserve to be in spaces and relationships that make you happy—that feed your soul and help you grow," https://www.instagram.com/p/CRXcTeENlqZ/.

4. Charlotte Perkins Gilman, "The Yellow Wallpaper" (1892), *Project Gutenberg*, https://www.gutenberg.org/files/1952/1952-h/1952-h.htm.

5. Michael R. Hill, "Introduction," in *Charlotte Perkins Gilman on Families, Marriages, and Children*, ed. Michael R. Hill (New Brunswick, NJ: Transaction Publications, 2011), xvii, https://digitalcommons.unl.edu/cgi/viewcontent.cgi?article=1321&context=sociologyfacpub.

6. Ruth Abbey, "Marriage as Friendship in the Thought of Mary Wollstonecraft," *Hypatia* 14.3 (1999), https://muse.jhu.edu/article/14064.

7. Emily Dumler-Winckler notes that Wollstonecraft contrasts the ideal of marriage as passionate, egalitarian friendship with the reality of

222 NOTES

eighteenth-century marriage. See her *Modern Virtue: Mary Wollstonecraft and a Tradition of Dissent* (New York: Oxford University Press, 2022).

8. Olive Banks, *Faces of Feminism: A Study of Feminism as a Social Movement* (New York: Basil Blackwell, 1986), 195: "Right into the twentieth century, the organized feminists were respectable, even puritan, in their attitude to marriage."

9. Tera W. Hunter, *Bound in Wedlock, Slave and Free Black Marriage in the Nineteenth Century* (Cambridge, MA: Harvard University Press, 2017), 301; Toinette Eugene, "While Love Is Unfashionable: An Exploration of Black Spirituality and Sexuality," in *Women's Consciousness, Women's Conscience: A Reader in Feminist Ethics*, ed. Barbara Hilkert Anderson, Christine E. Gudorf, and Mary D. Pellaur (San Francisco: Harper & Row, 1985), 121–142.

10. Patricia Hill Collins, *Black Feminist Thought: Knowledge, Consciousness, and the Politics of Empowerment* (New York: Routledge, 1991), 181–187.

11. Kecia R. Johnson and Karyn Loscocco, "Black Marriage through the Prism of Gender, Race, and Class," *Journal of Black Studies* 46.2 (2015): 164, http://www.jstor.com/stable/24572942.

12. Kathryn Edin and Maria Kefalas, *Promises I Can Keep: Why Poor Women Put Motherhood before Marriage* (Berkeley: University of California Press, 2005).

13. Quoted in Collins, *Black Feminist Thought*, 184.

14. Leah Libresco Sargeant, "What Is Other Feminisms?," https://otherfe minisms.substack.com/about. See also Erika Bachiochi, ed., *Women, Sex, and the Church: A Case for Catholic Teaching* (Boston: Pauline Books and Media, 2010).

15. Simone de Beauvoir, *The Second Sex*, trans. and ed. H. M. Parshley (New York: Vintage, 1989), 642.

16. Estelle B. Freedman, *No Turning Back: The History of Feminism and the Future of Women* (New York: n, 2002), 262; Banks, *Faces of Feminism*, 199; and Dorothy Sue Cobble, Linda Gordon, and Astrid Henry, *Feminism Unfinished: A Short, Surprising History of the American Women's Movement* (New York: Liveright, 2014), 14–15.

17. Catherine MacKinnon, *Feminism Unmodified: Discourses on Life and Law* (Cambridge MA: Harvard University Press, 1987).

18. Adrienne Rich, *Of Woman Born: Motherhood as Experience and Institution* (New York: Norton, 1986), 194.

NOTES 223

19. Adrienne Rich, "Compulsory Heterosexuality and Lesbian Existence," *Signs* 5.4 (1980), https://www.jstor.org/stable/3173834?seq=1#metadata_info_tab_contents.

20. Jack Halberstam, *Gaga Feminism: Sex, Gender, and the End of Normal* (Boston: Beacon, 2012), xiv.

21. Halberstam, *Gaga Feminism*, 111–129.

22. Judith Butler, "Is Kinship Always Already Homosexual?," *differences* 13.1 (2002): 21, https://muse.jhu.edu/article/9630.

23. Saidiya Hartman, *Wayward Lives, Beautiful Experiments: Intimate Histories of Social Upheaval* (New York: Norton, 2019), xv.

24. Hartman, *Wayward Lives, Beautiful Experiments*, 221.

25. Thelanthia Nikki Young, *Black Queer Ethics, Family, and Philosophical Imagination* (London: Palgrave Macmillan, 2016).

26. R. Marie Griffith, *Moral Combat: How Sex Divided American Christians and Fractured American Politics* (New York: Basic, 2017).

27. On development of Catholic teaching, see Joseph A. Selling, "Magisterial Teaching on Marriage 1880–1986: Historical Constancy or Radical Development?," in *Change in Official Catholic Moral Teachings*, ed. Charles E. Curran (Mahwah, NJ: Paulist, 2003), 248–252; and Michael Lawler, *Marriage and Sacrament: A Theology of Christian Marriage* (Collegeville, MD: Liturgical, 1993), 18–20.

28. John Paul II, *Man and Woman He Created Them: A Theology of the Body*, trans. Michael Waldenstein (Menlo Park, CA: Pauline Books and Media, 2006. Pope Francis continued this trajectory in *Amoris laetitia* (2016), nos. 120–152.

29. John Paul II, *Familiaris consortio* (1981), no. 25. Compare Pius XI, *Casti connubii* (1931), nos. 26 and 29. Even if the analogy is progressive in its context, it remains problematically hierarchical.

30. John Paul II, *Familiaris consortio*, nos. 17–64. Four tasks of the family provide the structure of the document. Except for nos. 23–25, the language is mostly gender neutral.

31. Julie Hanlon Rubio, *A Theology of Christian Marriage and Family* (Mahwah, NJ: Paulist, 2003), 25–42.

32. Karl Rahner, SJ, "Marriage," in *Theological Investigations*, vol. 10 (New York: Herder and Herder, 1973), 207. Compare to Halberstam, *Gaga Feminism*: "Marriage pits the family and the couple against everyone else" (110).

33. John Paul II, *Familiaris consortio*, nos. 28, 42, 44.

34. Francis, *Amoris laetitia*, no. 181.

224 NOTES

35. Francis, *Amoris laetitia*, nos. 291–312, 297.

36. Stanley Hauerwas, *A Community of Character: Toward a Constructive Christian Social Ethic* (Notre Dame, IN: University of Notre Dame Press, 1981), 155–174.

37. Julie Hanlon Rubio, "Families in the Bible Weren't Perfect, but We Can Still Learn from Them," *America*, June 9, 2016, https://www.americam agazine.org/issue/ordinary-holy-families.

38. Julie Hanlon Rubio, "Family Ethics: Beyond Sex and Controversy," *Theological Studies* 74.1 (2013): 138–161.

39. Pope Francis, *Laudato sî* (2015) and *Fratelli tutti* (2020).

40. Sidney Callahan, "Feminism at Fifty," *America*, December 2, 2013, https://www.americamagazine.org/issue/feminism-fifty.

41. Callahan, "Feminism at Fifty."

42. Mary J. Henold, *Catholic and Feminist: The Surprising History of the American Catholic Feminist Movement* (Chapel Hill: University of North Carolina Press, 2008), 62.

43. Henold, *Catholic and Feminist*, 18.

44. Marian Ronan, "A Brief History of the Grail in the United States," http://www.grail-us.org/wp-content/uploads/2011/07/Brief-History-of-the-US-Grail-Marian-Ronan-6-2013.pdf, 2. By the end of the 1960s, the Grail movement had become involved in the women's liberation movement and Christian feminist theology.

45. Quoted in Henold, *Catholic and Feminist*, 28.

46. Gertrude von le Fort, *Eternal Woman: The Timeless Meaning of the Feminine* (1934), trans. Marie Cecilia Buehrle, new ed. (San Francisco: Ignatius Press, 2010), 11.

47. Chuck Gallagher, *The Marriage Encounter: As I Have Loved You* (New York: Doubleday, 1975), 27.

48. Gallagher, *The Marriage Encounter*, 29, 30.

49. Jeffrey M. Burns, *Disturbing the Peace: A History of the Christian Family Movement, 1949–1974* (Notre Dame: University of Notre Dame Press, 1999).

50. Sally Cunneen, *Sex: Female, Religion: Catholic* (New York: Holt, Rinehart and Winston, 1968), 37.

51. Jose de Vinck, *Virtue of Sex: Pleasure and Holiness in Marriage* (New York: Hawthorn, 1966), 245.

52. Mary Daly, *Beyond God the Father: Toward a Philosophy of Women's Liberation* (New York: Houghton Mifflin, 1973), 122.

NOTES   225

53. The only anomaly was the Fitzgeralds. Robert left Sally for a younger woman. Elaine Woo, "Sally Fitzgerald: Flannery O'Connor's Friend, Editor, and Literary Steward," *Los Angeles Times*, July 14, 2000, https://www.lati mes.com/archives/la-xpm-2000-jul-14-me-52965-story.html#:~:text=Fit zgerald%2C%20a%20homemaker%20and%20occasional,short%20stor ies%20and%20other%20writings.

54. Cuneen, *Sex: Female, Religion: Catholic*, 113.

55. Sidney Callahan, *Beyond Birth Control: The Christian Experience of Sex* (New York: Sheed and Ward, 1968), 134–135.

56. See, e.g., Patricia Beattie Jung, *Sex on Earth as It Is in Heaven: A Christian Eschatology of Desire* (New York: SUNY Press, 2017); Elizabeth L. Antus, "'Was It Good for You?' Recasting Catholic Sexual Ethics in Light of Women's Sexual Pain Disorders," *Journal of Religious Ethics* 46.4 (2018): 611–634.

57. Todd A. Salzman and Michael G. Lawler, *The Sexual Person: Toward a Renewed Sexual Anthropology* (Washington, DC: Georgetown University Press, 2008), is the most comprehensive argument.

58. Julie Hanlon Rubio and Jason King, eds., *Sex, Love, and Marriage: Catholic Perspectives* (Collegeville, MN: Liturgical, 2020).

59. See Simcha Fisher, *A Sinner's Guide to Natural Family Planning* (Huntington, IN: Our Sunday Visitor, 2014) and Kate Bryan, *Living the Feminist Dream: A Faithful Vision for Women in the Church and in the World* (New York: New City Press, 2021).

60. Stephanie Coontz, *Marriage, a History: How Love Conquered Marriage* (New York: Penguin, 2006), 313.

61. Francis, *Amoris laetitia* (2016), no. 66.

62. Bridget Burke Ravizza and Julie Donovan Massey, *Project Holiness: Marriage as a Workshop for Everyday Saints* (Collegeville, MD: Liturgical, 2015).

Chapter 5

1. Anemona Hartocollis and Yamiche Alcindor, "Women's March Highlights as Huge Crowds Protest Trump: 'We're Not Going Away,'" *New York Times*, January 21, 2017, https://www.nytimes.com/2017/01/21/us/womens-march.html.

2. See Emma Green, "These Pro-Lifers Are Headed to the Women's March in Washington," *The Atlantic*, January 16, 2017, https://www.theatlantic. com/politics/archive/2017/01/pro-lifers-womens-march/513104/. Green

226 NOTES

reports that the group's partner status was subsequently withdrawn. I favor the terms most people use to describe themselves: "pro-life" and "pro-choice."

3. Julie Hanlon Rubio, *Hope for Common Ground: Mediating the Personal and the Political in a Divided Church* (Washington, DC: Georgetown University Press, 2016), 159–192.

4. John T. Noonan, "Abortion: An Almost Absolute Value in History," in *The Morality of Abortion: Legal and Historical Perspectives*, ed. John T. Noonan (Cambridge, MA: Harvard University Press, 1970), 1–59. Despite inconsistencies in enforcement and debates over ensoulment, culpability, and legality, direct abortion has always been understood as unethical killing. On the complexity of public opinion, see Tricia C. Bruce, "How Americans Understand Abortion," McGrath Institute, University of Notre Dame, 2020, https://triciabruce.com/2020/07/15/how-americans-und erstand-abortion/.

5. R. Marie Griffith, *Moral Combat: How Sex Divided American Christians & Fractured American Politics* (New York: Basic, 2017). Griffith views opposition to sexual freedom as the key to Christian pro-life advocacy, but Daniel K. Williams, *Defenders of the Unborn: The Pro-life Movement before Roe v. Wade* (New York: Oxford University Press, 2016) characterizes the movement as a continuation of 1960s struggles for justice.

6. US Conference of Catholic Bishops, "Forming Consciences for Faithful Citizenship," https://www.usccb.org/issues-and-action/faithful-citizens hip/forming-consciences-for-faithful-citizenship-title, nos. 31–35.

7. After *Dobbs*, advocates renewed calls for support. See Holly Taylor Coolman, "The 12 Things Pro-Lifers Must Do If Roe Is Overturned," *America*, December 3, 2021, https://www.americamagazine.org/politics-society/2021/12/03/abortion-pro-life-post-roe-catholic-241959.

8. Joseph Cardinal Bernadin, *Consistent Ethic of Life* (Kansas City: Sheed & Ward, 1988).

9. John Paul II, *Evangelium vitae* (1995). See also US Jesuits, "Protecting the Least among Us: A Statement of the Society of Jesus in the United States on Abortion," https://www.jesuits.org/wp-content/uploads/2021/01/Prote cting_the_Least_ENGLISH-FINAL-1-18-2018.pdf, and US Conference of Catholic Bishops, "Pastoral Plan for Pro-life Activities," https://www. usccb.org/prolife/pastoral-plan-pro-life-activities.

10. Frances X. Rocca, "With a Few Words on Abortion, Pope Francis Shows a New Way to Be Pro-life," *Catholic News Service*, January 10, 2014,

https://www.ncronline.org/news/vatican/few-words-abortion-pope-fran cis-shows-new-way-be-pro-life.

11. See US Conference of Catholic Bishops, "Forming Consciences."
12. Congregation for the Doctrine of the Faith, *Declaration on Procured Abortion* (1974), no. 14.
13. US Conference of Catholic Bishops, "Forming Consciences," nos. 27–32. See also Cathleen Kaveny, *Law's Virtues: Fostering Autonomy and Solidarity in American Society* (Washington, DC: Georgetown University Press, 2012), 219–242.
14. "Pregnancy Week by Week," Mayo Clinic, https://www.mayoclinic.org/ healthy-lifestyle/pregnancy-week-by-week/in-depth/prenatal-care/art-20045302.
15. Sanger's sympathy for eugenics taints her social justice legacy, as Planned Parenthood has recently recognized.
16. Estelle B. Freedman, *No Turning Back: The History of Feminism and the Future of Women* (New York: Ballantine, 2002), 229–252.
17. This stance reflects the race and class privilege of its advocates, who could reasonably expect abstinence to work for them.
18. Linda Gordon, "Why Nineteenth-Century Feminists Did Not Support 'Birth Control and Twentieth Century Feminists Do,'" in Rethinking the Family: Some Feminist Questions ed. Barrie Thorne with Marilyn Yalom, rev. ed. (Boston: Northeastern University Press, 1992), 142–147. See also Tracey A. Thomas, "Misappropriating Women's History in the Law and Politics of Abortion," *Seattle Law Review* 36.1 (2013): 1–68, https://dig italcommons.law.seattleu.edu/cgi/viewcontent.cgi?article=2111&cont ext=sulr.
19. See Rebecca Todd Peters, *Trust Women: A Progressive Christian Argument for Reproductive Justice* (Boston: Beacon, 2018).
20. Sidney Callahan, "A Case for Pro-life Feminism," *Commonweal*, April 1986, 232–238. See also Feminists for Life, "Abortion Is a Reflection That We Have Not Met the Needs of Women," https://www.feministsforl ife.org/.
21. Maggie Astor, "On Abortion Rights, 2020 Democrats Move Past 'Safe, Legal, and Rare,'" *New York Times*, November 25, 2019, https://www.nyti mes.com/2019/11/25/us/politics/abortion-laws-2020-democrats.html.
22. See https://shoutyourabortion.com/.
23. See "Birthing Reproductive Justice: 150 Years of Images and Ideas," https:// apps.lib.umich.edu/online-exhibits/exhibits/show/reproductive-justice.

228 NOTES

24. See Dolores Williams's account in *Sisters in the Wilderness: The Challenge of Womanist God-Talk*, 20th anniversary ed. (Maryknoll, NY: Orbis, 2013), 32–74.

25. In *Women, Race, & Class* (New York: Vintage, 1983), Angela Davis notes that women of color driven by desperation to abortion did not see abortion as a sign of freedom. She laments, "What was demanded as a 'right; for the privileged came to be interpreted as a 'duty' for the poor" (210). Yet she holds that birth control (including abortion) "is a fundamental prerequisite for the emancipation of women" (202).

26. See https://www.newwavefeminists.com/; https://www.rehumanizeintl. org/; Damon Linker, "Donald Trump and the Moral Decline of the Pro-life Movement," *The Week*, January 24, 2020, https://theweek.com/articles/891179/donald-trump-moral-decline-prolife-movement.

27. Susan Bigelow, "From the Site of the Empty Tomb: Approaching the Hidden Grief of Prenatal Loss," *New Theology Review* 28.2 (2016): 52. See also Jennifer Beste, "Limits to the Appeal to Women's Experience Reconsidered," *Horizons* 33.1 (2006): 54–77.

28. Sarah Stage, *Female Complaints: Lydia Pinkham and the Business of Women's Medicine* (New York: Norton, 1979), 64–88.

29. Rachel Reed, Rachel Sharman, and Christian Inglis, "Women's Descriptions of Childbirth Trauma Relating to Care Provider Actions and Interactions," *BMC Pregnancy Childbirth* 17.1 (2010): 21. See also Diana Bowser and Kathleen Hill, "Exploring Evidence for Disrespect and Abuse in Facility-Based Childbirth: Report of a Landscape Analysis," *Harvard School of Public Health University Research*, 2010, https://www.mhtf.org/document/exploring-evidence-for-disrespect-and-abuse-in-facility-based-childbirth-report-of-a-landscape-analysis//.

30. Jeanne L. Alhuesen et al., "Intimate Partner Violence during Pregnancy: Maternal and Neonatal Outcomes," *Journal of Women's Health* 24.1 (2015), https://www.ncbi.nlm.nih.gov/pmc/articles/PMC4361157/. This includes up to 50 percent of low-income single mothers.

31. Boston Women's Health Book Collective, *Our Bodies, Ourselves* (1973), excerpted in *The Essential Feminist Reader*, ed. Estelle B. Freedman (New York: Modern Library, 2007), 298.

32. Margaret Sanger, "Woman and the New Race," excerpted in *The Essential Feminist Reader*, ed. Estelle B. Freedman (New York: Modern Library, 2007), 210.

33. National Marriage Project and Center for Marriage and Institute for American Values, "When Marriage Disappears" (2010), http://national marriageproject.org/blog/resources/when-marriage-disappears/.

34. Kathryn Edin and Maria J. Kefalas, *Promises I Can Keep: Why Poor Women Put Motherhood before Marriage* (Berkeley: University of California Press, 2005), 46.

35. These were collected by Pat and Patty Crowley of the Christian Family Movement and other members of the papal birth control commission that met from 1965 to 1967 to advise Pope Paul VI. As I note in "Beyond the Liberal-Conservative Divide on Contraception," *Horizons* 32.2 (2005): 270–294, faithful Catholics testified to the rhythm method's negative effects on marriage.

36. Robert McGlory, *Turning Point: The Inside Story of the Papal Birth Control Commission* (New York: Crossroad, 1995), 92.

37. See Angela Franks, "The Gift of Female Fertility: Church Teaching on Contraception," in *Women, Sex, and the Church: A Case for Catholic Teaching*, ed. Erika Bachiochi (Boston: Pauline, 2010), 97–120.

38. Emily Reimer-Barry, *Catholic Theology of Marriage in the Era of HIV and AIDS: Marriage for Life* (Lanham, MD: Lexington, 2015).

39. Gretchen Livingston, "They're Waiting Longer but U.S. Women Today More Likely to Have Children Than a Decade Ago," *Pew Research*, January 18, 2018, https://www.pewresearch.org/social-trends/2018/01/18/the yre-waiting-longer-but-u-s-women-today-more-likely-to-have-children-than-a-decade-ago/.

40. Adrienne Rich, *Of Woman Born: Motherhood as Experience and Institution*, 10th anniversary ed. (New York: Norton, 1986), 26.

41. Chris Barcelos and Aline Gubrium, "Bodies That Tell: Embodying Teen Pregnancy through Digital Storytelling," *Signs* 43.4 (2018): 907.

42. Barcelos and Gubrium, "Bodies That Tell," 915.

43. Barcelos and Gubrium, "Bodies That Tell," 918.

44. Barcelos and Gubrium, "Bodies That Tell"; see also Myra L. Betron et al., "Expanding the Agenda for Addressing Mistreatment in Maternity Care: A Mapping Review and Gender Analysis," *Reproductive Health* 15.1 (2018), https://pubmed.ncbi.nlm.nih.gov/30153848/.

45. John Paul II, *Mulieris dignitatum* (1988), no. 18.

46. Bonnie Miller-McLemore, *Also a Mother: Work and Family as Theological Dilemma* (Nashville: Abingdon, 1992).

47. Carrie Frost, *Maternal Body: A Theology of Incarnation from the Christian East* (Mahwah, NJ: Paulist, 2019).

230 NOTES

48. Colleen Carroll Campbell, *My Sisters, the Saints: A Spiritual Memoir* (New York: Image, 2014). See also Kathryn Lila Cox, "Toward a Theology of Infertility and the Role of *Donum Vitae*," *Horizons* 40.1 (2013): 28–52.

49. Dorothy Day, *The Long Loneliness* (San Francisco: Harper, 1952), 136.

50. Day, *The Long Loneliness*, 135.

51. Susan Bigelow Reynolds, "From the Site of the Empty Tomb," *New Theology Review* 28.2 (2016): 47; Rachel K. Jones, Elizabeth Witwer, and Jenna Jerman, "Abortion Incidence and Service Availability in the United States," Guttmacher Institute, 2017, https://www.guttmacher.org/report/abortion-incidence-service-availability-us-2017.

52. "New Zealand Approves Paid Leave after Miscarriage," *New York Times*, March 25, 2021, https://www.nytimes.com/2021/03/25/world/asia/new-zealand-miscarriage-paid-leave.html; E. Joanne Angelo, "The Psychological Aftermath of Three Decades of Abortion," in *The Cost of Choice: Women Evaluate the Impact of Abortion*, ed. Erika Bachiochi (San Francisco: Encounter, 2004), 87–100.

53. Thia Cooper, "Race, Class, and Abortion: How Liberation Theology Enhances the Demand for Reproductive Justice," *Feminist Theology* 24.3 (2016): 227.

54. Cooper, "Race, Class, and Abortion," 238.

55. Reynolds, "Site of the Empty Tomb," 51. Reynolds uses "prenatal loss" rather than "pregnancy loss" because it better captures women's accounts of miscarriage and stillborn birth. See also Emily Reimer Barry, "A New Prolife Movement Is Possible," *Catholic Theological Society of America Proceedings* 74 (2019): 21–41; Amelia Bonow and Emily Nokes, eds., *Shout Your Abortion* (Oakland, CA: PM Press, 2018).

56. "I Believe My Daughter Will Wait for Me," *Shout Your Abortion*, https://shoutyourabortion.com/writing/i-believe-my-daughter-will-wait-for-me/.

57. Jennifer Baumgardner, *Abortion & Life* (New York: Akashic Books, 2008), 104.

58. Lawrence B. Finer, "Reasons U.S. Women Have Abortions: Quantitative and Qualitative Perspectives," *Perspectives on Sexual and Reproductive Health* 37.3 (2005): 110–118, https://www.guttmacher.org/journals/psrh/2005/reasons-us-women-have-abortions-quantitative-and-qualitative-perspectives.

59. Rubio, *Hope for Common Ground*: 168–172.

NOTES 231

60. Elizabeth Dias, "Inside an Evangelical Pregnancy Center," *New York Times*, August 23, 2019, https://www.nytimes.com/2019/08/23/us/abortion-evangelical-pregnancy-center.html.

61. Angela Kelly, "Full Disclosure: An OB/GYN's Personal Experience of Pregnancy Loss," *JAMA* 318.13 (2017): 1223–1224, https://jamanetwork.com/journals/jama/fullarticle/2656172?resultClick=1. See also Emily R. M. Lind and Angie Deveau, *Interrogating Pregnancy Loss: Feminist Writings on Abortion, Miscarriage, and Stillbirth* (Bradford: Demeter Press, 2017).

62. Bigelow, "Site of the Empty Tomb," 53.

63. Bigelow, "Site of the Empty Tomb," 54.

64. Bigelow, "Site of the Empty Tomb," 57.

65. Eve Ensler, "I Was There in the Room," *The Vagina Monologues*, 1996. Among many performances available on YouTube, see https://www.youtube.com/watch?v=kLalrZ6Qa_U. It is worth noting that Ensler's show used to be viewed as radical feminist, but today is often characterized as essentialist in its focus on women's experience.

66. Carroll, *My Sisters, the Saints*.

67. Dorothy Day, "Having a Baby," https://www.catholicworker.org/dorothyday/articles/583.pdf, differs from, Day, *The Long Loneliness*, 138–139.

68. Quoted in Caritas McCarthy, "Cornelia Connelly and the Incarnation," in *Women & Theology*, ed. Mary Ann Hinsdale (Maryknoll, NY: Orbis, 1995), 46.

69. McCarthy, "Cornelia Connelly," 46.

70. Clarie Cain Miller and Margot Sanger-Katz, Despite State Bans, Legal Abortions Didn't Fall Nationwide in Year After Dobbs," *New York Times*, Oct. 24, 2023, https://www.nytimes.com/2023/10/24/upshot/abortion-numbers-dobbs.html.

Chapter 6

1. See Ines San Martin, "Pope Calls Gender Theory a 'Global War' against the Family," *Crux*, October 1, 2016, https://cruxnow.com/global-church/2016/10/01/pope-calls-gender-theory-global-war-family/, and "Pope Francis, 'It's Terrible Children Taught They Can Choose Their Gender,'" *Catholic Herald*, August 3, 2016, http://www.catholicherald.co.uk/news/2016/08/03/pope-francis-its-terrible-children-taught-they-can-choose-gender/.

2. Francis, *Amoris laetitia* (2016), nos. 56–57; Congregation for Catholic Education, "'Male and Female He Created Them': Towards a Path of

232 NOTES

Dialogue on the Question of Gender Theory in Education" (2019), http://www.educatio.va/content/dam/cec/Documenti/19_0997_INGLESE.pdf; Peter Feuerherd, "Francis Still Falls Short with Women, Feminist Scholars Say," *National Catholic Reporter*, April 19, 2018, https://www.ncronline.org/news/people/francis-still-falls-short-catholic-women-feminist-scholars-say.

3. See, e.g., Abigail Favale, "The Eclipse of Sex by the Rise of Gender," *Church Life Journal*, March 1, 2019, https://churchlifejournal.nd.edu/articles/the-eclipse-of-sex-by-the-rise-of-gender/; Matt Loffman, "New Poll Shows Americans Overwhelmingly Oppose Anti-transgender Laws, *PBS*, April 16, 2021, https://www.pbs.org/newshour/politics/new-poll-shows-americans-overwhelmingly-oppose-anti-transgender-laws.

4. "Gender" came into usage as a word to describe what earlier scholars had called "sex roles" (influenced by cultures or learned rather than innate or natural) in the mid-1950s. Psychoanalyst Robert Stoller, in 1968 the first American to use "gender," worried about the "loss of gender roles." In the 1970s, feminists began questioning the validity of gender roles. In the 1980s, feminists expanded discussion on gender through dialogue with French poststructuralists. Joanne Meyerowitz, "History of Gender," *American Historical Review* 113.5 (2008): 1354–1355. In the 1990s, postmodern thinkers like Judith Butler challenged feminists and posited gender as identity rather than expression.

5. John Paul II, *Letter to Women* (1995). On early feminism, see Olive Banks, *Faces of Feminism: A Study of Feminism as a Social Movement* (New York: Basil Blackwell, 1981), 13–27. On care work, see Kirsten Swinth, *Feminism's Forgotten Fight: The Unfinished Struggle for Work and Family* (Cambridge, MA: Harvard University Press, 2018), 134–155.

6. Lisa Sowle Cahill, *Sex, Gender and Christian Ethics* (New York: Cambridge University Press, 1996) is a fountainhead text.

7. Lisa Sowle Cahill, "Renegotiating Aquinas: Feminist Ethics, Postmodernism, Realism, and Faith," *Journal of Religious Ethics* 43.2 (2015): 193–217.

8. Mary Anne Case, "After Gender: The Destruction of Man? The Vatican's Nightmare Vision of the 'Gender Agenda' for Law," *Pace Law Review* 31.3/2, http://digitalcommons.pace.edu/plr/vol31/iss3/2.

9. Cahill, *Sex, Gender, and Christian Ethics*, 82–90, exemplifies critical Catholic feminist engagement with postmodern theory.

10. See Evelyn Wheaton Whitehead and James D. Whitehead, *Fruitful Embraces: Sexuality, Love, and Justice* (Bloomington: iUniverse, 2012).

NOTES   233

11. For a history, see Mary Ann Case, "The Role of the Popes in the Invention of Complementarity and the Vatican's Anathematization of Gender," *Religion and Gender* 6.2 (2016), https://brill.com/view/journals/rag/6/2/article-p155_2.xml?language=en.

12. See John Paul II, *Letter to Women* (1995), on complementarity as pertaining to acting and being (no. 7), Mary (no. 10), and women's genius (no. 12). Still, women and men share responsibility for world and home (no. 8).

13. Francis, *Amoris laetitia*, no. 56. See also http://en.radiovaticana.va/news/2014/11/17/pope_francis_marriage_and_the_family_are_in_crisis/1111371.

14. Francis, *Amoris laetitia*, no. 54.

15. See, e.g., Peggy Orenstein, *Girls and Sex: Navigating the Complicated New Landscape* (New York: Harper, 2017).

16. Boys routinely report pressure to avoid feelings of sadness, vulnerability, fear, and joy. See The Men's Project & M. Flood, "The Man Box: A Study on Being a Young Man in Australia," Jesuit Social Services: Melbourne (2018), https://jss.org.au/wp-content/uploads/2018/10/The-Man-Box-A-study-on-being-a-young-man-in-Australia.pdf. See also Richard Reeves, *Of Boys and Men: Why the Modern Male Is Struggling, Why It Matters, and What to Do about It* (New York: Brookings, 2022).

17. Francis, *Amoris laetitia*, no. 286. See also John Paul II on machismo, *Familiaris consortio* (1981), no. 25.

18. Judith Butler, "Performative Acts and Gender Constitution: An Essay in Phenomenology and Feminist Theory," *Theatre Journal* 40.4 (1988): 519–531.

19. Butler, "Performative Acts," 526.

20. Judith Butler, *Gender Trouble: Feminism and the Subversion of Identity* (New York: Routledge 1990), 7. She further claims that "perhaps the distinction between sex and gender turns out to be no distinction at all" (7), and "sex, by definition, will be shown to have been gender all along" (8).

21. Butler, *Gender Trouble*, 140, 147.

22. Hannah Roberts, "Women Theologians Are 'the Strawberry on the Cake,' Says Pope Francis," *The Tablet*, December 11, 2014, http://www.thetablet.co.uk/news/1508/0/-women-theologians-are-the-strawberry-on-the-cake-says-pope; Emma Seppala, "Are Women Really More Compassionate?," *Psychology Today*, June 20, 2013, https://www.psychologytoday.com/us/blog/feeling-it/201306/are-women-really-more-compassionate.

234 NOTES

23. Cahill, Sex, *Gender, and Christian Ethics*, 85.

24. Francis, *Amoris laetitia*, no. 54.

25. Elizabeth M. Bucar, "Bodies at the Margins: The Case of Transsexuality in Catholic and Shia Ethics," *Journal of Religious Ethics* 38.4 (2010): 604. Factors contributing to maleness or femaleness (chromosomes, gonads, sex hormones, internal reproductive organs, and genitalia) do not perfectly align for intersex persons.

26. Estimates vary from one in one hundred to 1 in five thousand. Stephanie Dutchen, "The Body, The Self: The Care of People with Intersex Traits Evolves as Clinicians and Researchers Listen More," *Harvard Medicine*, Winter 2020, https://hms.harvard.edu/magazine/lgbtq-health/body-self.

27. Intercultural comparison shows variety, raising questions about the objectivity of medical judgments. Some intersex persons advocate for accepting their bodies as they are rather than imposing a sex via surgery at birth that may or may not fit the person they become.

28. See "How Many Adults and Youth Identify as Transgender in the United States?," *UCLA School of Law Williams Institute*, June 2022, https://williamsinstitute.law.ucla.edu/publications/trans-adults-united-states/ ; Esther L. Meerwijk and Jae M. Sevelius, "Transgender Population Size in the United States: A Meta-regression of Population Based Probability Samples," *American Journal of Public Health* 107.2 (2017), https://www.ncbi.nlm.nih.gov/pmc/articles/PMC5227946/. Pew Research numbers are significantly higher (1.6 percent of adults and higher for young adults); see Anna Brown, "About 5 percent of Young Adults in the U.S. Say Their Gender Is Different from Their Sex Assigned at Birth," *Pew Research*, June 7, 2022, https://www.pewresearch.org/fact-tank/2022/06/07/about-5-of-young-adults-in-the-u-s-say-their-gender-is-different-from-their-sex-assigned-at-birth/.

29. Cahill, *Sex, Gender, and Christian Ethics*, notes that the distinction between sex and gender is integral to feminism in many disciplines (psychology, history, and philosophy) (83–34).

30. Katie Grimes, "Butler Interprets Aquinas: How to Speak Thomistically about Sex," *Journal of Religious Ethics* 42.2 (2014): 187–215; Craig Ford, "Transgender Bodies, Catholic Schools, and Queer Natural Law: A Theology of Exploration," *Journal of Moral Theology* 7.1 (2018): 70–98. For an alternative view, see John S. Grabowski and Christopher K. Gross, "An Analysis of the GSUSA's Policy of Serving Transgender Youth: Implications for Catholic Practice," *Journal of Moral Theology* 5.1 (2016): 86–110.

NOTES 235

31. See, especially, Todd A. Salzman and Michael G. Lawler, *The Sexual Person: Toward a Renewed Catholic Anthropology* (Washington, DC: Georgetown University Press, 2008).

32. John Paul II, *Man and Woman He Created Them: A Theology of the Body*, trans. Michael Waldenstein (New York: Pauline Media, 2006).

33. Carl Anderson and Jose Granados, *Called to Love: Approaching John Paul II's Theology of the Body* (New York: Doubleday, 2009). Many Catholic theologians question whether the pope's theology is authentically grounded in experience.

34. Elizabeth Johnson, *She Who Is: The Mystery of God in Feminist Theological Discourse* (New York: Crossroad, 2002).

35. Valerie Saiving, "The Human Situation: A Feminine View," *Journal of Religion* 40.2 (l960): 100–112.

36. See e.g., Linda F. Hogan and A.E. Orobator, eds., *Feminist Catholic Theological Ethics: Conversations in the World Church* (Maryknoll, NY: Orbis, 2014).

37. Heribert Jone, *Moral Theology*, trans. Urban Adelman (Westminster, MD: Newman, 1945).

38. Cristina L. H. Traina, "Papal Ideals, Martial Realities: One View from the Ground," in *Sexual Diversity and Catholicism: Toward the Development of Moral Theology*, ed. Patricia Beattie Jung with Joseph Andrew Coray (Collegeville, MN: Liturgical, 2001), 269–288.

39. Bryan Massingale, "Has the Silence Been Broken? Catholic Theological Ethics and Racial Justice," *Theological Studies* 75.1 (2014): 133–155.

40. Ibram X. Kendi, *Stamped from the Beginning: The Definitive History of Racist Ideas in American History* (New York: Bold Type Books, 2017); Willie James Jennings, *The Christian Imagination: Theology and the Origins of Race* (New Haven: Yale University Press, 2011).

41. M. Shawn Copeland, *Enfleshing Freedom: Body, Race, and Being* (Minneapolis: Fortress, 2009), 24.

42. Margaret A. Farley, "The Role of Experience in Moral Discernment," in *Changing the Questions: Explorations in Christian Ethics*, ed. Jamie Manson (Maryknoll, NY: Orbis, 2015), 47–68.

43. Patricia Beattie Jung, *Sex on Earth as It Is in Heaven: A Christian Eschatology of Desire* (New York: SUNY Press, 2017).

44. Kate Blanchard, "Who's Afraid of 'The Vagina Monologues'? Christian Responses and Responsibility to Women on Campus and in the Global Community," *Journal of the Society of Christian Ethics* 30 (2012): 99–122.

236 NOTES

See also Roxane Gay, *Bad Feminist: Essays* (New York: Harper, 2014) and *Difficult Women* (New York: Grove, 2017).

45. The Mudflower Collective, *God's Fierce Whimsy: Christian Feminism and Theological Education* (Cleveland, OH: Pilgrim, 1985), from a racially diverse group of feminists.

46. Margaret A. Farley, *Just Love: A Framework for Christian Sexual Ethics* (New York: Continuum, 2006), 156–158.

47. Kate Bornstein and S. Bear Bergman, eds., *Gender Outlaws: The Next Generation* (Berkeley: Seal Press, 2010).

48. Julia Serano, "Performance Piece," in Bornstein and Bergman, *Gender Outlaws*, 85.

49. Serano, "Performance Piece," 87.

50. Audre Lorde, "The Uses of the Erotic: The Erotic as Power," in *Sister Outsider: Essays and Speeches* (Berkeley: Crossing, 2007), 57.

51. Lorde, "Uses of the Erotic," 58.

52. Serene Jones claims baptism is the most significance performance for Christians in *Feminist Theory and Christian Theology: Cartographies of Grace* (Minneapolis: Fortress, 2000), 66–68.

53. Edith Stein, "The Separate Vocations of Man and Woman," in *Essays on Woman*, vol. 2., rev. ed., trans. Freda Mary Oben (Washington, DC: ICS Publications, 2017).

54. Gendered passages in Francis, *Amoris laetitia*, nos. 168–77, are not unproblematic.

55. Francis, *Amoris laetitia*, no. 130.

56. Francis, *Amoris laetitia*, no. 183.

57. James Martin, SJ, "A Good Measure: Showing Welcome and Respect in Our Parishes for LGBT People & Their Families," *The Tablet*, August 23, 2018, https://www.thetablet.co.uk/texts-speeches-homilies/4/1180/a-good-measure-showing-welcome-and-respect-in-our-parishes-for-lgbt-people-and-their-families.

58. Christine Firer Hinze, "Catholics and Feminists on Work, Family, and Flourishing," in *Sex, Love, and Families: Catholic Perspectives*, ed. Julie Hanlon Rubio and Jason King (Collegeville, MD: Liturgical, 2020), 258.

59. See, e.g., Amy Hollywood, "Queering the Beguines: Mechthild of Magdeburg, Hadewijch of Anvers, Marguerite Porete," in *Queer Theology: Rethinking the Western Body*, ed. Gerard Loughlin (Malden, MA: Blackwell, 2007), 163–175.

60. Hollywood, "Queering the Beguines, 172.

NOTES   237

61. Sarah Coakley, *God, Sexuality, and the Self: An Essay 'On the Trinity'* (Cambridge: Cambridge University Press, 2013), 300.
62. Katie Grimes, "Theology of Whose Body? Sexual Complementarity, Intersex Conditions, and La Virgen de Guadalupe," *Journal of Feminist Studies in Religion* 32.1 (2016): 84.
63. Cornwall, *Un/familiar Theology: Reconceiving Sex, Reproduction, and Generativity* (London: Bloomsbury T&T Clark, 2017), 20.
64. Cornwall, *Un/familiar Theology*, 22.
65. David Albert Jones, "Truth in Transition? Gender Identity and Catholic Anthropology," *New Blackfriars* 99.104 (2018): 756–774, https://doi.org/10.1111/nbfr.12380; Abigail Favale, *The Genesis of Gender: A Christian Theory* (San Francisco: Ignatius, 2022).

Chapter 7

1. Naomi Alderman, *The Power* (New York: Little, Brown, 2016), 370.
2. Simcha Fisher, "Pope Francis Has Done Many Great Things, but on Sex Abuse, He Hasn't Done Enough," *America*, March 10, 2023, https://www.americamagazine.org/faith/2023/03/10/francis-ten-years-women-abuse-reflection-244886.
3. Pius XI, *Ad catholici sacerdotii* (1935), nos. 16–17.
4. *Lumen gentium* (1964), no. 18.
5. Julie H. Rubio and Paul J. Schutz, " 'Beyond Bad Apples': Understanding Clergy Perpetrated Sexual Abuse as a Structural Problem and Cultivating Strategies for Change," 35, https://www.scu.edu/ic/programs/bannan-forum/media—publications/beyond-bad-apples-/.
6. Rosemary Radford Reuther, "Christian Understandings of Human Nature," in *Religion, Feminism, & the Family*, ed. Anne Carr and Mary Stewart Van Leeuwen (Louisville: Westminster John Knox, 1996), 95–110.
7. John XXIII, *Gaudium et spes* (1965), nos. 52, 60.
8. Paul VI, *Inter insigniores* (1976).
9. Paul VI, *Inter insigniores*.
10. John Paul II, *Ordinatio sacerdotis* (1994).
11. John Paul II, *Mulieris dignitatum* (1988), nos. 25–26.
12. John Paul II, *Mulieris dignitatem*, no. 26.
13. Elisabeth Schüssler Fiorenza, "The Twelve and the Discipleship of Equals," in Schüssler Fiorenza, *Discipleship of Equals: A Critical Feminist Ekklesia-logy of Liberation* (New York: Crossroad, 1993), 80–90, is the classic argument.

238 NOTES

14. Schüssler-Fiorenza, "The Twelve," 112–113.
15. Susan A. Ross, "God's Embodiment and Women: Sacraments," in *Freeing Theology: The Essentials of Theology in Feminist Perspective*, ed. Catherine LaCugna (New York: Harper, 1993), 197.
16. Mary Catherine Hilkert, "Experience and Tradition: Can the Center Hold? Revelation," in *Freeing Theology: The Essentials of Theology in Feminist Perspective*, ed. Catherine LaCugna (New York: Harper, 1993), 68.
17. Michele M. Schumacher, ed., *Women in Christ: Toward a New Feminism* (Grand Rapids, MI: Eerdmans, 2004), 201–231, explicitly engages feminist critics.
18. Pia de Solenni, "Should Catholic Women Preach at Mass? Here's a Better Question," *America*, September 9, 2019, https://www.americamagazine.org/faith/2019/09/09/should-catholic-women-preach-mass-heres-better-question.
19. Clericalism is seen as a key cause by many scholars and advocates. Sarah Salvadore, "Clericalism Cited as Root Cause of Sex Abuse Crisis," *National Catholic Reporter*, February 4, 2020, https://www.ncronline.org/news/accountability/clericalism-cited-root-sex-abuse-crisis.
20. "Authentic and Lasting Reform," https://www.scu.edu/jst/resources/authentic-and-lasting-reform/.
21. Pope Francis's discussion of clericalism sometimes treats it as a vice rather than a structure. Paul-André Durocher, "Clericalism," in *Pope Francis Lexicon*, ed. Cindy Wooten and Joshua L. McElwee (Collegeville, MD: Liturgical, 2017), 21–24.
22. Rubio and Schultz, "Beyond 'Bad Apples.'"
23. Amy Harmon and Sabrina Tavernise, "One Big Difference about George Floyd Protests: Many White Faces," *New York Times*, June 12, 2020, https://www.nytimes.com/2020/06/12/us/george-floyd-white-protesters.html; and Nicole Narea, "How Two Weeks of Protest Have Changed America," *Vox*, June 10, 2020, https://www.vox.com/2020/6/10/21283966/protests-george-floyd-police-reform-policy.
24. Daniel K. Finn, "What Is a Sinful Social Structure?," *Theological Studies* 77.1 (2016): 136–164, especially 139–142.
25. Bryan N. Massingale, *Racial Justice and the Catholic Church* (Maryknoll, NY: Orbis, 2010).
26. Bryan N. Massingale, "Racism Is a Sickness of the Soul. Can Jesuit Spirituality Help Us Heal?," *America*, November 20, 2017, https://www.americamagazine.org/politics-society/2017/11/20/racism-sickness-soul-can-jesuit-spirituality-help-us-heal.

NOTES 239

27. Finn, "Sinful Social Structure," 151–152.

28. James F. Keenan, "If We Want to Reform the Church, Let's Make Women Cardinals," *National Catholic Reporter*, September 8, 2018, https://www.ncronline.org/news/accountability/if-we-want-reform-church-lets-make-women-cardinals; and Phyllis Zagano, ed., *Women Deacons? Essays with Answers* (Collegeville, MD: Liturgical, 2016).

29. "Pope Names 1st Woman to Vatican's Top Management Position," *PBS*, January 15, 2020, https://www.pbs.org/newshour/world/pope-names-1st-woman-to-vaticans-top-management-position, and Gerard O'Connell, "For the First Time, Pope Francis Appoints a Woman with the Right to Vote as Undersecretary of the Synod of Bishops," *America*, February 6, 2021, https://www.americamagazine.org/faith/2021/02/06/pope-francis-women-synod-voting-nathalie-becquart-239941.

30. Bryan N. Massingale, "Anti-Blackness and Christian Ethics," *Political Theology Network*, June 16, 2020, https://politicaltheology.com/anti-blackness-and-christian-ethics/.

31. Compare Francis, *Spiritus domini* (2021) to US Conference of Catholic Bishops, "Extraordinary Ministers of Holy Communion at Mass," http://www.usccb.org/prayer-and-worship/the-mass/order-of-mass/liturgy-of-the-eucharist/extraordinary-ministers-of-holy-communion-at-mass.cfm. The *General Instruction of the Roman Missal* assumes an ordained male acolyte and lector, while making provisions for lay ministers to fulfill these roles (98–101), http://www.vatican.va/roman_curia/congregations/ccdds/documents/rc_con_ccdds_doc_20030317_ordinamento-messale_en.html#I._THE_DUTIES_OF_THOSE_IN_HOLY_ORDERS.

32. Sally Cunneen, *Sex: Female, Religion: Catholic* (New York: Holt, Rinehart & Winston, 1968), 131–134.

33. Michael O'Loughlin, "The Altar Girls Debate: Do They Kill Vocations, or Feel Valued?," *Crux*, February 4, 2015, https://cruxnow.com/church/2015/02/the-debate-over-altar-girls-does-it-kill-vocations-or-value-girls/.

34. Christine Schenk, "Why Are We Silencing Women (and Lay) Preachers?," *National Catholic Reporter*, August 28, 2020, https://www.ncronline.org/blogs/simply-spirit/why-are-we-silencing-women-and-lay-preachers.

35. Natalia Imperatori-Lee shows how Rebecca Solnit's use of "mansplaining" is operative in church contexts where men silence women. "Father Knows Best: Theological Mansplaining and the Ecclesial War on Women," *Journal of Feminist Studies in Religion* 31.2 (2015): 89–107.

36. John Paul II, *Redemptoris mater* (1987), *Mulieris dignitatem* (1988), no. 4.

240 NOTES

37. Chung Hyun Kyung, *Struggle to Be the Sun Again: Introducing Asian Women's Theology* (Maryknoll, NY: Orbis, 1990), 75.

38. John Paul II, *Letter to Women* (1995), no. 10.

39. Kyung, *Struggle to Be*, 76.

40. Elizabeth A. Johnson, *Truly Our Sister: A Theology of Mary in the Communion of the Saints* (New York: Continuum, 2003).

41. Johnson, *Truly Our Sister*, 22.

42. Johnson, *Truly Our Sister*, 247–271.

43. See Rose Marie Berger, "Three Years after 'Radical Feminist' Charge, U.S. Sisters and Vatican Reach Peace Agreement," *Sojourners*, April 16, 2023, https://sojo.net/articles/three-years-after-radical-feminist-charge-us-catholic-sisters-and-vatican-reach-peace.

44. Mary J. Henold, *Catholic and Feminist: The Surprising Story of the American Catholic Feminist Movement* (Charlotte: University of North Carolina Press, 2008).

45. Sandra M. Schneiders, *Prophets in the Their Own Country: Women Religious Bearing Witness to the Gospel in a Troubled Church* (Maryknoll, NY: Orbis, 2011).

46. Sarah Vincent, "Report: Many women serve as 'de facto deacons'; Does the church recognize their gifts?," *America*, October 18, 2021, https://www.americamagazine.org/faith/2021/10/18/called-contribute-report-catholic-women-deacon-241648.

47. Francis, *Praedicate evangelium* (2002); Colleen Dulle, "Women Are Rising to New Heights at the Vatican. Could It Change the Church Forever?," *America*, September 16, 2021, https://www.americamagazine.org/faith/2021/09/16/vatican-top-women-change-smerilli-becquart-scaraffia-241413.

48. For an accessible account of René Girard's famous theory in the work of James Alison, see "Violence Undone: James Alison on Jesus as Forgiving Victim," *Christian Century*, September 5, 2006, https://www.christiancentury.org/article/2006-09/violence-undone.

49. Beverly Wildung Harrison, "The Power of Anger in the Work of Love," in *Making the Connections: Essays in Feminist Social Ethics*, ed. Carol S. Robb (Boston: Beacon, 1986), 224.

50. Harrison, "Power of Anger," 223. See also Brittany Cooper, *Eloquent Rage: A Black Feminist Discovers Her Superpower* (New York: St. Martin's, 2018).

51. Audre Lorde, "Poetry Is Not a Luxury," in *Sister Outsider: Essays and Speeches* (Berkeley: Crossing, 1984), 36–37, 39.

NOTES 241

52. Audre Lorde, "The Transformation of Silence into Action," in *Sister Outsider: Essays and Speeches* (Berkeley: Crossing, 1984), 41.

Chapter 8

1. Michael P. Jaycox, "Black Lives Matter and Catholic Whiteness: A Tale of Two Performances," *Horizons* 44 (2017): 306–341.
2. Ada María Isasi-Díaz, *Mujerista Theology* (Maryknoll, NY: Orbis, 2001), 192–202.
3. Margaret Talbot, "The Women Who Want to Be Priests," *New Yorker*, June 21, 2021, https://www.newyorker.com/magazine/2021/06/28/the-women-who-want-to-be-priests.
4. *The Duty of Delight: The Diaries of Dorothy Day*, ed. Robert Ellsberg (Milwaukee: Marquette University Press, 2008), 458.
5. Olive Banks, *Faces of Feminism* (New York: Blackwell, 1986), 13–27.
6. Susan Ross, *Extravagant Affections: A Feminist Sacramental Theology* (New York: Continuum, 2001), 19–42.
7. Isasí-Díaz, *Mujerista Theology*; Natalia Imperatori-Lee, *Cuéntame: Narrative in the Ecclesial Present* (Maryknoll, NY: Orbis, 2018). See also, e.g., Robert Orsi, *Madonna of 115th Street: Faith and Community in Italian Harlem* (New Haven: Yale University Press, 1988).
8. Experiences of women of color are, of course, complex. See, e.g., Frances E. Wood, "'Take My Yoke upon You': The Role of the Church in the Oppression of African-American Women," in Wood, *A Troubling in My Soul: Womanist Perspectives on Evil & Suffering* (Maryknoll, NY: Orbis, 1993), 37–47.
9. See https://thecatholicfeminist.com/.
10. Claire Swinarski's guide to being a Catholic feminist is available at https://static1.squarespace.com/static/58952390e3df28d5835174d9/t/5ddece9b51c72e2c5ee12c02/1574882972797/40+Days+to+a+Feminist+Faith+Final.pdf.
11. Morgan E. Knobloch, "Framing Femininity: How Catholic Women Use Blogging to Navigate a 'Secular' Discourse on Feminism through a Religious Lens," undergraduate research thesis, 2019, https://oaktrust.library.tamu.edu/handle/1969.1/175412. See also Claire Swinarski, *Girl, Arise: A Catholic Feminist's Invitation to Live Boldly, Love Your Faith, and Change the World* (Notre Dame, IN: Ave Maria, 2019), 1–20.
12. Michele Dillon, "Survey of U.S. Catholics Shows Refreshed Enthusiasm among Women," *National Catholic Reporter*, January 11, 2018, https://

242 NOTES

www.ncronline.org/news/parish/survey-us-catholics-shows-refreshed-enthusiasm-among-women.

13. Mark M. Gray and Mary L. Gautier, CARA, "Catholic Women in the United States: Beliefs, Practices, Experiences, Attitudes," 2018, https://www.americamagazine.org/sites/default/files/attachments/Catholic WomenStudy_AmericaMedia.pdf.

14. Ross, *Extravagant Affections*, 55–56, drawing on Ricoeur.

15. Ross, *Extravagant Affections*, 46–47.

16. *Code of Canon Law*, 766, 767.

17. M. Therese Lysaught, "Love and Liturgy," in *Gathered for the Journey: Moral Theology in Catholic Perspective*, ed. David Matzko McCarthy and M. Therese Lysaught (Grand Rapids, MI: Eerdmans, 2007), 33.

18. This theme emerges both in the new orthodox circles (e.g., a Catholic Feminist podcast, which stresses the import of prayer and a relationship with Jesus), and liberal religious feminist spaces, e.g., Gina Messina et al., eds., *Faithfully Feminist: Jewish, Christian, and Muslim Feminists on Why We Stay* (Ashland, OR: White Cloud Press, 2015).

19. Sandra M. Schneiders lays out the key issues in "The Bible and Feminism," in *Freeing Theology: The Essentials of Theology in Feminist Perspective*, ed. Catherine Mowry LaCugna (San Francisco: Harper, 1993), 34–35.

20. Schneiders, "The Bible and Feminism," 50.

21. Elizabeth A. Johnson, *She Who Is: The Mystery of God in Feminist Theological Discourse* (New York: Crossroad, 1993), 4–5. Among many others, see Rosemary Radford Reuther, *Sexism and God-Talk: Toward a Feminist Theology* (Boston: Beacon, 1983).

22. Johnson, *She Who Is*, 45.

23. Elisabeth Schüssler Fiorenza, *In Memory of Her: A Feminist Theological Reconstruction of Christian Origins* (New York: Crossroad, 1989), 105–204.

24. Schüssler Fiorenza, *In Memory of Her*, 205–218.

25. Elisabeth Schüssler Fiorenza, "Saints Alive Yesterday and Today," in Schüssler Fiorenza, *Discipleship of Equals: A Critical Feminist Ekklesia-logy of Liberation* (New York: Herder & Herder, 1995), 40.

26. Elizabeth A. Johnson, *Friends of God and Prophets: A Feminist Theological Reading of the Saints* (New York: Continuum, 2005).

27. See, e.g., Sarah Bessey, ed., *A Rhythm of Prayer: A Collection of Meditations for Renewal* (New York: Convergent, 2021), and Shannon Evans, *Feminist Prayers for My Daughter: Powerful Petitions for Every Stage of Her Life* (Ada, MI: Brazos, 2023).

NOTES   243

28. Mary Daly, *Outercourse: The Be-Dazzling Voyage* (San Francisco: Harper, 1992), 7–11.

29. Rosemary Radford Reuther, *Women-Church: Theology & Practice* (San Francisco: Harper, 1985).

30. Elise M. Edwards, "The Faith of My Mothers and Sisters," in *Faithfully Feminist: Jewish, Christian, and Muslim Feminists on Why We Stay*, ed. Gina Messina et al. (Ashland, OR: White Cloud Press, 2015), claims "arguments have never been convincing enough to outweigh my experiential knowledge" (21).

31. This argument is made by bloggers (Amanda Bambury, "It's Time to Reclaim Feminism, and It's Up to Catholics to Do It," *FemCatholic*, November 12, 2018, https://www.femcatholic.com/post/its-time-to-recl aim-feminism-and-its-up-to-catholics-to-do-it), and academics, most significantly, Michele M. Schumacher, ed., *Women in Christ: Toward a New Feminism* (Grand Rapids, MI: Eerdmans, 2004).

32. Mary Catherine Hilkert, "Experience and Tradition: Can the Center Hold?," in *Freeing Theology: The Essentials of Theology in Feminist Perspective*, ed. Catherine Mowry LaCugna (San Francisco: Harper, 1993), 59–82.

33. The radical group of female seminary professors (the Mud Flower Collective) who wrote *God's Fierce Whimsy: Christian Feminism and Theological Education* (New York: Pilgrim, 1985) noted that they found "rituals that promote racist, sexist, or classist power relations . . . not merely offensive . . . [but] evil" (176).

34. See, e.g., Helen LaKelly Hunt, *Faith and Feminism: A Holy Alliance* (New York: Atria, 2004); and Dorothy Sue Cobble, Linda Gordon, and Astrid Henry, *Feminism Unfinished: A Short, Surprising History of American Women's Movements* (New York: Norton, 2014).

35. Mary J. Henold, *Catholic and Feminist: The Surprising History of the American Catholic Feminist Movement* (Chapel Hill: University of North Carolina Press, 2008); and see Marjorie Procter Smith, *Praying with Our Eyes Open: Engendering Feminist Liturgical Prayer* (Nashville: Abingdon, 1995).

36. Ross, *Extravagant Affections*, 34–41.

37. Lysaught, "Love and Liturgy," 26–32.

38. William T. Cavanaugh, "Pilgrim People," in *Gathered for the Journey: Moral Theology in Catholic Perspective*, ed. David Matzko McCarthy and M. Therese Lysaught (Grand Rapids, MI: Eerdmans, 2007), 96–105.

244 NOTES

39. David Cloutier, "Human Fulfillment," in *Gathered for the Journey: Moral Theology in Catholic Perspective*, ed. David Matzko McCarthy and M. Therese Lysaught (Grand Rapids, MI: Eerdmans, 2007), 143.

40. Tobias Winright, "Gather Us In and Make Us Channels of Your Peace," in *Gathered for the Journey: Moral Theology in Catholic Perspective*, ed. David Matzko McCarthy and M. Therese Lysaught (Grand Rapids, MI: Eerdmans, 2007), 293–298.

41. María Pilar Aquino, *Our Cry for Life: Feminist Theology from Latin America* (Maryknoll, NY: Orbis, 1993), 150–151. See also Leah Libresco, *Arriving at Amen: Seven Catholic Prayers Even I Can Offer* (Notre Dame, IN: Ave Maria, 2015), 1–18.

42. Lysaught, "Love and Liturgy," 33.

43. Sandra M. Schneiders, *The Revelatory Text: Interpreting the New Testament as Sacred Scripture* (Collegeville, MD: Liturgical, 1999).

44. Lisa Sowle Cahill, "On Being a Catholic Feminist," *Santa Clara Lecture* 9.3 (2003), https://www.scu.edu/media/ignatian-center/pdf-files/Cahill-Lecture.pdf.

45. Lysaught, "Love and Liturgy," 35.

46. Aquino, *Our Cry for Life*, 152.

47. Ross, *Extravant Affections*, 213.

48. Anne Arabome, "Dreams from My Mother, Prayers to My Father: Rethinking the Trinity of God, Woman, and Church," in *Feminist Catholic Theological Ethics: Conversations in the World Church*, ed. Linda Hogan and A. E. Orobator (Maryknoll, NY: Orbis, 2014), 14–25.

49. *Sacrosanctum concilium* (1963), no. 14.

50. Robert David Sullivan, "Survey: A Third of Young Catholics Expect to Attend Mass Less Often after the Pandemic," *America*, November 10, 2021.

51. Pauline Boss, *Ambiguous Loss: Learning to Live with Grief with Unresolved Grief* (Cambridge, MA: Harvard University Press, 2000).

52. Catholic Women Preach has over seven thousand followers on Facebook, https://www.catholicwomenpreach.org/about.

53. @BlessedIsShe has over 200,000 followers on Instagram, https://blessedisshe.net/about.

54. @CatholicFeminist (thirty-three thousand followers) and @FemCatholic (sixteen thousand followers) are similar theologically, but more explicitly feminist and less focused on prayer.

55. *Lumen gentium* (1964), no. 11.

56. Anne E. Carr, *Transforming Grace: Christian Tradition and Women's Experience* (San Francisco: Harper, 1988), on mysticism (212).

NOTES 245

57. Evelyn Underhill, *Worship*, excerpted in *Essential Writings*, ed. Emilie Griffin (Maryknoll, NY: Orbis, 2003), 118.

58. Evelyn Underhill, *The Spiritual Life*, excerpted in *Essential Writings*, ed. Emilie Griffin (Marynoll, NY: Orbis, 2003), 26, 28.

59. Underhill, *Spiritual Life*, 36.

60. Elizabeth A. Johnson, *Truly Our Sister: A Theology of Mary in the Communion of the Saints* (New York: Continuum, 2005), 324–325.

Chapter 9

1. Hart Research Associates, "The Shriver Report Snapshot: Catholics in America," http://www.shrivermedia.com/wp-content/uploads/2015/09/Key-Findings-from-Poll-of-Catholics.pdf, 7.

2. CARA, "Frequently Asked Questions: U.S. Data over Time," https://cara.georgetown.edu.

3. See, e.g., Rebecca Bratten Weiss, "Who Speaks for the Church?," *Patheos*, January 31, 2021, www.patheos.com, on owning the complicity of being a practicing Catholic.

4. See, e.g., Jim McDermott, "A Place for Us: On Being Gay in the Priesthood," *National Catholic Reporter*, January 26, 2021, www.ncronline.org; and Diana L. Hayes and Cyprian Davis, eds., *Taking Down Our Harps: Black Catholics in the United States* (Maryknoll, NY: Orbis Books, 1998).

5. Barbara Hilkert Andolsen, Christine E. Gudorf, and Mary D. Pellaur, eds., *Women's Consciousness, Women's Conscience: A Reader in Feminist Ethics* (San Francisco: Harper & Row, 1985).

6. Mary Catherine Hilkert, "Experience and Tradition: Can the Center Hold?," in *Freeing Theology: The Essentials of Theology in Feminist Perspective*, ed. Catherine Mowry LaCugna (San Francisco: Harper, 1993), 59–82.

7. Andrew Prevot, "Sources of a Black Self: Ethics of Authenticity," in *Anti-Blackness and Christian Ethics*, ed. Vincent W. Lloyd and Andrew Prevot (Maryknoll, NY: Orbis Books, 2017), 85.

8. For a more systematic treatment of these question, see Julie Hanlon Rubio, "Moral Cooperation with Evil and Social Ethics," *Journal of the Society of Christian Ethics* 31.1 (2011): 103–122.

9. Cathleen M. Kaveny, "Tax Lawyers, Prophets and Pilgrims: A Response to Anthony Fisher," in *Cooperation, Complicity and Conscience: Problems in Healthcare, Science, Law, and Public Policy*, ed. Helen Watt (London: Linacre, 2005), 65–88.

246 NOTES

10. James F. Keenan, "Redeeming Conscience," *Theological Studies* 76.1 (2015): 133–135.
11. John XXIII, *Gaudium et spes* (1965), no. 16.
12. Francis, *Amoris laetitia* (2015), no. 37.
13. Virginia Woolf, *A Room of One's Own* (New York: Harcourt Brace, Jovanovich, 1929), 54.
14. Woolf, *Room of One's Own*, 58.
15. Tillie Olsen, *Silences* (New York: Dell, 1965).
16. Betty Friedan, *The Feminine Mystique* (New York: Dell, 1963).
17. Anne E. Patrick, *Liberating Conscience* (New York: Continuum, 1996), 178.
18. Linda Hogan, *Confronting the Truth: Conscience in the Catholic Tradition* (Mahwah, NJ: Paulist, 2000), 189–90.
19. For "only in the mystery of the incarnate Word does the mystery of man take on light" (John XXIII, *Gaudium et spes*, nos. 16, 22).
20. Francis, *Amoris laetitia*, no. 37.
21. Vincible ignorance can be overcome, but invincible ignorance is excusable. On the authority of an erroneous conscience, see Bernard Häring, *The Law of Christ: Moral Theology for Priests and Laity* (Westminster, MD: Newman, 1961), 154–157.
22. Bryan N. Massingale, "Conscience Formation and the Challenge of Unconscious Racial Bias," in *Conscience and Catholicism: Rights, Responsibilities, & Institutional Responses*, ed. David E. DeCosse and Kristin E. Heyer (Maryknoll, NY: Orbis, 2015), 53–68.
23. Kristin E. Heyer, "Catholic Public Witness on Health Care Reform: Toward a More Capacious Model of Conscience," in *Conscience & Catholic Health Care: From Clinical Contexts to Government Mandates*, ed. David E. DeCosse and Thomas A. Nairn (Maryknoll, NY: Orbis, 2017), 79–90; and Elizabeth Sweeny Block, "A Call to Action: Global Moral Crises and the Inadequacy of Inherited Approaches to Conscience," *Journal of the Society of Christian Ethics* 37.2 (2017): 79–96, 90.
24. Friedan, *Feminine Mystique*, 26–27.
25. Friedan, *Feminine Mystique*, 356. "Drastic steps must now be taken to re-educate the women who were deluded or cheated by the feminine mystique."
26. M. Shawn Copeland, "Toward a Critical Feminist Theology of Solidarity," in *Women & Theology*, ed. Mary Ann Hinsdale and Phyllis H. Kaminski, (Maryknoll, NY: Orbis, 1995), 3–38.
27. Mary J. Henold, *Catholic and Feminist: The Surprising History of the American Catholic Feminist Movement* (Chapel Hill: University of North Carolina Press, 2008), 83–115.
28. Patrick, *Liberating Conscience*, 210–211.

NOTES   247

29. Sandra M. Schneiders, *Beyond Patching: Faith and Feminism in the Catholic Church*, rev. ed. (Mahwah, NJ: Paulist, 2004), 98. See also Carolyn Osiek, *Beyond Anger: Being a Feminist in the Church* (Mahwah, NJ: Paulist, 1986), on how staying entails suffering for the sake of a better church.

30. Sandra M. Schneiders, interview by the author, April 11, 2023.

31. Gracie Morbitzer, "St. Catherine of Siena, Patron Saint of Women Who Are 'Too Much,'" *FemCatholic*, April 28, 2022, https://www.femcatholic.com/post/st-catherine-of-siena-patron-saint-of-women-who-are-too-much.

32. Kathleen Cummings Sparrow, quoted in Julie Hanlon Rubio, "Honoring Our Mothers in Theology," *CatholicMoralTheology.com*, May 11, 2014, https://catholicmoraltheology.com/honoring-our-mothers-in-theology/.

33. Joan Chittister, *The Time Is Now: A Call to Uncommon Courage* (New York: Convergent, 2019).

34. Thomas Merton, *Conjectures of a Guilty Bystander* (Garden City, NY: Doubleday, 1966), 140–142

35. Dorothy Day, *The Long Loneliness* (San Francisco: Harper, 1952), 284.

36. Margaret A. Farley, "Ethics, Ecclesiology, and the Grace of Self-Doubt," in *A Call to Fidelity: On the Moral Theology of Charles E. Curran*, ed. James J. Walter et al. (Washington, DC: Georgetown University Press, 2002), 55–76.

37. Stephanie Deprez, "Musician Audrey Assad Seeks 'Permission and Freedom for All to Feel at Home,'" *National Catholic Reporter*, September 24, 2021, https://www.ncronline.org/news/culture/musician-audrey-assad-seeks-permission-and-freedom-all-feel-home.

38. See, e.g., his interview with Krista Tippet of *On Being*, March 2017, https://soundcloud.com/onbeing/padraig-o-tuama-belonging-creates-and-und oes-us-both.

39. Nick Ripatrazone, "That's What Language Can Do: *The Millions* Interviews Padraig O' Tuama," *The Millions*, June 14, 2021, https://themillions.com/2021/06/thats-what-language-can-do-the-millions-interviews-padraig-o-tuama.html.

40. James Alison, "Letter to a Young Gay Catholic," http://jamesalison.com/let ter-to-a-young-gay-catholic/.

41. M. Shawn Copeland, *Enfleshing Freedom: Body, Race, and Being* (Minneapolis: Fortress, 2010), 127.

42. "Sr. Thea's Address to the U.S. Bishops," (1989), https://www.youtube.com/watch?v=uOV0nQkjuoA.

Index

For the benefit of digital users, indexed terms that span two pages (e.g., 52–53) may, on occasion, appear on only one of those pages.

abortion, 4–5, 7, 92–99, 105–8, 109–10, 111–13, 114
accompaniment, 45, 114, 155, 177, 204
agency, 26–27, 28, 93, 100–2, 103–5, 109–10, 111–12, 113–14, 123–24, 185–86, 191
authenticity, 23–25, 28, 53, 57, 59–60, 89–90, 113–14, 115–16, 118, 134, 136–37, 140, 161–62, 175–76, 179, 185–86, 189–90, 193, 194–95, 200–5
autonomy, 42–43, 56, 57–59

Beauvoir, Simone de, 14, 74
Bowman, Thea, 203–4
Butler, Judith, 76, 120–21, 122–23, 130–31

Cahill, Lisa Sowle, 120–21, 178
Callahan, Sydney, 83, 87–88, 97–98, 99–100
Campbell, Colleen Carroll, 15–16, 17–18, 23, 104–5
Catholic social teaching (also Catholic social thought)
  abortion, 94–95
  family, 35–36, 50, 64, 86
  gender, 133
  human dignity, 38–39, 41, 79–80
  immigration, 35
  racism, 148
  sex, 40–41

solidarity, 28–29, 44–45
  work, 55, 60, 61, 67
clericalism, 140, 146–48, 150, 151–52, 158, 159, 183–84
common good, 61, 62, 63, 65, 68, 79–80, 199
complementarity, 7, 11–12, 78–79, 115–16, 119–20, 134, 145
conscience, 7, 187–89, 190–91, 192–93, 194–95, 197–99, 201–2
consciousness-raising (also feminist consciousness), 13, 18, 21, 26–27, 84, 127–28, 131–32, 168, 174, 188–89, 190–91, 194–95, 197–98, 202
Copeland, M. Shawn, 28–29, 126–27, 198–99, 203

Daly, Mary, 14, 87, 174, 181
Day, Dorothy, 1–2, 87, 105, 111, 157–58, 164–65, 200
domestic labor, 50–51, 53, 54–55, 83, 194
domestic workers, 42–43, 49–50, 51, 54–55, 125–26

embodiment, 6–7, 97, 120–21, 123–24, 143–44
empowerment, 6–7, 11–12, 21–22, 64, 68, 139, 140, 151–53, 155, 156–57, 158, 159
Ensler, Eve, 110–11, 127–28

250 INDEX

experience
in Christian ethics, 124–29, 191,
200–1, 205
of women, 6–7, 9–10, 11, 14, 23,
33–34, 39, 41–42, 68, 71–72,
75–76, 86–88, 100, 103–11,
134, 148, 163–64, 168, 174–
75, 179, 182–83, 188–89
of workers, 56–57, 59–61

family, 7, 35–36, 107–8, 114, 132–33
duties beyond, 21, 89–91, 199–200
marriage and, 69–71, 72–75, 77–
78, 80, 81–82, 84–85, 86, 88
planning, 101–3, 117
religious practice and, 165, 166–
67, 169, 173–74, 180, 181
sacrifice for, 11–12, 13, 15–16
violence, 36–37
work and, 49–50, 51–55, 62, 63,
64–65, 66–68
Farley, Margaret, 27–28, 46–47, 127,
130, 200–1
feminine genius, 37, 50, 120–21, 138
feminism
definition, 2–3, 167–68
history, 13, 54–55, 130–31
types, 5–6
Asian feminism, 42–43
Black feminism, 21–22, 64, 73, 194
Latina Feminism, 26
liberal, 14, 52, 122, 192
new orthodox, 16, 42, 50, 53–
54, 63, 73–74, 88–89, 116,
127–28, 132, 145, 152–53,
165–66, 182–83
postmodern, 14–15
radical, 14, 42, 74, 75
socialist, 49–50, 52, 74–75, 96
waves, 5
first-wave, 52, 71–72, 96–97
second-wave, 21, 22–23, 50, 53,
63, 71, 75, 96, 100, 103, 117,
156, 175–76, 194

third-wave, 49–50, 127–28
new wave, 92–93
flourishing, 2–3, 6–7, 47, 60, 63, 74,
79–80, 89–90, 119–20, 133,
135, 145–46, 151–52, 167–
68, 198
Francis, Pope, 35, 36–38, 79–81, 82,
90, 95, 116, 119–21, 132–
33, 139–41, 149, 165–66,
191, 193
Friedan, Betty, 13, 14, 21, 53–54, 83,
192, 194

gender, 1, 5, 11–12, 14, 70–71, 75,
139, 146, 149, 151–52, 153–
54, 166–67, 169–70, 189,
198–201
binary, 117–18, 120, 121–
22, 143–44
Catholic theology and, 16–17, 26,
35–37, 78–79, 83, 115–17,
118, 132–33, 141, 143–
44, 172
definition, 117–18
differences, 98
identity, 4–5, 116, 120, 121–22,
123–24, 130–32, 133, 134–36
ideology, 116
queer theory and, 76–77, 88–89,
117–18, 124, 129–30, 131–32,
133, 134
race and, 21–22, 43–44
roles, 71–74, 85–86, 103
sex, as related to, 118–24, 128–29,
133, 134
theory, 7, 116, 121–23
transgender, 121–22, 130–
31, 135–36
violence and, 31–32, 34–35, 88
Gilbert, Elizabeth, 13, 14–15, 17–
18, 21
Grimes, Katie Walker, 87, 122–23

Hinze, Christine Firer, 62

INDEX 251

human dignity, 32, 38, 39, 44, 45–46,
70–71, 96, 98, 112, 119–20,
131–32, 133, 141, 198, 203

intersex, 118, 121–22, 123–24, 135–36

John Paul II, Pope, 11–12, 17, 36–37, 38–
39, 41, 44–45, 47, 50, 55, 60, 62,
78, 79–80, 94–95, 104–5, 117,
124, 126, 140–41, 142–43, 152
Johnson, Elizabeth, 153–54, 171–72,
173–74, 185–86, 196–97

Lay ministry, 157–58, 170–71, 178
Leo XIII, Pope, 38–39, 43, 47
Lorde, Audre, 21–22, 27, 46, 47, 131–
32, 161–62

marriage, 4–5, 6–7, 9, 20, 22–23, 35–
37, 51–52, 53, 69–77, 82–91,
132–33, 139, 155, 156–57,
189, 199–200, 201
Catholic teaching on, 77–81
same-sex, 76, 80, 88, 123
Mary (Mother of Jesus), 16, 81, 84,
85–86, 104–5, 152–55, 163,
166, 169–70, 172–73, 185–
86, 196–97
Massingale, Bryan, 148, 193
MeToo Movement, 4, 31, 32–34, 35,
37–38, 46, 47, 48
ChurchToo Movement, 4, 31, 47, 48
miscarriage, 15–16, 105–6, 107–10,
111–12, 113, 114
motherhood, 6–7, 21, 50, 51–52, 73–
74, 75–76, 83, 96–97, 101–2,
103, 105–6, 152–53, 155,
156–57. See also parenthood
mutuality, 6–7, 74, 84–85, 86, 88–
89, 156

natural family planning, 102

O'Connor, Flannery, 1–2, 87, 157–58

Olsen, Tillie, 14, 192
ordination, 120–21, 140, 141–42,
145–46, 149, 150, 151, 156–
57, 158, 159, 162, 163–64, 166

parenting (and parenthood), 9, 15–
16, 22–23, 49–51, 53, 72–73,
76, 86, 97, 98–99, 101, 102–3,
107, 192, 199
participation, 22–23, 61, 63, 146,
149, 168, 169, 176, 180–81,
182–83, 185–86, 203–4
patriarchy, 14, 76, 88–89, 171
Paul VI, Pope, 141–43
prayer, 6, 7–8, 29–30, 35, 78–79,
150–51, 155–56, 157, 171–76,
177–83, 184, 185–86, 189,
200, 201, 204–5
Adoration, 172–73, 178
Eucharist, 9, 28–29, 78, 142–43,
145, 150–51, 177–78, 203
liturgy, 7, 9, 28–29, 79, 140–41,
142, 155–56, 163–67, 169–73,
174–78, 179, 180, 182–83
rosary, 172–73, 178, 181
pregnancy loss, 93, 99–100, 108–9
Prevot, Andrew, 25, 190

racism, 2, 5–6, 26, 45–46, 48, 85,
92–93, 94–95, 98–99, 126–
28, 147–48, 149, 150, 193,
200, 203–4
relationality, 27–28, 63, 93, 101–2,
103–5, 111–12, 113–14, 125,
140–41, 179
reproductive justice, 4–5, 98, 112–13
Rich, Adrienne, 75–76, 103

saints, 1, 15–16, 78, 82, 83, 111, 134,
144, 163, 166, 169–70, 173–
74, 196–97, 205
Saiving, Valerie, 11, 12, 16, 22, 25–
26, 125–26
Schneiders, Sandra 196–97, 205

252 INDEX

Schüssler Fiorenza, Elizabeth, 143, 172
sex, 86–88, 102, 116–17, 120, 125–26
  sexism, 32, 41–42, 167–69, 174–75
  sexual binary, 117, 118, 119–21
  sexual ethics, 27–28, 37, 88
  sexual intimacy, 33–34, 41–42, 86, 103
  sexual revolution, 32, 42, 53–54, 75, 86–89
  sexual violence, 31–32, 38, 39, 41–44
    bad sex, 33–34, 39–40, 127–28
    Clergy Perpetrated Sexual Abuse, 31, 32, 37–38, 47–48
sin, 4, 7, 11, 22, 27, 176–77, 200–1
  hookup culture, 40
  rape culture, 31–32, 40–41
  social sin, 41–43, 148–49, 187
sisters (religious), 1, 9–10, 37–38, 63, 82, 113, 155–57, 158, 175–76

Sojourner Truth, 25, 73
solidarity, 28–29, 44–45, 67, 199–200, 203

Taylor, Charles, 24, 179, 190
Theology of the body, 124
Traina, Christina, 126

Vatican II, 1, 78, 84, 86, 140–42, 144, 148, 150–51, 176–77, 178, 180, 183, 191
virtue, 18, 28–29, 37, 45, 125–26, 142, 177
vulnerability, (and vulnerable), 19–20, 31–32, 37, 39, 42, 45, 67, 73–74, 93, 94–95, 96, 98, 100, 101–2, 112–14, 119–20, 133, 139–40, 151, 154, 161, 180, 194, 198

Woolf, Virginia, 14, 27, 49, 192